MIND ABUSE

Nov. 10/99

George,

I cannot begin to fully express how fortunate I feel to have had, in completing this work, the benefit of your guidance as a media scholar, leadership as a community activist and warmth as a friend.

Once again, thank you for all your help and encouragement and, especially, your endorsement. Rose

To community activists, media scholars, parents, teachers, health professionals and abuse survivors everywhere who valiantly try to push our human evolution forward.

MIND ABUSE

Media Violence
in an
Information Age

Rose A. Dyson

Montréal/New York
London

Black Rose Books No. CC282
Hardcover ISBN: 1-55164-153-4 (bound)
Paperback ISBN: 1-55164-152-6 (pbk.)

Canadian Cataloguing in Publication Data
Dyson, Rose A. (Rose Anne), 1940-
Mind abuse : media violence in an information age

Includes bibliographical references and index.
Hardcover ISBN: 1-55164-153-4 (bound)
Paperback ISBN: 1-55164-152-6 (pbk.)

1. Violence in mass media. I. Title.

P96.V5D98 1999   302.23   C99-900471-9

Cover design by Associés libres, Montréal

BLACK ROSE BOOKS

C.P. 1258
Succ. Place du Parc
Montréal, H2W 2R3
Canada

2250 Military Road
Tonawanda, NY
14150
USA

99 Wallis Road
London, E9 5LN
England
UK

To order books in North America:
(phone) 1-800-565-9523 (fax) 1-800-221-9985
In Europe: (phone) 0181-986-4854 (fax) 0181-533-5821

Our Web Site address: http://www.web.net/blackrosebooks

A publication of the Institute of Policy Alternatives of Montréal (IPAM)
Printed in Canada

The Canada Council | Le Conseil des Arts
for the Arts | du Canada

TABLE OF CONTENTS

ACKNOWLEDGMENTS

IT WOULD BE IMPOSSIBLE TO acknowledge everyone who contributed to this book. First and foremost, of course, I am indebted to those who guided me through the process of completing a doctoral thesis on the subject of media violence at the Ontario Institute for Studies in Education at the University of Toronto. I was fortunate to have Alan Thomas, Angela Miles and Deanne Bogdan as my supervising committee. George Gerbner, now at Temple University in Philadelphia, complimented us all when, as my external examiner, he recommended quick book publication and wide dissemination. Since then he has continued to provided me with inspiration, guidance and support, both through his renowned scholarship on the subject of mass media and his leadership within the Cultural Environmental Movement.

Very special gratitude is felt for all members, past and present, of Canadians Concerned About Violence In Entertainment (C-CAVE) but Valerie Smith in particular must be singled out as my extra-ordinary research assistant. As communications co-ordinator for C-CAVE, her collaborative activities not only enriched the contents of this book immeasurably but her initiative and vigilance on behalf of the public interest, along with a wonderful sense of humor, lightened the gravity of my commitment considerably.

Metta Spencer, Eric Fawcett, Elayne Harris, Dorothy Goldin Rosenberg, Jody Macdonald, Dolina Smith, Nancy Torin-Harbin, Priscilla de Villiers and Daphne White assisted in the data collection on the topic of cultural violence through their own organizations, publications and scholarship. My colleague, Bill McQueen, who first taught me how to use my computer and enjoy the technology has come to my rescue on more than one occasion.

My husband Norman provided cherished feedback on legal issues. I was also fortunate in having the support of my two children, Anna and Arthur. Their own interest in cultural studies and youthful perspective on the topic of media violence greatly embellished the project.

Finally, I am extremely grateful to my publishers at Black Rose Books for their interest and confidence in my manuscript. Jean Nataf and Dimitri Roussopoulos have both provided invaluable guidance and it has been a real joy to work with Linda Barton.

PREFACE

MEDIA VIOLENCE IS ONE of the most widely researched and hotly debated social issues to ever dominate the public agenda. Although intense scrutiny within the mainstream media has waxed and waned in popularity for several decades now, violence as a theme in popular culture continues to proliferate along with innovations in communications technology. Parents, teachers, health professionals and researchers have frequently voiced concerns, which have spawned numerous public inquiries and recommendations, but the conventional wisdom on the part of policy makers tends to be that any interference with these trends poses grave threats to our basic freedoms. In short, powerful media interests have capitalized on the fact that our collective ability to understand the impact of new information technology on our lives has not kept pace with innovations.

One of the most thorough and significant inquiries on the subject of violence in the media ever conducted was published in Canada, in 1977. It was chaired by the late Honorable Judy LaMarsh who served in the federal cabinet during the Pearson administration. Also known as the *Report of the Ontario Royal Commission on Violence in the Communications Industry*, it is still lauded as one of the best public inquiries into the causes and effects of media violence ever undertaken anywhere in the western world.[1] However, both before and since 1977 most of the research, as well as the production and distribution of popular culture involving media violence, has been done in the United States.[2]

The LaMarsh Commission concluded that the great weight of research into the effects of violent media content indicates potential harm to society. Its prevalence in the North American intellectual community was compared to potentially dangerous food and drug additives and air or water pollutants such as lead, mercury, and asbestos: all known to be hazardous to humans. Unfortunately, as a major study on the subject, the LaMarsh Report has tended to be overlooked, trivialized and dismissed by critics who have argued, instead, for maintaining the status quo.

Although some of its conclusions and recommendations are now dated, many remain both relevant and urgent, and continue to surface in subsequent studies. In an era of shrinking budgets, when duplication of public inquiries on critical social and economic problems must be avoided, the need to rekindle interest and discussion on its extraordinary depth and breadth is obvious. That is, if the public will exists to responsibly address rapidly converging forms of communications technology as the most powerful educational force the world has ever known.

Framework for the Book

This book is primarily about policy trends and developments on issues involving media violence, particularly as these have unfolded since 1990. Discussion revolves around five broad categories; a new system or framework for communications management; legislation; financial incentives; research, education, and public awareness; and the role of parents. Inevitably, some aspects of this enormous topic have been left out and others have been examined only peripherally.

On the whole it is based on over fifteen years of scholarship in the area. This includes completion and defense of a doctoral thesis at the Ontario Institute for Studies in Education at the University of Toronto in 1995, leadership of the community based organization, Canadians Concerned About Violence In Entertainment (C-CAVE), founded in 1983 for the purpose of providing public education on research findings, and membership on the executive committee of the Cultural Environment Movement (CEM), based in Philadelphia and founded by George Gerbner in 1996. It is a sincere attempt to provide an historical overview of how this subject has been approached in the past in order to provide some insights into how we might more effectively address what is becoming an increasingly urgent social and cultural problem, in the future.

My observation and analysis of a myriad of responses since the LaMarsh Commission Report in 1977 indicate how a combination of social, political, and economic conditions continues to cloud public debate on civil liberties, censorship and freedom of expression. These conditions, in turn, underscore the growing need for educators, as well as for the public at large, to address the fundamental consciousness-forming nature of materials in the mass media and the question of who has the right to disseminate them. The Commission recognized the damage caused by media violence and took a clear position in the "cause and effects" debate. It demonstrated a firm commitment to democratic principles of civil liberties pertaining to freedom of expression and speech, but rejected the notion that these include protection for violence in the media.

So far, initiatives for change have been concentrated primarily in the area of supporting and encouraging individual responsibility. In fact, the greatest tension involved in recent public initiatives for corporate accountability and government vigilance exists in hegemonic attempts within industry, in cooperation with government, to shift responsibility back onto the individual and into the teaching community. I argue that the predominant emphasis from government and industry in supporting and encouraging individual responsibility will continue to be relatively ineffective as long as these institutions themselves resist reform. Because of these prevailing tendencies, the basic and crucial understandings that the LaMarsh Commission articulated, have been lost as parameters for meaningful public debate.

Industry structure, social and economic forces, and Canadian-American media relations, are still key aspects of the "problem." These, however, are multiplying in an era of globalization and structural change that favors the interests of capital. Powerful economic and social interests determine market forces that influence and shape media content, structure, and control while the need to resist them grows increasingly urgent.

Notes

1. Sauvageau, et al., 1991.
2. Huston, Donnerstein, Fairchild, Feshbach, Katz, Murray, Rubinstein, Wilcox, and Zuckerman were appointed to the task force by the APA to review and integrate existing research on the positive and negative effects of television advertising on programming on particular segments of the United States population; specifically women, children, minorities, and the elderly. Published in 1982, their report was entitled *Big World, Small Screen: The Role of Television in American Society*. It placed special emphasis on research conducted since the report from the National Institute of Mental Health in 1982.

INTRODUCTION

A FEW WORDS NEED to be said about the context in which I use many popular concepts in this book. I refer to popular culture as that aspect of our socialization that is shaped and dominated by mass media in the form of information, entertainment and public education. I am among those who believe that, partly on the basis of the "synergism" in the production of popular culture today, isolated studies on the impact of certain aspects of the media to the exclusion of others are relatively meaningless and that there is a need to look at the interconnectedness of the entire field. The various forms are linked and they reinforce each other.[1] Also, it is possible to extrapolate from the research on one medium to the effects or impact from another medium.[2]

In general, the boundaries between "culture" and "society" are collapsing as we move away from modernity. As a component of postmodernizing change, the kind of tensions that facilitate differentiation and the negotiation of meaning within the cultural realm between commodification and its denial are being reduced through fragmentation. Consequently, distinctions between commodities, their use-value and subsequent value systems are also being reduced.[3]

Postmodernism, in my view, is regarded as the condition of rapid change from modernity to an era of postindustrialism. Large scale enterprises, ushered in during the industrial revolution, are being displaced by an increasingly globalized economy that includes commodification of communications technology, information and services as useful products for trade in the profit-driven marketplace. The subsequent penetration into various social and cultural realms underscores the growing importance of the cultural arena as the source of new and powerful economic forces.

On the whole, postmodernists have produced arguments that offer a substantial challenge to the assumptions of traditional western thought. These have tended to defy all allegedly authoritative criteria which purport to guide how we should understand, describe and act in the everyday world and hence how we should go about creating or recreating our institutions. In the process, attention has been focused on the struggles of disempowered groups to be heard and the potential authority of many different voices.

Although postmodernism has contributed useful analytical perspectives for unsettling the dominant discourses of the status quo, its tendency has been to undermine any aspirations for deriving rational grounds on which to reconstruct educational theory and practice. Because of a reluctance to draw conclusions for the purposes of policy development, it must, in turn, be viewed with scepticism. The focus should now be on "re-construction" and integration of insights with, for example, those initiated by feminist critique which continues to rely on the categories of truth, values and ethics that postmodernist theorists themselves have tended to reject.[4]

This orientation toward re-construction is, inevitably, most compatible with principles involving health and healing. Because of my early background in health sciences as a psychiatric nurse and group therapist, the subject matter in this book has been approached primarily from a health-orientated perspective. As a result, many trends away from the centrality and stability of modernity to the decentralization and fragmentation of multidirectional and unpredictable processes of transformation are regarded as frequently harm-based. I have also examined some of the limitations in the literature on representation and the negotiation of meanings—so central to the constructs for curriculum development on media literacy in schools—where the impact of the content, itself, particularly as it relates to media violence, is often trivialized.[5]

Inevitably, some areas of this enormous topic involving the role of media in our lives have received more attention than others. My references to media violence are based on the kinds of media content that researchers in child and adult development have hypothesized to have harmful or negative effects. These include graphic horror, violence, the exploitation of sex, and the combination of sex and violence as they surface in television programming, film, rock and rap music, videos, sports, advertising, pornography, toys, computer programming, video games, comic books, print and the Internet. In addition, particularly as communications technologies and various forms of content converge, harmful influences involving the celebration of drug and alcohol abuse, suicide, Satanism and cult worship, racism, sexism, and bigotry are included along with commodities such as war toys. It should be noted that the latter are frequently described in promotional material as "action-filled" in order to avoid being labeled as *violence*-filled.

Interpretations of media violence are based primarily on media produced specifically for entertainment purposes. However, the overlap with advertising, news, and other forms of information as the boundaries between these different forms fade, is discussed as an inevitable characteristic of the existing cultural climate. In the process, *institutionalized* violence through dominant social and political forces that reinforces a culture of violence in the broadest context, is also addressed.

To some extent, my outlook has been influenced by the debate on morals and values education, which in the 1960s became an international movement that redefined teaching methods in schools. There is some evidence that its central tenets—values clarification and Kohlberg's moral reasoning approach—helped to create a learning environment that has led us into the battle over control of popular culture which we now face in the nineties.[6] Some argue that the pendulum swing away from teaching based on conventional foundations for standards and ethics toward moral relativism and emphasis on individual rights have contributed to the present dilemma.

Tolerance and open-mindedness are always of paramount importance in any school curriculum, but these components are overtaking fundamental principles on what is right and what is wrong and, themselves, becoming the chief virtues in school curricula. Good example and character formation are becoming secondary. In the process, *values* often become synonymous with *feelings* with a tendency for the classroom teacher to adopt the role of facilitator. In an era of rapid conversion to more and more computer based learning in schools, the role of teacher as facilitator is becoming the norm. All of this is helping to create a scenario where school instruction is now often on par with television or computer programming with emphasis on popular appeal or individual student preferences.

In North America, the growing uneasiness that we have gone too far in emphasizing individual rights and the idea that all values are relative has, for example, helped to spawn the creation of charter schools. On the whole, there is some evidence that the emphasis is beginning to shift back to more traditional models of morality for the collective well-being of society. Growing levels of violence in schools throughout North America are forcing teachers and administrators to develop and implement values-based policies on what is right and what is wrong simply in order to avert chaos. In the process, these developments have begun to eclipse the philosophical discourse over less traditional approaches to morals and values education.[7]

Notes

1. Gerbner, 1991, 1993, Schiller, 1989.
2. American Psychological Association, 1993, Centerwall, 1992, Comstock, 1991.
3. Crook, Pakulski & Waters, 1992, Fiske, 1987.
4. McCallum, 1992, Eisler, 1996.
5. Gerbner, 1991.
6. Beck, 1990; Gow, 1985; Kilpatrick, 1992.
7. Valpy, 1994, Feb. 10, *The Globe and Mail*, p.2; Galt, 1996, Feb. 2, *The Globe and Mail*, p.A1.

Chapter 1

TEACHERS TODAY—WHO ARE THEY?

FORMAL EDUCATION, PARTICULARLY in early childhood, is a necessary component in shaping our social fabric, but at this critical juncture in our human history, some of the most powerful educational forces in society are exerted through the mass media. Inevitably, the increasing importance of cultural commodities in the current information-based economy, which include more and more "action-filled" or violence-filled forms of entertainment, helps to foster and reinforce a broadly based culture of violence. Most thinking adults would agree that it is neither desirable nor possible to eradicate all violence from society; but that rising levels, as well as the fear of violence—real or imagined—call for mitigation.

Media violence may be only one of many contributing factors but it is one that, if we choose to, we can ameliorate. Aggression, itself, in its most primitive form is an act of creation that expresses itself in infancy with the birth of a child. It evolves into a force that enables the child to grow and develop. Without it children could not cope with their environment. Parenting and childhood education operate to mold and shape this force into a form compatible with the norms of a given culture. Canada has a historical tradition based on peace, order, and good government. The extent to which this tradition has been adequately developed, or ever could be in a way that conforms with the expectations of all citizens, is a moot point. However, as a collective vision, anywhere in the world today, it is becoming more and more obscured in an increasingly centralized, globalized and mass-marketed media environment with growing emphasis on violent content.

Community Erosion and Countervailing Forces
Community is usually regarded as arising from the preservation and enhancement of a widespread sense of belonging, trust and responsiveness among its members who hold common purposes, interests, and belief systems. These bonds have traditionally provided a base for social security and stability. This has changed.

As communications technology pervades the entire global community, children everywhere are being born into an environment of images and messages that are largely independent of their home, school, spiritual leaders, neighborhood, and in many cases, even their native country. Today, storytellers are seldom parents, aunts, uncles, grandparents, teachers, or the clergy. Instead, they are a handful of distant conglomerates with something to sell.

Our contemporary storytellers still enlighten, entertain, and occasionally even challenge us, but this tends to happen only if their stories fit into marketing strategies and priorities. Within a market driven, global economy the tendency is for images of life to be presented in saleable packages.

American media scholar, George Gerbner, has referred to the "teaching" images inherent in this process as the "hidden curriculum."[1] He also calls attention to heavy reliance on the "cheap industrial ingredients of sex and violence" because they translate easily into any language and sell well on a global market.[2] In the process, as cultural commodities driven by communications technology proliferate, societies around the world are becoming detached from physical reality and any responsibility for it. Personal and community values are being eroded. On an individual level there is growing evidence of diminishing commitment, self esteem, social bonding, media absorption of more and more time, indiscriminate consumption, and political alienation.

Feminist scholars are among those who have now argued for several decades that many of the lifestyles promoted in the mass media are controlling, manipulating and often health destroying. Photographs of digitally enhanced female models set impossible standards for body weight, skin texture, hair thickness and eye color. The health costs that manifest themselves in the form of bulimia and anorexia among young women in particular, are well known and serve to underscore the systemic violence in our social, political and economic order.[3]

What needs to be better understood is that everyone pays for these extra "lifestyle" dividends, regardless of gender and age. The costs involved in advertising products are always, in the end, passed on to the consumer. Those who manage to resist seduction into compulsive purchasing habits or crippling health problems, still bear the costs through tax dollars which contribute to health care delivery and social rehabilitation programs.

Despite trends toward fragmentation of community stability, the mass media, as vehicles of communication, will undoubtedly continue well into the future to provide services to society such as information, education, entertainment, advertising, and a means of political and social mobilization. What is apparent and must be addressed, however, is that these essential services have become intertwined with harmful effects, among them reality distortion. These effects are multiple and varied. They go far beyond the conventional action-filled imagery commonly associated in the public mind with "media violence" and include media exploitation which results in any one or many symptoms such as desensitization, intimidation, fear, anxiety, terror, hyperactivity in young children and, particularly in the case of adolescents and young adults, a growing disregard for civil liberties.[4] As these economic forces gather momentum, they encourage neglect of vital cultural and social systems and the silent crumbling of democratic infrastructures.[5]

What are the possibilities of critical and independent thought on the basis of current trends in communications industries? A number of points need to be considered. First, research on the subject of "effects" demonstrates that actual effects differ for different people. For example, on the subject of pornography, some people are sexually stimulated while others are appalled by the explicitness of the depictions. Violent entertainment, can either sensitize or desensitize a viewer. Many variables such as age, gender, expectations, social context, peer pressure, level of education, and parental role modeling can intervene and in turn either mitigate or accelerate the influence of any or all of the foregoing.

Fortunately, because of the multiplicity of ways in which we are affected by media, there is evidence of prosocial developments, as well, within the broad spectrum of what makes up the mass media. We have what is frequently referred to as the "alternative or independent" media.[6] In a pluralist society, always shifting and in the process of transformation, these countervailing possibilities ensure a degree of diversity and help to create *spaces* for critical intervention. In addition, there are the individual judgment calls made on the part of producers, editors, and other members of the mainstream media, at both the lowest and the highest levels of hierarchal structures. Now the Internet also offers unprecedented opportunities for grassroots involvement in social and political issues. Still, the majority of the mass media are dominated by the consolidation of media ownership to serve economic imperatives and these trends are accelerating for all industries.

One has only to observe current trends toward more liberalized global trading patterns in every sector of society. The U.S./Canada Free Trade Agreement, signed in 1988 and followed by the North American Free Trade Agreement (NAFTA) in 1993, set the stage for the controversial Multilateral Agreement on Investment (MAI), drafted by the 29 industrial countries of the Organization for Economic Co-operation and Development (OECD). Although it was defeated at that stage in 1998, by widespread citizen opposition, modifications have already reincarnated at the World Trade Organization (WTO).[7]

What is unique about the media industries within the context of globalization and increasing corporate domination is that they are so central to our identity, cultural sovereignty and, in turn, to democracy itself. Throughout negotiations for more liberalized trading patterns in each one of these free trade agreements, despite efforts on the part of Canadian officials to ensure exemptions for the protection of cultural industries, there is increasing evidence that these are rapidly eroding. In fact, cultural nationalists all over the world are sounding alarms about these trends. Advances in intrusive technologies, privatization, deregulation, and commercialization of electronic media are making it more and more difficult not only for governments, but for families and teachers as well, to compete with the global media for the attention of the next generation.[8]

Examining the Medium for the Message

Frequently, the view that technology itself is neutral is challenged on the basis that the very idea of value-free technology of any kind confirms a formidable pro-technology mind-set. Marshall McLuhan urged us to think of all technology in environmental terms because of the way in which it envelops us as we live out our lives in reconstructed, human-created environments, literally *inside* manufactured goods.[9]

Evolution was once an interactive process between human beings and a natural, unmediated world. Now, it is largely an interaction between us and our own artifacts. Technology is the grounded practice in which we have always worked and lived together. What is new is the scale of its intervention in everyday life. The emphasis on precision in the organization of work has resulted in its control being taken over by the organizer, boss or manager. As a result, most of our technologies have become designs for human compliance.[10]

In his book, *Four Arguments for the Elimination of Television*, published in 1978, former advertising executive Jerry Mander, argued that the medium is not reformable at all because of problems inherent in the technology itself. Any effective television advertisement, he explained, is contingent upon shattering an existing mind set on the part of the viewer and then restructuring an awareness along lines that are more useful to persuasion. "You do this with a few very simple techniques like fast-moving images, jumping among attention focuses, and switching moods. There's nothing to it."[11]

This results in television addiction, sense deprivation, disorientation and confusion. Like Mander, many scholars have issued the warning that television encourages mass passivity and trains people to accept authority. Also, that it accelerates our alienation from nature and, in turn, the destruction of nature by moving us farther inside an already pervasive artificial reality.[12]

Marshall McLuhan, Harold Innis, Ursula Franklin and Jerry Mander are among many who have pointed out that we have not yet grasped the fact that many technologies determine their own use, their own effects and even the kind of people who control them. We have to think of technology as having ideology built into its very form. It helps to remind ourselves that, in the early 1950s, television was introduced to shift a wartime economy to one based on consumerism.[13]

Once any technology of a certain scale is introduced, it effectively becomes the environment of our awareness. The very idea that technology is neutral blinds us to the ultimate direction in which we are heading and directly serves the promoters of the centralized technological pathway.[14] In this context, although he acknowledges that the chances of eliminating television entirely are slim and next to none, Mander cautions that positive changes in television programming from the present violent, antisocial tendencies to the more "prosocial" visions of educators and health professionals will never fully compensate for the training in passivity and other inherently destructive qualities that extended exposure to all kinds of programming inevitably produces. In terms of better managing our responses to the seductive powers of all technology, however, communications technology must be addressed both as part of the solution as well as the problem.

In his book, *The Closing of the American Mind,* published in 1987, Allan Bloom's assessment of the crisis includes a profile of a thirteen-year-old boy sitting in the living room of his family home doing his homework alternatively wearing Walkman head-phones and watching Music Television. With his body throbbing to the rhythmic, orgasmic sounds and articulations of onanism or the "killing of parents," his ambition, explained Bloom, is to win fame and wealth by imitating those who make the music.[15]

Such a child has been provided with comfort and leisure by the most productive economy ever known to mankind. Science has penetrated the secrets of nature in order to provide him with the marvelous, lifelike electronic sound and image reproduction that he enjoys. Yet in the end, life is reduced to a nonstop, commercially prepackaged masturbational fantasy—the culmination of liberties hard won over centuries by the alliance of philosophic genius and political heroism, often consecrated by the blood of martyrs.[16]

All of this has occurred under the guise of 'progress' while youth, socialized by concentrated diets of unfocused thematic material laced with violent imagery and lyrics, often revels in 'resistance' for its own sake. Unable to find radical potential in the politics of parties or mass movements, their resistance is expressed in subcultures and popular styles as an achievement in and of itself and accorded dignity alongside life threatening work against environmental degradation, fascism or political repression.

While the relationship between the portrayal of violence and the practice of it remains both complex and subtle there is no doubt that scientific evidence of one has grown increasingly in the past four decades. Public concern about it, on the other hand, has remained fairly constant for over four decades. In the aftermath of the Littleton Colorado highschool shooting in April, 1999, *USA Today* reported relatively consistent levels of belief in a link between the two since 1954 of 70 percent and over.[17] The debate now needs to turn to an examination of what the relationship between these two phenomena should be. In other words, how trends in the communications industries should be balanced in deference to public opinion and preferences.

The Broad Picture

Attempts to define what is meant by "communications research" vary. There has always been a tendency toward strong views regarding the power of communications to influence society, however, political involvement in financing and initiating mass communications research has occurred for various reasons. A great deal of the research has been concentrated on social problems which have been funded in response to political pressures based on public outcries, with academic and theoretical rigor often secondary considerations.

More recently, there have been the economic implications of new communications technologies in an increasingly globalized market. All of these trends have, despite the volume of literature on the subject, somewhat retarded the development of a coherent body of theory. Because political forces have been dominant in providing money for research, and he who pays the piper calls the tune, public inquiries have predominated since the late 1920s.[18]

Communications research has always, by nature, been multi-disciplinary, drawing upon studies in the social sciences, humanistic psychology, linguistics and economics. In recent years new technologies such as computers have begun to dismantle the frontiers between mass and individual communication, further compelling researchers in all disciplines to reconsider old methods of examining their impact on society. A more holistic approach has been one result as the possibilities for analysis of data have multiplied. These have led to new insights into the limitations of certain methodologies and the need for a multiplicity of approaches. Nevertheless, while the need to address content as well as transmission patterns is acknowledged in scientific research, given the growing evidence of overlap between these two spheres of activity, content still tends to get very little attention in the development of policy.

In Canada, governments over the years have looked to the mass media to help create and express a sense of unity and identity, to weld together a vast and disparate nation. The additional concern that the media be free of government patronage so they can act as vehicles of open and informed discussion and criticism has contributed to private ownership patterns that have helped to foster a very large foreign presence in our media. More recently, this has reinforced a scenario involving control by both foreign and domestic economic elites whose interests are often contrary to those of Canadian society as a whole.

One example involves entry of New York based shock jock radio talk show host, Howard Stern, into two of Canada's largest radio markets in the fall of 1997 in order for Canadian conglomerates to bump up sagging ratings on two stations in particular. When his broadcast first began in Toronto on CILQ-FM, owned by Western International Communications, and in Montreal on CHOM-FM, owned by CHUM Ltd., thousands of complaints from Canadians poured into Ottawa. The Canadian Radio-television and Telecommunications Commission's (CRTC) response was to turn the matter over to the industry run Canadian Broadcast Standards Council (CBSC). The Council ruled in October, 1997, that the show violated its code of ethics and sex role portrayal code.[19] In August, 1998, he was removed from the air in Montreal and CHUM Ltd. made a decision not to bring him to late night television in Toronto, but he can still be heard throughout the Greater Toronto Area on Q107-FM Radio.

Because of our large common border, no country has been or continues to be affected by the influx of American culture more than Canada. Increasingly the problem of American cultural encroachment is creating widespread concern on a global basis. By January, 1996, American media scholar, George Gerbner, reported that the U.S. controlled over 50 percent of the world's television screens, dumping mostly "action-packed" products onto the global market while importing less than 2 percent.[20]

Common Themes

Over the years, themes that have attracted the most attention from both researchers and the public at large, are obscenity, pornography, violence and delinquency. Certainly there are many others, such as consumer-driven ethics, racism, bigotry, antisemitism, discrimination, inequality for women and gender stereotyping, the breakdown of the family, illiteracy, eating disorders, decline in both high and popular culture, substance abuse, copycat actions from news reports, disrespect for authority—the list goes on. The more positive contributions of communications technology to the fields of education, information provision, leisure possibilities and expansion of cultural experiences have also been studied, but as the LaMarsh Commission Report on Violence in the Communications Industry, released in Canada in 1977, and others since have discovered, there is still a need for variety in the research on effects in order to avoid endless repetition on how matters are investigated.[21]

On the whole, discussion of mass media has expanded tremendously in the past twenty years. Courses now offered at various universities present a bewildering picture of diversity ranging from the "how-to" studies of journalism and broadcasting to the more theoretically based studies in culture and communications. Centers in communications still tend to be influenced by sociology departments with the total social communications process under examination. This diversity reflects the variety of approaches and orientations between the practical, professional and theoretical emphasis of communications study as it pervades various disciplines and expands their boundaries.

Responses from within the educational community, particularly from those directly responsible for teaching children, have veered toward increasing criticism of the medium of television and violent content, although this is now beginning to shift to the Internet. In the late 1970s, strong criticism, regardless of the nature of the programming aired, began to appear in the United States. Those who had applied themselves to the improvement of children's television had become discouraged. The focus shifted to adult education and the intrinsic nature of the industry itself.

This is, of course, where a significant portion of the current emphasis is being placed with the focus of responsibility primarily on parents. Most public discussion tends to revolve around calls for public service announcements, warning labels, blocking devices, parental advisories and violence symbols on programming introductory visuals. There is some evidence, however, that this is starting to change. In the United States the industry is once again under the critical spot light due to a new round of inquiries initiated in Washington and the proliferation of civil lawsuits for damages brought forward by the families of victims against various media outlets being charged with fostering violence and the subsequent death of their loved ones.[22]

In 1977, American educator and critic Marie Winn argued that concerned parents and educators who had pinned their hopes on the reform of programming designed for children were misguided in their efforts and beliefs.

According to her, the television experience is at best irrelevant and at worst detrimental to children's needs, because viewing of any kind leads to increased reliance on the medium by parents as an electronic babysitter.

This is problematic because there are subtle differences in how adults as opposed to children process information. Adults transform the material into particular needs on the basis of present and past relationships, experiences, dreams and fantasies. For the young child, who has barely emerged from the proverbial fog of infancy, life experiences are limited. If hour after hour of television watching constitutes a primary activity, the child's subsequent real-life experiences will stir memories of television experience, not, as for the adult watcher, the other way around.

To some extent, said Winn, the child's early television experiences will serve to dehumanize, mechanize, and make less real the realities and relationships encountered in life. Real events will always carry subtle echoes of the television world. In fact, the preponderance of offensive and banal programs, she postulated, could act as a natural check on television viewing since conscientious parents would be more likely to limit their children's television intake if only unsavory programs are available. What Winn did not consider was the desensitizing component in television viewing which has now socialized more than one generation into accepting these kinds of programs as part of the norm and, in the process, desensitized a whole generation of parents.

Harmful effects from any kind of television viewing such as reduced attention spans, temporary crankiness or misbehavior because of energy absorbed from the television set, hyperactivity, and lazy reading, continue to be identified in subsequent studies. Only now, they tend to be more pronounced because of the steady increase in the media diet for children with the proliferation of additional, related commodities due to new technology.

There is also evidence that child specific programs such as *Sesame Street*, one early example of a serious programming alternative to commercial exploitation of children by television, was not as successful as had originally been anticipated. The gap between middle class and poor children has not been closed. If anything, it has widened because middle class children, for a variety of reasons of privilege, are better able to benefit from the more positive aspects of the program. Schools have not found it necessary to readjust their curricula in the first grade as had first been enthusiastically anticipated.

Winn was among the first to comment on evidence that heavy viewers demonstrate fewer gains in cognitive skills than light viewers. Other studies dealing with the actual comprehension of television material have found that, while children enjoy programs intended for their age group and are thoroughly attentive while they watch, their understanding of what is actually happening on the screen is very small.[23]

Further limitations to *Sesame Street* and similar programs surfaced in 1993 from studies conducted by Dorothy and Jerome Singer for Connecticut Public Television at Yale University. *Sesame Street* was contrasted with the "theme-based approach"[24] in the television show, *Barney & Friends*, which they developed, widely criticized by some parents for being too repetitive and dull. Children, Dorothy Singer countered, can better absorb new ideas when they are repeated frequently during a half hour segment. However "sweet and syrupy" the dialogue may seem to adults, *Barney & Friends*, she pointed out, was created to meet the need in children for a secure environment and to instil confidence and trust. *Sesame Street*, by contrast, tends to "jump around from one idea to another."

Like the Ontario Government initiated LaMarsh Commission conclusions in 1977, both Winn's and the Singers' observations underscore the complicated range of effects that television viewing can have quite apart from the component of violence in the programming. The trance-like result from television viewing can be compared with the use of drugs and, as Winn pointed out, the addiction is as serious for parents as it is for children. In fact, in her book, *The Plug-In Drug*, Winn described one instance in which pediatricians studied the "tired child syndrome." Treatment involved withdrawal of television viewing with a prescription of mild doses of chlorpromazine as a form of sedation to counteract symptoms of hyperactivity. When treatment was over and regarded a success, rather than continue to restrict television viewing, parents opted instead to have the chlorpromazine prescribed again. Life without television was deemed to be too drastic a solution.

Another component to the arsenal of harmful effects has been contributed by Alvin Toffler who made parallels between the arrival on the American scene of both television and drugs in the early 1970s. To him and others it was beginning to appear that the widespread use of drugs was not so much one of decadence as one of adaptation. Toffler assessed the United States as a nation in which tens of thousands of young people would continue to flee reality by opting for drug-induced lethargy. By blindly stepping up the rate of change, the level of novelty, and the extent of choice, we were condemning millions, he said in his book about the subject, to future shock and warned us that we were thoughtlessly tampering with the environmental preconditions of rationality.

In Canada, there was a certain irony to the fact that, in the summer of 1995, while Government officials enthusiastically promoted the benefits of technology in classrooms and lauded partnership models with the education community through projects such as *Schoolnet*, at the annual Lake Couchiching Institute on Public Affairs Conference on *Media and Society*, the American Psychological Association was holding its annual conference in Toronto with delegates reporting growing evidence of adolescent addiction to the Internet.

Television viewing impinges significantly upon viewers' perceptions of reality. In studies first undertaken by Gerbner and his associates in the 1970s, they found that heavy viewers of television chose television-based answers in questionnaires far more often than the correct ones while light viewers did the opposite. Questions involved such things as the likelihood of encountering personal violence in real life.

Gerbner refers to these distorted perceptions as "the mean world syndrome."[25] Those afflicted demonstrate a predisposition toward preferences for strict measures of law and order in dealing with real life violence. Education appears to play no significant role in ameliorating these distortions. College-educated subjects are just as vulnerable as those with only grade school education.

Confusion over Educational Goals

It is frequently pointed out in the literature on the effects of media violence that conflict-resolution skills which do not include violence have been largely overlooked in media diets for youth, particularly boys, from a very early age. Instead, they have been de-glamorized in favor of bullying tactics where the aim is "to kick major butt." These trends help to sustain, perpetuate and reinforce a culture of violence as the norm.[26] As a result, teachers often feel helpless.

In her book on breaking the links between violence and masculinity published in 1991, Miedzian referred to evidence that children are becoming increasingly obsessed with "war" play. She issued a warning of widespread evidence that it is becoming harder to manage, or ban, and is invading the school curriculum in a way that is eroding the teachers' sense of control.

In Canada, by the end of 1997, widespread news coverage was focused on the growing incidence of violence among girls as well as boys in the aftermath of 12 year old Reena Virk in British Columbia being beaten up and left to die on a deserted beach by seven of her peers. All of them were girls except for one boy.

By early 1999, waves of violent outbursts reverberated throughout North America following the massacre of fifteen people in a highschool in Littleton, Colorado. A similar shooting which occurred soon after in Taber, Alberta, precipitated a new round of speculation on causes, effects and solutions.

Strong and growing contradictions exist between our professed goals and beliefs for unity and interdependence and our reality. Indeed, in 1990 George Bush appointed Arnold Schwarzenegger as chairman of the President's Council on Physical Fitness and Sports. When over 200 groups protested, asking for a kinder, more gentle nominee as a role model for young males, Bush simply stated that he asked Arnold to chair the Council because he believed him "uniquely qualified" to address and influence national health and fitness issues among youth.[27] For Canadians concerned about American threats to our cultural identity, a particularly bitter pill had to be swallowed in November, 1997, when, despite widespread protest, George Bush, himself, was awarded an honourary doctorate at the University of Toronto.

These sorts of contradictions underscore a kind of social psychosis that characterizes public policy when cultural initiatives are undertaken in isolation from pressing social problems and often in ways that exacerbate them. The counter-productivity in such initiatives is amplified around the globe when one considers the world-wide fascination with American habits and mores.[28] It is now virtually certain that thousands of people worldwide are being adversely affected by violent, action-filled forms of entertainment.[29]

My community-based activities have demonstrated evidence of confusion among well-meaning and committed parents on how to deal with the avalanche of popular cultural commodities involving innovations in communications technology aggressively marketed for youth. On one hand, there is a growing gap between privileged and underprivileged children in society because of the different ways in which they use the technology made available to them.[30] Middle-class homes are likely to have more parental supervision and activities unrelated to communications technology, such as music or dance lessons, that enable the child to integrate more effectively the positive aspects of television and related forms of popular culture.

On the other hand, because of more disposable income, these homes are more easily targeted and pressured into purchasing the commodities. The media diet for privileged children may be more varied, but in most cases it is equally heavy. Considerable evidence, for example, suggests that the number of television sets per household has increased dramatically in recent years. Many children now have their own television sets and, as a result, are further removed from the viewing guidance of their parents.[31] The problem is compounded by the marginally supervised time these same children spend with computer games and the Internet—new forms of popular cultural commodities which are beginning to compete with television for the attention of children but which are still, in many instances, thematically linked.

The literature frequently demonstrates that the hours children spend in school are minimal compared to the hours spent with new and increasingly varied forms of communications technology designed to amuse, entertain, and occasionally educate them. Upon completing grade 12, the average child will have spent between 3,000 and 4,000 more hours watching broadcast television alone than in the classroom. Similarly, by the time they leave elementary school, children will have witnessed 8,000 murders and 100,000 acts of violence on the television screen.

The problem of media violence and how it should be addressed must be considered within the context of certain attitudes within the educational community. These responses vary from denial to lack of awareness on the part of many educators about their diminishing role and sphere of influence on the way children learn when compared to the impact of television and related technologies. At times, these responses manifest themselves in a kind of intellectual dishonesty, particularly in the "effects" debate, with teachers dismissing the magnitude of media influence by adopting the attitude that the results are "inconclusive." At other times they appear in the form of naive and arrogant criticisms of government intervention, of rare examples of industry self-regulation.

One example occurred in 1994 when the children's program, *Mighty Morphin Power Rangers* was ruled too violent for Canadian television. Some media literacy experts argued that the problem can and should be addressed exclusively by parents and teachers.

Classroom teachers, however, are not alone in their intellectual dishonesty, as Metta Spencer, Professor Emeritus in the Department of Sociology at the University of Toronto pointed out in her remarks at the American Sociology Association Conference in Toronto in August, 1997. The problem of denial, in her view, is still endemic throughout academia.

Television and related technologies are now the main, if largely unacknowledged, educators in society. Schools are no longer the primary socializers of the young. Radio, television and related cultural products have taken over this integrative socializing function. David Olson at the Ontario Institute for Studies in Education has argued that the tendency on the part of educators to overlook the form of "educational enterprise" and the goals for which it is intended, has led to a certain "blindness" to the effects of the medium of instruction.

Meanwhile, the incidence of maladjustment among children throughout North American schools continues to rise. At a conference on school violence in Toronto in 1993 sponsored by *The Canadian Institute*—one of many on the subject since then—numerous experts spoke about the links between media violence and violence in the schools. Dan Offord, Professor of Psychiatry at McMaster University and director of the Center for the Studies of Children at Risk; Robert Heath, Superintendent of the Scarborough Board of Education; Joanna Santa Barbara, Child Psychiatrist in Dundas, Ontario; Detective Paul Goldenberg, Attorney General's Office, New Jersey; Stuart Auty, Executive Director, Canadian Association for Safe Schools; and Robert Horner, Member of Parliament for Mississauga West were among those who stressed the role of the media in exacerbating problems of violence in the schools.

It was frequently pointed out that, although violence in schools is nothing new, there was a growing tendency toward the use of weapons. As a result, the learning environments in schools are becoming significantly impaired because fewer and fewer staff members are expected to cope with more and more children with a growing number of problems. In an era of structural change and budget cutbacks these problems are being compounded.

Market-Place Values Invading the Classroom

Many environmentalists point out that technology is frequently designed to serve the interests of capital in ways that lead to violence and repression of all life on earth. This is often reinforced by the education system both in classrooms and beyond them through the mass media. As a result, important information has been mixed with the trivial. Quite apart from the complex challenges this creates in terms of the whole business of filtering out misinformation and disinformation and teaching children how to distinguish between the various forms, it adds yet another dimension to the looming problem of super-consumerism, waste disposal and long term sustainability.

The extent to which our formal educational system has become interlocked with the needs of capitalist economics can be observed through growing corporate initiatives to direct and supplement state-supported educational facilities and systems. Long-term relationships for research and development are being established between major companies—or consortia—and leading universities through grants and contracts for specific projects that tend to skew the mandate and purposes of these institutions to be of most benefit to business interests. In fact, an intrinsic part of the process of economic globalization is the rapid homogenization of global culture both within and beyond the university community.

An example of this kind of encroachment within the university campus surfaced in the summer of 1997 when on July 31st American shock rock band, Marilyn Manson, whose members adopt the names of serial killers and celebrate their activities and life styles in music lyrics, performed at Varsity Arena at the University of Toronto. The band was brought to Canada, despite widespread controversy over their music and performance antics throughout North America, by two Canadian consortiums, Shaw Communications and MCA Music owned by Seagrams.

Bruce Kidd, director of athletics and recreation at the University, not only refused to cancel the booking—as did, for example, officials at the Max Bell Centre in Calgary, Alberta once they learned more about the nature of the band's entertainment—but he made it clear that another, similar band could end up performing at Varsity Arena in the future. The University needed the money. Besides, he added when I met with him in November, 1997 on behalf of C-CAVE and a number of other organizations who had protested the booking, "the students like Marilyn Manson's music."

Beyond these growing links between corporate business and the academic community, more direct ties between education and the corporate community have been noted. In 1989, Herbert Schiller pointed out that, for the training and education of their employees, American corporations were rapidly approaching the total annual expenditure of all colleges and universities with four-year and graduate programs.[32] These corporations often see themselves as creating global classrooms to meet the "real" needs of an interdependent global community. For them, community is synonymous with economy.

In Canada, another example of corporate encroachment upon the classroom has been the controversial Youth News Network, modeled after a similar television service in the United States called Channel One. Since 1993 it has been trying to gain entry into schools across the country with TV sets, satellite dishes and a twelve minute public affairs package, which would include two and a half minutes of mandatory commercials, that would be shown daily. Initially the potential benefits for educators and students alike from an infusion of modern communications technology in an era of shrinking education budgets was welcomed by many parents, teachers and school trustees. In any event, a campaign of opposition launched by John Pungente, president of the Canadian

Association of Media Literacy Organizations (CAMEO) managed to keep the network out of the schools anywhere in the country until the fall of 1998 when school and provincial ministry education officials paved the way for a pilot project in Peel County in Mississauga, Ontario.

This intrusion symbolizes an additional step in the corporate takeover of public expression with many children further reduced to passive recipients, programmed to meet short-term business goals. The preparation of young people to work within a vibrant and healthy economy will always, to some extent, require cooperation and input from the corporate sector but the concurrent objective in public education for community stability and well-being in public education is becoming more and more obscured.

The growing urgency for collective pressure for a more democratic cultural policy on a global basis is being exerted by an increasing number of scholars from a variety of disciplines.[33] However, before this kind of reform is likely to gain widespread popularity, it is essential that concerned citizens who are leaders in the community—in government, legal circles, and education—become more conscious of the growing sophistication that industry demonstrates with hegemonic attempts to reduce any restrictions on their freedom of enterprise. As I point out in the next chapter, strategies used by the industry which tend to focus the public debate on the issue of censorship, in an abstract and undefined manner, have been among the main obstacles to meaningful public dialogue on the subject.

Notes

1. Gerbner, 1973, 1980, 1981.
2. Gerbner, 1991a, 1993.
3. Berkoff, 1993, Faludi, 1992, Wolf, 1990.
4. Comstock, 1991, Miedzian, 1991.
5. Gerbner, 1991c, 1993.
6. Examples in print include *Edges Magazine, PEACE Magazine,* and *Mediacy* published in Toronto, *Adbusters* published in Vancouver and *Media and Values* published in California.
7. Clarke and Barlow, 1997; OECD, 1997; Directorate for Financial, Fiscal and Enterprise Affairs Negotiating Group on the MAI, Feb. 25, 1997; Graham and Speller, 1997, HSSFC, 1999 (June 6-8).
8. Barnet and Cavanagh, 1996.
9. Mander, 1991, p.31.
10. Franklin, 1990, p.23.
11. Mander, 1978, p.197.
12. Mander, 1978, p.348-9.
13. Mander, 1978, p.355.
14. Mander, 1991, p.36.
15. Bloom, 1987, p.74.
16. Bloom, 1987, p.74.
17. Oldenburg, 1999
18. Howitt (1983, p.5) has provided the following historical overview: In the late 1920s and early 1930s the Payne Fund published book length accounts of research they had commissioned from famous psychologies and social scientists (Blumer, 1933, Blumer and

Hauser, 1933; Cressey and Thrasher, 1933, Foreman 1935; Peterson and Thurstone, 1933; Suttleworth and May, 1933). During the 1940s the American Army used Carl Hoyland's research skills to investigate the effects of army propaganda on the morale of U.S. troops (Hoyland, 1954;Hoyland, Lumsdaine, and Sheffield, 1949). During the 1950s in Great Britain the Nuffield Foundation provided funds for research into the impact of television on children's education, attitudes and behaviour, partly as a response to the introduction of commercial television into the country (Himmelweit, Oppenheim, and Vince, 1958.) In Great Britain in the 1960s, the Home Office persuaded commercial television to provide funds which led to the establishment of a television research committee as a response to the feeling that delinquency was increasing due to television. In the USA the Eisenhower Commission into the causes and prevention of violence included a section on Television Violence as a possible contribution to the urban violence associated with demonstrations and riots (Baker and Ball, 1970); in 1969-70 the United States Surgeon General spent about two million dollars on research into the effects of television violence, and about the same time the American Presidential Committee on Obscenity and Pornography initiated and reviewed research (Commission on Obscenity and Pornography, 1970). Throughout the 1970s money was available for research into the use of the mass media in social policy research of one kind or another.

19. CBSC, 1997.

20. Gerbner, Jan. 29, 1996, ggerbner@nimbus.ocis.temple.edu

21. Howitt, 1983; Withey & Abeles, 1980.

22. Quill, 1999, June 6, *The Toronto Star*, p.D16.

23. Winn, 1977.

24. Lender, 1993, Oct. 26, *The Toronto Star*, p.E8.

25. Gerbner, 1994a.

26. Eisler, 1988, 1996, O'Connor, 1985, Miedzian, 1991.

27. NCTV, Press release, Dec. 28, 1990.

28. UNESCO, 1991.

29. ICAVE, 1990.

30. Comstock, 1991.

31. Comstock, 1991.

32. Schiller, 1989a&b.

33. Barron, 1992; Gerbner, 1991;Gostin, 1988; Herman & Chomsky, 1988; Miedzian, 1991; Nelson, 1989; Schiller, 1989.

Chapter 2

MEDIA IN CONTEMPORARY CAPITALISM

IT IS IMPOSSIBLE TO DISCUSS media violence without taking into account some of the deeper and broader manifestations of dominant media interests in every aspect of social, political and cultural life. These developments are transforming traditional modes of democratic thought and challenging conventional wisdom on such basic notions as the public interest, censorship, freedom of expression and the free marketplace of ideas. Throughout the literature on mass media there is a recurring theme of indignant campaigns and suppressions, of shading and emphasis on certain meanings to the exclusion of others, and selection of context, premises and a general agenda which is highly functional for established power.

One example involves the publicity—or rather the lack of it—surrounding negotiations for a Multilateral Agreement on Investment (MAI), now back for a second time at the World Trade Organization as a result of worldwide opposition to it from citizen's groups. Despite the fact that it amounts, basically, to a global charter of rights for transnational corporations, print coverage has been sporadic and appears usually in the form of opinion pieces from columnists rather than hard, front page news.

Meanwhile, with a minimum of transparency, business rights are in the process of being transformed into moral rights with the political rights of corporations taking precedence over the rights of nation states and their citizens. If this Agreement or some other incarnation of it is ratified in its currently drafted form, for the first time in history, corporations will be granted equal legal standing with nation states along with access to domestic courts. They will be able to challenge any legislation such as copyright protection and content rules—literally anything that would be seen to be contrary to the interests of foreign investment.[1]

In Canada, this was evident in the struggle waged by Federal Heritage Minister, Sheila Copps, to salvage some portion of the country's magazine industry under the rules of the North American Free Trade Agreement (NAFTA) while constantly being threatened by an all out *trade war* between Canada and the U.S. In the end, a "compromise" was reached on May 25, 1999, with U.S.

publications gaining limited access to Canadian advertising markets and Canadian publications promised subsidies to offset their shrinking protection. Needless to say, the Canadian taxpayer will be expected to absorb the cost of these generous concessions. Bill C-55, the controversial magazine-protection bill now before the Senate, will evidently be amended to include "relaxed foreign-ownership restrictions."[2]

A key assumption in classic capitalist ideology is that economic activity should be separated from the control of the state. Politics is regarded as the sphere of interest that deliberates over the good of society as a whole. Conflict of interest occurs when economic self-interest takes precedence over the public interest. States where this kind of separation has not taken place, or where it is not regarded as legitimate, tend to be severely criticized for the suppression of individual rights. These are taken to mean the economic right to the pursuit of individual wealth, personal religious beliefs, freedom of speech and participation in democratic self-government.

Supporters of classic liberalism seldom acknowledge, however, that some state intervention is necessary to ensure the preconditions for any kind of a capitalist economy to flourish. Monopoly control of the market must, for example, be avoided, and money has to be printed and circulated by somebody. Now, at this critical juncture in our social, political and economic history, the pendulum has swung almost completely in favor of free, unimpeded, trans-border flows of capital with the role of national governments skewed in the direction of ensuring maximum mobility at the expense of the public interest. Contributions to the economy made by the volunteer sector are ignored entirely along with such things as the full cost of environmental devastation.

American author and historian David Korton urges us to compare this development to a cancerous bodily condition in which rogue cells, without the foresight to anticipate and avoid the inevitable deadly outcome, ultimately destroy their own host along with themselves by expropriating and consuming energy through an incessant demand for unlimited growth. Living economies, he explains, like human bodies with immune systems do have mechanisms to control or eliminate elements that do not serve the whole.[3]

Since the rise of the modern press, the acknowledged function of the media of communication has been to assist in mediating among competing interests. In most western jurisdictions, freedom of the press has been carefully enshrined for this purpose. The news media are expected to keep the general public informed of the facts as they surface in current events on the basis of responsible, objective journalism practices and ethics. The extent, however, to which the facts in most media are manipulated and presented to the public for self-serving economic and political purposes is seldom acknowledged.

Consequently, there is a growing lack of credibility to the conventional wisdom that freedom for all media of communication automatically ensures more freedom of expression for everyone else as well. There is increasing evidence that knowledge and information are organized for the benefit of dominant groups at the expense of marginalized groups.[4] If, for profit-driven reasons, on a world-wide basis, the number of television networks, cable companies, film and television production and distribution studios shrinks through mergers and conglomeratization of mass media, with fewer independent newspaper chains and wire services, how can the discourse in the media really be considered free?

What are the consequences for democracy in societies dominated by market-driven forces where only a few corporate voices are heard? The traditional role assigned to the media is only tenable where there is widespread access to the media along with diverse opinion within them. Anything less creates a climate for a combination of both public and private censorship, particularly when government authorities regulate or deregulate aspects of media industries only on the basis of economic considerations. In fact, it is becoming apparent that the media now constitute an additional branch of government.

Noam Chomsky has pointed out how mainstream coverage of world events mobilizes public support for the special interests that dominate the government and the private sector, by "manufacturing consent."[5] As a result, a climate for private censorship is established because attention is focused on serving dominant media interests to the exclusion of other interests. These conditions make the presupposition that the spheres of economy and politics are separate from the process of mediation in communication less applicable today than ever before.

The Manufacture of Consent

An underlying characteristic in the changing global economy is the growing importance of cultural commodities and marketing of lifestyles. The merger of American giant Time Warner Turner, for example, has created a number of corporate divisions to ensure that the exploitation of its intellectual properties goes far beyond the traditional magazine and movie theatre to ultimately include such popular items as clothing and toiletries. The result is what it calls "synergies" among these divisions.

Media educators argue that legislation to protect intellectual property is usually designed solely for the advantage of producers and publishers. This, in turn, is creating a closed social system in which the economic cycle of production and consumption is validated and steered by the political order in such a way that the needs, desires and participation of individuals are internalized and rationalized to become synonymous with the needs of the system as a whole.

More recently, concern over copyright issues has surfaced within the industry itself. Freelance writers and publishers are now seeking to protect their rights and profits for their own creations as these are repackaged and resold in electronic products such as database services, CD-ROMs and on-line magazines.[6] But as Tony Clarke and Maude Barlow have argued in their book on the MAI and its threat to Canadian sovereignty, if this Agreement is ratified Canada's copyright legislation, tabled in the House of Commons in April, 1997, will be marginalized before it ever gets off the ground.

A postmodern analysis of cultural trends indicates that as the code of signs that influences our attitudes is sustained, reinforced, produced, exchanged, negotiated, and consumed, it tends to become the main cultural determinant in a monopolistic, capitalist way of life. This code is what predisposes us to a collective, common outlook as the mass media are expanded from their mediational function to become the major determinant in how we think.[7]

One approach used to deflect criticism about the "effects" component in mass media arises from what is called the "transportation" or "mathematical" model of communication in which information is simply transferred from one location to another. This reasoning keeps the debate over media causes and effects directed toward insoluble dead-ends as questions swing back and forth along a pendulum of examination as to whether society affects media or media affects society.

Enlarging on Marshall McLuhan's observation that "the medium is the message" Judge Beaulieu, one of the LaMarsh Report commissioners, pointed out in a position paper published soon after the Commission completed its work in 1977 that "...the medium is also the 'money'." In his own response to this line of reasoning, former CRTC chairman Keith Spicer was among those who point out that "common sense" tells us media affect us all. Why else would companies spend billions of dollars advertising their various commodities?[8]

Another aspect of communications today includes television programming and related entertainment media with sponsorship designed to market commodities to middle class consumers. As a result, the emphasis has tended to be predominantly on middle class views of status, social conscience and moral responsibility. This occurs whether these messages are beamed into developing countries, the far north, city slums or remote villages in developed countries and regardless of who watches.[9]

More recent analysis, however, demonstrates that what conventional wisdom has hitherto defined and accepted as traditional middle class values, such as moral responsibility and accountability, are themselves under attack. Los Angeles film critic Michael Medved has discussed popular culture and what he sees as the war on traditional values in his book *Hollywood Vs. America,* published in 1992. In his view, popular culture seems bent on attacking religion, glorifying brutality, undermining the family and authority figures, deriding patriotism and, in the process, exacerbating serious social problems ranging from teenage pregnancies to violence in the streets.

There is no doubt that Medved's observations and others like them—frequently advanced by the Religious Right—have helped to complicate and confuse thematic approaches to analysis of popular culture. However, traditional, middle-class views, or more transitional modifications of them, have hitherto formed the basis of most meanings and pleasures offered and negotiated within the mass media.

Furthermore, because the current information based economy is still largely profit-driven, it is by corollary dominated by middle class values, regardless of whether demand is created or negotiated. Acquisition of material goods, equated with successful lifestyle, is still the prevailing standard for middle-class status notwithstanding the growing calls for new value systems for a sustainable future. In fact, the main message going out is that consumerism is desirable and essentially the definition of democracy. In short, one practices democracy when one consumes and selects products from an ever widening range of choices.

Economic Trends

During the 1980s there were two major economic developments within the modern American media system as it mushroomed into a world-wide system. These were deregulation and conglomeratization. One outgrowth of the trend toward deregulation, initiated in 1982 during the Reagan administration, was a relaxation of standards in children's television programming. The result was that up to 80 percent of all new children's programming essentially became 30-minute commercials funded by various toy companies.[10] According to the National Coalition on Violent Entertainment (NCTV) newsletters, published in the late 1980s, the incidence of sales in military toys increased 600 percent between 1982 and 1986 in Canada, and in the United States, by 800 percent.

The second major development involving mergers and conglomeratization of information and cultural capital has led to an increasing reliance on violence as a cheap industrial ingredient because it commands attention easily and, for the global market, translates well into any language.

An example of the symbiosis that is occurring within the industry at large was given by George Irwin of the Irwin Toy Ltd., Canada's largest domestic toy maker, at the closing of the annual Canadian toy fair held in Toronto in 1994. Said Irwin, "The re-emergence over the past few years of combat-style action figures as hot sellers is a progression from the heightened interest in video games, which are also filled with fighting themes." According to Peter Turvey, president of Playmates Toys Canada Inc., the majority of the estimated $70 to $80 million in annual sales of action figures and related toys for that year was driven by popular television series and films.[11]

The harmful side effects to these economic trends are multi-faceted. One aspect to the problem emerges in the seductive career paths available to youth in what is an increasingly glamorized and lucrative sector of the global economy. Socialized from an early age by "action-packed" thrillers, their options and potential rewards are later reflected in the production of these cultural commodities. Similarly, skill development in visual image animation, taught at postsecondary levels in community colleges such as Sheridan College in the Greater Toronto Area, tends to focus on violence or action-filled thematic material. Mastery in box office hits such as *Terminator II*, *The Abyss*, *Silence of the Lambs* and *Natural Born Killers* considered problematic by many elementary and highschool teachers, are, in turn, celebrated as outstanding artistic achievements with the nature and impact of the content itself ignored.[12]

This was especially evident during a series of screenings and discussions on provocative issues in Canadian and international television production hosted in March, 1996, by The Canadian Film Centre in Toronto in association with Atlantic Communications Inc., at the time one of Canada's largest film and television producers. It concluded with a screening of "THE OUTER LIMITS" and the "Wild Wild World of SPECIAL EFFECTS." Viewers were invited to "step into the madness…a world of paranormal occurrences and unnerving effects." Canadians, the hosts explained, have become masters in the art of special effects as relationships between writers, producers and special effects companies merge. As a result, there is increasing evidence that the "script" is being driven by special effects with dialogue itself becoming less and less important.

In 1982, media analysis indicated that, in the United States, the information industries accounted for about 10 percent of the gross national product and comprised its third largest export.[13] By 1990, it was reported in *Fortune Magazine* that cultural commodities alone, including promotional items such as T-shirts, cereals and toothbrushes along with paperback books, movies, television programs and computer game software, were the country's leading export. Calculated on their own, electronic components made up the second leading export with the arms industry or *aerospace* industry as it is now called, still firmly in first place.

In fact, attention is frequently drawn to the similarities between popular cultural commodities designed to entertain us, products of the military and related foreign policy. In 1993, Alvin and Heidi Toffler described research conducted by the United States Army on protective suits for soldiers. Capability, they said, would be integrated into a suit "right out of a Hollywood special effects department." The aim, evidently, was to equip soldiers with an exoskeletal suit that would allow them to leap tall buildings with a single bound—just like Superman.

With the sharp cutback in defense spending following the end of the Cold War, a new dimension of cross pollination occurred within the military-entertainment complex with indications that some aerospace companies and engineers were applying their expertise to areas such as movie special effects. It was first reported in 1997 that the U.S. Marine Corps were using "shoot-'em-up computer games like Doom" to help in training.[14] On June 4, 1999, *Entertainment Weekly* provided further evidence of this cross pollination with examples of how guns like any other commodities with brand names get product placement in film and television scripts.

The dominance of American cultural exports in the international market means that, increasingly, they set the standard for entertainment in other countries as well.[15] Sometimes this includes evidence of fusion between military operations and popular culture. In 1993, with the help of the main movie theatre owner in Mogadishu, Canadian journalist Paul Watson described movie preferences in the midst of heavy firefights. "Mohammed's formula is simple," he said, "Play the soppy stuff first when the customers are still arriving in the darkness and then give them what they came for: war movies." The top two favorites at that time were Sylvester Stallone's *Rambo* and Chuck Norris in *Delta Force Commando*.

Additional ways in which our stories, either in fictional form or as real life events, have become dominated by the prerogatives of market forces in conjunction with defense policies were observed in the nature of news coverage during the Gulf War in 1991. Canadian media literacy education pioneer Barry Duncan, along with many others, helped to focus public attention on ways in which coverage of the war was skewed to serve American foreign policy for a "just war to liberate Kuwait." At the time, George Bush, borrowing from the vernacular of the cult developed around cultural commodities for children from the extremely popular as well as violent films on teenage mutant ninja turtles, vowed that American soldiers were determined to "kick major butt."

There are other kinds of alterations in our learning and living patterns that underscore the growing influence of mass-marketed popular culture in our lives. Demands from the film and television production industry to use public facilities such as subways, court houses, museums, hospitals, schools and libraries are increasingly inconveniencing and infringing upon the rights of the average citizen. One Los Angeles producer, originally denied a permit from the Toronto Transit Commission in the summer of 1992 because his script was considered too violent and thus contravened its policy to make the system safer for riders, especially women, was required to make revisions. As a result he had a number of criticisms and complaints about restrictions in the provincial attorney-general's office about shooting in provincial courts and tough guidelines set by the Toronto Historical Board.

By 1993, in an attempt to better accommodate the burgeoning film and television production industry, it was reported in *The Toronto Star* that members of the city's film liaison committee had appealed to Metro police to reduce the price of hiring an officer to direct traffic during filming, which is required by law. A further demonstration of this general trend surfaced in 1995 when the Economic Development Committee in Toronto supported the proposition put forth by the film location caucus of the Director's Guild of Canada in asking the province for permission to enact a bylaw prohibiting disruption of film crews.[16] It was also evident in Ontario's provincial budget brought down on May 7, 1996. In the aftermath of merciless cuts in social spending, finance minister Ernie Eves deemed it appropriate to award a tax break for film and television production, "to ensure that Ontario remains a player in the North American industry."[17]

As local economic activity involving the production of cultural commodities becomes more and more dominated by market-driven forces on a global basis, enormous pressure is being exerted on decision-makers at all levels of government. The public at large is being collectively seduced, not only into buying particular products, but into adopting a way of life that places a high priority on paving the way for their production as well. Increasingly, life is consumer-driven and happiness is equated with materialism, possession of commodities and the production of them.

Meanwhile, public policy dealing with economic issues continues to be made in isolation from issues dealing with health and safety. In Toronto, while teachers and administrators criticize the role of media violence in fostering crime among youth, debate the feasibility of video surveillance cameras in schools as deterrents, and implement zero tolerance programs for violence in conflict resolution, elsewhere, policy makers exacerbate their problems. In 1996 their deliberations at a conference in Toronto on these topics coincided with municipal and provincial authorities paving the way for the development of virtual reality theme parks which promised game players new "space-aged, shoot-'em-up adventures." Right on schedule, the 'Sega City Playdium' opened in Mississauga, Ontario, in August of that yea,r without any objections from anywhere.

Violent Underpinnings

In their 1988 collaboration on *Laws of the Media*, Marshall and Eric McLuhan pointed out that "radical changes of identity, happening suddenly and in very brief intervals of time, have proven in the past to be more deadly and destructive to human values than wars fought with hardware weapons." Throughout history it has been demonstrated that any new service environment, such as that created by the alphabet, railways, motor cars, telegraph or radio, deeply modifies the very nature and image of people who use it.

Changes in habits and mores, always integral to patterns of social organization, are now occurring with increasing rapidity and we are starting to witness more frequent eruptions of violence on a global basis. These occurrences underscore both the existence of institutionalized violence in society and the powerful potential of communications technology for either destructive or constructive change.

Fundamental changes are occurring in our habits and mores as we become more and more reliant in our day to day work and play habits on video games, television, and computers, along with other technological innovations.[18] Walkmans now appear on heads of all ages, on the street and on the treadmill in the fitness room. Along with the assembly line and the freeway they are all part of an acceleration process that spins our lives faster and faster, making it appear more exciting when it is actually only more hyperactive.

The prevailing paradigm in which speed is considered inherently good benefits some aspects of society more than it does others. Those most likely to benefit are large institutions that can translate speed of transactions and travel directly into money and power. Television is especially effective for this purpose because it is in our homes and has become such a dominant part of our lifestyles. It is uniquely suited to implant and continuously reinforce dominant ideologies which enslave us all. In the process, it is effectively producing a new form of human being which is less creative, less able to make subtle distinctions, although speedier, and more interested in "things" like high-speed computers, faxes, lasers, satellites, robotics and high tech war. The problem is magnified as our preoccupation with these proliferating forms of technology results in a further suppression of nature. Essentially, we become "redesigned" to be compatible with a high-tech future that involves a further retreat into a man-made world.[19]

Television, in particular, implants and reinforces dominant ideologies through other, thematically related cultural commodities. Like children's half-hour television programs that link up with theme-related toys, rock and rap music videos on television are often little more than commercials for compact discs and records. More conventional advertising commercials not only dominate the scripting and pace of television programming but now frequently show up in the form of product identification right in the middle of film and television scripts themselves.

In the final analysis, one need only consider Time Warner's enthusiasm for the synergistic approach to doing business. The furtherance of balance sheets with an aim to enhance profits means that books turn into movies which turn into video-cassettes, then toys reflecting characters on these screens, then T-shirts, and now theme parks. Any one of these developments in itself may appear reasonably harmless, but looked at in their entirety they begin to offer a picture of homogeneity in popular culture which reduces the potential for diversity.

We also have the illusion of "choices" that television offers, particularly in large urban areas where the range can include hundreds of channels. But this ensures neither quality nor prosocial content. This irony was not lost on Canadians in the fall of 1997 when additional channels offered through cable in the Greater Toronto Area resulted in the deletion of programming in Chinese, heavily relied upon by many recent immigrants, and the relegation of the popular programming of Vision TV to the outer fringes of the spectrum. Commercial channels promoting commodities were installed in their previous spots instead.

The illusion of choice is further reinforced by industrial promises of classification criteria for various kinds of cultural commodities for the protection of children from harmful content. An early example manifested itself in 1993 during the distribution, in Canada, by Sega, of a video game called *Night Trap* which prompted widespread calls for boycotts. Objections were expressed by C-CAVE and other community based organizations as well as White Ribbon Campaign Organizer and Bell Canada vice-president James Osborne, and Ontario Attorney-General Marion Boyd. In response, Sega stated that its corporate obligation to the general public was fulfilled because the video game had been classified as adult entertainment and would not be sold to anyone below twelve years of age. There are problems inherent in this perception of suitability regarding the age of the player as well as with this kind of violent entertainment being defined as "adult" and therefore by corollary "mature."

In the literature on policy there is evidence that ratings and classification systems do little to protect children from restricted forms of entertainment. Once a commodity is on the market, particularly if it is available for home use, children of all ages usually end up with access to it. Furthermore, children inevitably pattern their behavior after that of adults whom they look up to as role models.

Trends toward greater homogeneity in the way popular cultural commodities including radio and television programming are produced and marketed are apparent in a number of ways. Statements in 1993 from both Sega and Nintendo, that new interactive forms of video games like *Mortal Kombat* and *Night Trap*, with extraordinarily high and extreme levels of violence, were being produced and distributed with the "older" player in mind are one of them.[20]

In other words, one generation of video game players has already been socialized into wanting these kinds of pastimes and this addiction continues to fuel a demand for ever more "challenging and stimulating" games and outrageous programs. As a spokesman for the virtual reality theme parks explained when their pending arrival in Canada was first announced, they were being planned for the entire family—children as young as three years of age as well as mature adults.[21] A visit to the 'Sega City Playdium' in Mississauga, Ontario, will quickly confirm that the prevailing emphasis in all of these games is on power, speed and violence. There is no evidence of any of the innumerable games identified as having mature themes because of excessive violence being restricted to anyone in particular because of age.

The success of these unimpeded profit driven initiatives is underscored by the popularity of radio show host Howard Stern whose listeners are predominantly between the ages of twelve and thirty-four. His regular flow of racist, homophobic and misogynist commentary, all under the guise of humor, is very popular among millions of fans across North America many of whom have been socialized from an early age by several decades of similar content in rock and rap music lyrics.

Ways in which market forces now dominate the production and distribution of popular cultural commodities, thus accelerating the assault on childhood, is implicit in the title itself of David Sheff's 1993 book, *Game Over: How Nintendo Zapped an American Industry, Captured your Dollars, and Enslaved your Children.* It is an illustration of how image management is giving rise to a bewildering quantity of misinformation, disinformation and seduction while adequate filtering techniques remain relatively underdeveloped.

Unfortunately, media literacy resource material, as a component in public education on the subject rarely includes a critique of market forces that are driving and shaping media production. The focus still tends to be on individual responsibility in the determination of media consumption habits, either on the part of the parent, the teacher or the child. In fact many experts on media literacy within schools make a conscious effort to avoid what they call "media bashing."

In any case, there is little that the education community can do on its own to address the problem. The volume of information being generated by the technology has dovetailed almost totally with the market-driven demands of an old-style economy predicated on factors involving endless growth and consumption. Manifestations of how government regulatory boards often end up working primarily in the interests of big business rather than the public at large are apparent in the ways, despite fundamental differences in approach, that the Federal Communications Commission (FCC) in the United States or the CRTC arrive at their decisions.[22] As demonstrated in negotiations of various free trade agreements now proliferating around the world, the public interest is being regarded more and more as synonymous with that of big business.

With the convergence of companies, technologies, and media, the time has come for new and more appropriate forms of regulation.[23] Innovations such as fibre optics and satellites alone, to the exclusion of considerations of quality and content in communications technology, do not constitute a viable culture. In his book, *Earth in the Balance: Ecology and the Human Spirit*, American Vice-President Al Gore argued that new approaches to regulation, which include calculations of pollution and health costs in profit and loss statements in every sphere of the economy, must be negotiated on a global basis if we are to even begin to move in the direction of a sustainable future.

We have yet, however, to see much evidence of implementation of recommendations based on his conclusions. Although factoring in social costs fostered by media violence makes obvious sense, no where is this being seriously considered. In fact, in the case of the MAI, the opposite approach is being sold to the public all over the world. Health, social programs, education and the environment as well as culture have yet to be declared exempt from transnational corporate privatization.

The outright war on cultural rights in this draft agreement raises the point that cultural sovereignty, so closely linked to diversity in expression and identity, is rapidly becoming the new battlefield for security and freedom in all countries being infiltrated by American cultural products. Remarkably, this is happening while the evidence of pollution in the cultural environment and its ominous consequences is being overlooked by proponents and critics alike.

Pollution of public airwaves is every bit as dangerous as global warming. In an economy increasingly dominated by communications technology on the basis of free market forces, conventional approaches to the practice of business without any apparent ethical considerations, quite simply paves the way for the choice of human extinction over evolution. New challenges now face educators. Public or "adult" education must be interpreted to go far beyond the television decoding techniques of the classroom curriculum on media literacy.

It requires acceleration of the Cultural Environment Movement, launched at the Founding Convention at Webster University in St. Louis, Missouri, in 1996 by George Gerbner and now supported by over 250 other concerned academics and community activists from around the world. In this context it becomes useful to look back at what was started in Canada over two decades ago by the LaMarsh Commission, still lauded as one of the most thorough and comprehensive public inquiries ever conducted anywhere in the western world.[24]

Notes

1. Clarke and Barlow, 1997; OECD, 1997; Graham and Speller, 1997.

2. Scoffield, 1999b, May 27, *The National Post*, p.A3.

3. Korton, 1999, yes@futurenet.org.

4. Kirby & McKenna, 1989; Razack, 1989, Herman and Chomsky, 1988.

5. Herman & Chomsky, 1998, National Film Board of Canada, 1992.

6. Ross, 1996, May 22, *The Globe and Mail*, p.B1.

7. Angus & Jhally, 1988; Schiller, 1989.

8. CRTC, 1992. On the other hand, John Ralston Saul in his book *Voltaire's Bastards* published in 1992 has questioned the fundamental western assumption that humanism, rational thought and common sense are naturally linked in the first place.

9. Huston, Donnerstein, Fairchild, Feshbach, Katz, Murray, Rubinstein, Wilcox, & Zucherman, 1992; UNESCO, 1991.

10. Huston et al., 1992; ICAVE, 1989.

11. "Toy makers," 1994, Feb. 3, *The Globe and Mail*, p.B5.

12. CBC Television, 1992, Nov. 17, Adrienne Clarkson Presents, Toronto, On: Author.

13. Chisholm, 1982.

14. Pollack, 1997, Oct. 14, *The Globe and Mail*, p.D1.

15. Ellis, 1992; Gerbner, 1994; Schiller, 1989; UNESCO, 1991.

16. Maloney, 1995, May 26, *The Toronto Star*, p.A6.

17. Ross, 1996, May 22, *The Globe and Mail*, p.C1.

18. Mander, 1991.

19. Mander, 1991.

20. CBC Television, 1993b July 15, Midday News hosted by Laurie Brown, Toronto, On: Author.

21. Rowan, 1994, Oct.26, *The Globe and Mail*, p.B1.

22. Angus & Jhally, 1988; Ontario, 1977; Vipond, 1989.

23. Ellis, 1992.

24. Sauvageau, F., Atkinson, D., & Gourdeau, M. (1991, June).

Chapter 3

THE LAMARSH COMMISSION MANDATE

CONSIDERABLE PUBLIC DEBATE surrounded initiation and appointment of the LaMarsh Commission. The press wondered why Ontario taxpayers needed to spend over two million dollars studying "television" violence in Canada when there had already been countless studies done in the United States. Surely it was possible, they argued, to act on the basis of what our neighbors already knew. Nevertheless, public demand for action meant that in May, 1975, Judy LaMarsh, a lawyer, journalist, writer, former federal politician, and cabinet minister for the Liberal Government was appointed to chair the Commission along with Judge Lucien Beaulieu and journalist Scott Young, at that time, with the *Globe and Mail* in Toronto.

The Commission was empowered and instructed to first, study the effects on society of increasing exhibition of violence in the communications industry; second, to determine if there is any connection or a cause-and-effect relationship between this phenomenon and the incidence of violent crime in society; third, to hold public hearings to enable groups and organizations, individual citizens and representatives of the industry to make known their views on the subject; and fourth, to make appropriate recommendations, if warranted, on any measures that should be taken by the Government of Ontario, by other levels of Government, by the general public and by the industry.[1]

Although organized and funded by the Government of Ontario, the consensus was that the Commission's inquiry would be best conducted within the larger Canadian context. Its mandate was to look at the entire Canadian communications industry with its deep penetration from the United States and to decide on the degree to which the existing climate of violence in the media within the public's popular intellectual environment was perceived by the public and the scientific community to be harmful to society.

This was considered a realistic investigative approach in that virtually everyone is a multi-media consumer with books, newspapers, magazines, television and film among the many different kinds of media that people rely upon both for news and entertainment purposes. In other words impressions people form are intermingled. On the whole, the Commission was required to decide what might be done about the problem of media violence, keeping firmly in mind that the majority of people in Canadian society abhorred the idea of censorship, the latter interpreted by the Commission as "having bureaucrats or politicians decide what people can or cannot see, read or experience."[2]

The Commission defined first the nature of violence and then the nature of media violence.[3] It said that violence itself, "is action which intrudes painfully or harmfully into the physical, psychological or social well-being of persons or groups" with effects that might range from "trivial to catastrophic." The violence might be real or symbolic, obvious or subtle, arise naturally or by human design, either suddenly or gradually, and "take place against persons or against property," be "justified or unjustified, or justified by some standards and not by others."

Media violence was defined as that "depicted in film, television, sound, print or live performance" but "not necessarily the same as violence in real life." Things, for example, not violent in real life might be violent in the way they are portrayed. Violence in media might reach large numbers of people, whereas real violence might not. In the media, artificial devices might be used to "lessen or to amplify its emotional and social effects." Depicted violence might do harm that real life violence might not have done or "it might have no impact at all."

Appointment of the Commission

Widespread criticism plagued the Commission from the very beginning. Why was the inquiry set up in Ontario? How were the commissioners selected for appointment? What were the objectives? Each of the major players interviewed, had a different perspective on the reasons. Bill Davis explained that LaMarsh had been appointed because of her high public profile, reputation for hard work, and commitment as a prominent Canadian.[4] Scott Young brought to the Commission the perspective of a journalist, and Lucien Beaulieu a background in social work, law and judicial process. The main reason, said Davis, that the Commission was appointed in Ontario was that he did not see anyone else in Canada undertaking the job and he was not impressed with American initiatives on the subject at the time.

Ken Marchant, the holder of five degrees including a doctorate in law, was appointed director of research. Despite the disadvantage of provincial appointment, he stressed, when interviewed, that there is a lot that can be done at both provincial and municipal levels of government through provincially mandated review boards for classification of films and videos, tax incentives and permits for film and television production crews.[5]

Roy McMurtry, a close advisor on the appointments, said that the government of Ontario was aware of its limited jurisdiction over the communications industry as a whole, but anticipated that the Canadian Radio-television and Telecommunications Commission (CRTC), as the federal government agency in Canada mandated to regulate broadcasting and telecommunications, might become interested in the problem. In any event, the Commission was expected to help focus public and moral pressure in response to the problem of violence used as entertainment. It was also meant to focus attention on American responses, such as boycotts, and to stimulate social activism.

McMurtry said, "We were a little naive about the degree of paranoia that existed in the media about their seeming 'God given right' to do what ever they want. We went ahead anyway and I think it was a useful process." He recalled how the media did their best in trying to discredit and bury the Report on the basis that government might possibly dictate standards and undermine their views regarding freedom of the press. The traditional approach to the definition of these freedoms, he said, sets up a smoke screen.[6]

Commissioner Lucien Beaulieu remembers public concerns then as being much the same as they are now. On criticisms from the media that the provincial government had no jurisdiction over major aspects of the communications industry he said, "That may be technically true but citizens of the province of Ontario, like anyone else, whether they were citizens in the community at large, parents or teachers in schools, had a right to express their concerns and to find out about the harmful effects of media violence."[7]

Scott Young said that from the time he first heard about the Commission he was keenly interested in becoming a part of it. "I had been a journalist since the age of eighteen, often reported on violent events and often wondered about the impact this had."[8] Sheila Kieran, a Toronto author and former reporter for the *Globe and Mail*, was hired as the production manager and director of public participation. After completing Volume One of the Report in June, 1977, she spoke of helping to publicize it for the following four months by speaking to interested groups.[9]

Six additional volumes were completed soon after. These included a bibliography, reports on foreign consultations conducted in Austria, Belgium, Finland, France, Germany, Hungary, Italy, the Netherlands, Norway, Poland, Sweden, Switzerland, the United Kingdom and the United States and detailed accounts of the commissioned research projects.

From the beginning, the intention was to make the Commission bilingual which accounted, in part, for Lucien Beaulieu's appointment. Young said that he had never intended to leave the *Globe and Mail*, but that Dick Doyle, then editor of the newspaper, made it clear that he "couldn't serve two masters." Once the Commission was set up to operate, he stopped writing for it but not before defending LaMarsh's appointment in print. According to Young, "The media were always firing off cracks at Judy. It was the first time I really became aware of discrimination against women. She received criticism for the money she was spending in a way that never seemed to happen to men heading Commissions who tended to spend a lot more. They kept referring to her as '300 dollar a day Judy'." *The Globe and Mail*, in its reports on the work of the Commission itself, "walked," said Young, "along the well trodden paths on the subject of censorship."

According to Marchant, the one million dollars allotted to, and spent on, the research component of the inquiry was the only part to escape criticism, partly because the twenty-eight projects undertaken were all within budget.

Although he does not consider himself an "expert" on the media, the multi-disciplinary aspects of the topic, he explained, have always interested him.

A common theme among those responsible for the inquiry was an interest in and fascination with the diversity of mass media, as well as its power and seeming omnipotence. The role of media in modern society was perceived by everyone to be not only a very complex problem but an extremely important and urgent one. This was a perception that also seemed to be shared throughout the province during the inquiry itself.

Young said, "As we went around the province it became obvious that we were touching a real raw nerve. Sometimes people worried more about sexual content than violence. In Toronto, at one hearing we conducted at the Royal Ontario Museum someone presented me with a piece of paper and then walked out. On it was one line from a song my son Neil Young wrote, 'Down by the river I shot my baby.' It was clear that we were all grappling with an extremely complex subject that was making everyone very uneasy."

Methods and Scope of the LaMarsh Commission Research

The Commission recognized that it had some traditions to follow. It considered movie and television production codes and the pressures that had brought them about, U.S. government studies of violence on television and its effects and studies of print media in Canada and other countries. But in their view, no one had ever been asked "to study the total media environment" before.[10] The task of assessing a condition in society and making recommendations that may or may not be acted upon, they recognized, would pose specific problems.

The Commission began its inquiry by first becoming familiar with all previous research on the subject. This dated as far back as 50 years. It was soon discovered, however, that most major research on specific effects of media depictions of violence began in the 1950s. Extensive foreign consultations were undertaken with people in the United States, but the Commission preferred first to consult with Europeans in order to find such commonalities in research, conclusions and remedial action as might exist.

The impression was that on the whole, countries in the western world, apart from the United States, had many problems similar to Canada's. It was also considered useful to compare these with experiences in Poland and Hungary. Although snippets of interesting information were available in South Africa, Japan, Israel, Mexico and the countries of the Caribbean and South America, European models were thought to be more relevant.[11]

Marchant commented that, at the time, Poland was doing some of the most interesting work on prosocial programs. Nevertheless, particular attention was paid to the American influence. Once again, it was determined that the United States, as the principal producer of violent content in films and television for international distribution, had also been the focal point for most of the research: "a mass," according to the Commission's Report, "involving nearly 4,000 titled studies."

The Commission's research decisions included both strengths and weaknesses. Although cumulative effects were addressed with the help of what was described as "surrogate approaches," longitudinal studies were not included because of the limited time frame allotted for the study.[12] It faced a management choice between commissioning research studies elsewhere and assembling staff to complete some or all of the studies internally.

A decision was made in favor of the former option enabling the Commission to draw upon the extensive research capacity available in universities or consulting firms. Duplication of facilities was thus avoided and specific research projects were more geographically diversified. It was also anticipated that this approach would give support to the ongoing development of communications research capacity at a number of Canadian universities. One resulting disadvantage was perceived to be the "diminution of overall cohesion."[13] The Commission's research methodology contrasted sharply with that adopted by the U.S. Surgeon General's Advisory Committee on Television and Social Behaviour which released its report in 1972. In that case the research was based on funding proposals submitted by academic research teams.

The LaMarsh Commission acknowledged previous difficulties encountered in making use of existing social science research for the development of public policy on the basis that related pieces of research did not always connect up well with each other. As a result, the Commission pioneered one of the first major attempts undertaken anywhere in the world to conduct a multi-disciplinary examination of violence in the media. Interrelationship of studies, where necessary, was undertaken. An example emerged in its attempts to relate content analysis specifically to studies of audiences and to relate either, or both, to certain kinds of effects studies. A further attempt was made to build in the perspectives of all relevant disciplines with the intent that news-related violence would be investigated as well.

In the interim report released in 1976 it was pointed out that most existing research had been conducted by social psychologists and sociologists. In the final Report it became evident that the Commission's research was unique because of its attempt to build in the perspectives of all relevant disciplines.[14] Developmental psychologists were included in order to take into account the different interactions there can be with media at different stages of a child's emotional, cognitive and physical development.

The perspectives of educators on the learning impact of media, particularly television, were considered along with those of lawyers on matters such as constitutional jurisdiction and the legal expression of philosophical and political values related to the media and public policy. Political scientists offered insights into the relationship of the media to collective conflict and political violence. Psychiatrists offered insights into deviant behavior and that of the mentally disordered. Anthropologists, contributed historic as well as contemporary interpretations of symbolic roles of violence in popular culture. Economists added insights into the economic structure, imperatives and motivations of the media industries.

Communications research, then still a relatively new discipline, was included within the context of areas such as content analysis. Attention to the discipline of engineering, spawned early references to future technologies of television distribution and blocking devices, such as the "V-chip." Medicine and physiology, yielded information on the physiological aspects of people's reactions to media presentations.

Literary, music and film criticism provided classical sources of analysis and scholarship on media content. Library science contributed to the breadth of major categories of literature. Journalism, through professional analysis, enhanced an understanding of the content and behavior of the news industries generally. The historical component was evident in the depth and breadth of the Commission's review of previous studies.

In the end, extensive medical and physiological studies were perceived to be beyond the budget of the Commission. Nevertheless, the social effects of media were investigated beyond aggression as a posited effect of exposure to depictions of violence to include possible effects such as exaggerated fears and anxieties, victimization, sensitization causing excessive defensiveness and desensitization causing tolerance of violence.

It was concluded that distorted images of reality and the spreading of conflict and confrontation are potentially very important constituents of public mental health. The prosocial possibilities of media content were investigated specifically as the relevant standard of comparison with the antisocial effects of media violence. Developing technology was examined, as well as the existing system because the Commission decided that, "a policy approach directed only to the existing system could become obsolescent as rapidly as the system itself."[15]

A detailed systems analytical framework was set up for media violence issues and research to be commissioned. These ranged from factors and imperatives operating in the media industries, to specific media conventions, practices and behavior reflected in the content. It was assumed that media conventions, practices and behavior affect audience choices and that these combine with audience exposure patterns which, in turn, lead to patterns of reactions, perceptions and effects. It was also assumed that attributes such as individual personality, as well as influences outside the media, can and do affect outcomes in terms of responses to media. In addition, patterns of attitudes and behavior that may result from these multifaceted variables, also become part of personal and social reality.

The Final Report

In total, the Commission held 61 hearings in 38 communities and received more than a thousand briefs: 600 in writing from Ontario, 100 from outside the province. It also heard from hundreds of people who got up to speak without the benefit of notes. The hearings began in October, 1975, and ended in May, 1976, during which time the Commission logged, according to its Report, about 10,000 air miles and heard from over 8,000 people. They included, teachers, parents, librarians, spokespersons for religious organizations, women's groups, service clubs, boards of education, nursery schools and communications departments of postsecondary institutions of learning, members of the media—both public and private—and researchers.

To advise the Commission and the director of research in the early weeks of the hearings, an academic panel was established. It was multi-disciplinary in nature and included a psychologist, a senior media sociologist, a political scientist specializing in communications, and a philosopher and professor of law. It was one of the first steps taken to facilitate the research involved and included University of Toronto lecturer and psychiatrist Vivian Rakoff and York University instructor on women's studies, Thelma McCormack. The group met regularly for a period of about ten weeks in 1975.

Said Marchant, "It had wide-ranging and sometimes combative discussions on the strengths, weaknesses and gaps in existing literature, and how the issues surrounding media violence might be disentangled for operational research purposes and policy impact."[16] In addition, professional and scholarly specialists in communications and communications effects were contacted and consulted from across Canada, the United States and Europe. This helped to put the Commission in touch with other, ongoing communications research projects reflecting the concerns of other nations around the world about the impact of the media environment.

One of the directives from the Commission was that any research projects undertaken by the Commission, itself, were to be done in Canada. However, the largest amount of the research undertaken was not done in Ontario at all. The reason, according to Marchant, was because the best expertise was found at the University of British Columbia in the person of Tannis McBeth Williams.

Several trips were made to various places in the U.S. such as Boston, New York and San Francisco for meetings with major American researchers. One or two, such as George Gerbner, then at the Annenberg School of Communications at the University of Pennsylvania in Philadelphia, came to Ontario and participated in seminars held. Said Marchant, "We mapped out a set of questions about both entertainment and news media and tried to use a number of different methodologies ranging from content analysis, experimental psychological research and surveys." These were later integrated with the political aspects.

The University of Windsor was particularly helpful because of a major center for communications studies. The University of Montreal, he explained, "had Jim Taylor and André Caron." The francophone element was different but important. Marchant felt that he had been successful in facilitating a synergetic approach to the research in a way that reinforced the positive aspects of the entire project.

Whenever possible all researchers took advantage of existing research already done. Two or three meetings were held involving everyone and others met more frequently among themselves. The intent was to respond to the ideas the researchers themselves brought forward. For example, Marchant said, "Eugene Tate from the University of Saskatchewan was interested in different personality types and the ways in which people responded differently to media. Caron and Taylor, at the University of Montreal, were interested in formularization."

In retrospect, he said, they tried to move the frontiers of research forward in ways that would connect better with public policy formation and public education. It was obvious to them that, despite the large number of U.S. studies that had already been done, the body of research was still being regarded as inconclusive. Said Marchant, "We wanted to change that. It was one of the broadest inquiries I'd ever been involved in."

He pointed out that different disciplines are often at war with each other. "Economists," he said, "have one way of looking at things and then there are others. Commissions or any kind of research can become the subjects of controversy in and of themselves especially with a highly politicized set of issues." He noted that this had happened in Canada in the case of the Royal Commission on Reproductive Technologies in the late 1980s. With the LaMarsh Commission there had been a minimum of dissent. One of the major positive outcomes of the inquiry, in his view, was that for several years after it stimulated a fair degree of interest in the subject of media violence within academic circles.

According to both the interim and final Reports, from the outset, the Commission recognized that definitive answers to the usual questions on the issue of media violence were impossible:

> Television, newspapers, films, books, magazines, live theatre, comic books, concerts, recorded music, radio—all offer violence as part of their normal messages. But then come the questions. Do they give us too much violence? How much *is* too much? What harm is there, if any, even in too much violence? If it can be proven that excessive depiction of violence by the communications industry causes damage to society by providing models or an aura of acceptability for criminal or antisocial acts, what should be done about it? And what weight should be given to the fact that a great deal of Canadian media violence is imported, constituting, in effect, the imposition of an alien culture on Canadians?[17]

Although it acknowledged that Canada's susceptibility to the influences of American culture was beyond the direct terms of reference for the Commission, it emphasized the widespread concern regarding this development. "It became part of every study...constantly introduced into testimony and opinion by scientist and citizen alike as an integral part of the problem."[18]

From the beginning it was intended that the Commission's broad definition of violence would include nonphysical forms such as psychological and social violence. This made the inquiry exceptional in that the problem of institutionalized violence was more fully addressed than has tended to be the case in subsequent public inquiries around the world: an observation since made by other researchers in Canada as well. In his *Summary and Analysis of Various Studies on Violence and Television*, released by the CRTC in 1992, Sauvageau, et al., contrasted the LaMarsh Report with two reports done in the 1980s: the Wyatt Committee Report (commissioned by the British Broadcasting Corporation (BBC) and another done by the Australian Broadcasting Tribunal. Two points were regarded as being of particular interest:

The LaMarsh Report clearly reflects the commonly-held assumptions of sociology and communications specialists in the 1970s. The authors of the report conclude that violence in the media is dangerous because it encourages real violence, and categorically reject the argument that violence can be cathartic. They also dismiss out of hand methodological arguments refuting analyses of the effects of media violence. While the LaMarsh Report attributed violence in the media to economic causes, the profit motive—in short, to capitalism—by the end of the 1980s, studies into media violence no longer focused on the motivating factors.[19]

A priority for the LaMarsh Commission was to build a bibliography and selective library that would comprehensively cover its total range of issues and become a permanent legacy of research and reference materials.

The LaMarsh Commission's Research Analysis
Content

The Commission's analysis of the data from its own studies confirmed that violence routinely predominates in entertainment: television, films, news, contemporary literature, children's books, magazines and some categories of popular music. Similarly, violence is a staple ingredient of media productions, including news presentations which in turn are rich sources of potential effects, providing audiences with a host of aggressive role models and norms of violence. These role models and norms used in media content help to determine approaches used for conflict resolution in the plot. Then, as now, it was found that American "action" film styles dominate the medium and suffuse our own feature films. Also, it was observed that values and conventions in news selection were defined in a way that heavily emphasized violent news.

It was determined that the content properties of mass media extensively reflect industrial and commercial imperatives and that this leads to a search for content that is focused on what nourishes that highly selective commercial interest. The Commission also concluded that, to the maximum extent possible, the experience of viewers is carefully managed for commercial ends in all dimensions. These include the emotional, cognitive and temporal.

The essence of commercial scheduling was deemed to work on the audience's interests in order to give them as little effective choice as possible, so that they would expose themselves to the messages of that station's or network's commercial sponsors. Consequently, the ratings measured not what people wanted, but the relative success in confining audience choice to the programs of a particular network or station.[20]

Formularization

In its analysis of all the data, "formularization" was identified, by the Commission, to be a key weapon in the commercial content arsenal.[21] Television crimes were written in a teaser and four-act format, with each act building to a mini-climax prior to a commercial break. In essence, the dramatic structure was designed around commercials. Little variety was provided purposely. The Commission said:

> It is known from experimental aesthetics that what attracts are combinations of familiarity and novelty. The research shows that the American television crime format offers aesthetically reassuring and attractive complexity of both kinds. The formula is the familiarity and the novelty is largely superficial.[22]

Formulas, the Commission concluded, were tried-and-true products that feed the commercial interest and lend themselves well to the factory-style production that was identified as characteristic of the U.S. and, increasingly, Canadian commercial television and movie industry.

Successful formats, it said, involve skillfully interweaving dramatic stylistic properties with socio-cultural metaphors about sex and violence in a way that reinforce life-and-death issues in very specific ways. It was observed that even the news is extensively formularized through selection values and presentational styles, further confusing what is real with what is fictional. The audience is drawn in and physically manipulated by the emotion-eliciting properties of content such as sound and extensive surface motion of action and rapid change in camera shots.

One result is that producers of commercials have refined similar techniques to a 30-second art.

At a primitive level, our eyes and ears, designed to respond *involuntarily* to movement and dramatic variation in sound, are exploited by the extensive surface motion of action and rapid change in camera shots and a sound track specially designed to get and keep our aural attention.[23]

People, the Commission observed, respond physiologically to emotional issues of life (sex, family) and death (violence, attack), including symbolic ones such as behavioral norms. That, in turn, is the basis for rooting television drama in structurally formularized myths. "For each emotional response, there is a physiological correlate, associated with a distinctive pattern of hormonal secretions. In colloquial terms, that is how we *feel*."[24] The mind and body respond to stimuli in one of two general ways: with raised or lowered activation and arousal, or with aversion and withdrawal.[25] As a result, media impact can be pleasant or cause discomfort. Television producers test programs to gauge potential reactions to sex, violence and action in their attempts to deliver an exciting product.

Because commercial considerations are paramount over social concerns, television is often sanitized so that we get death and violence without blood.[26] Although this approach is purported by the industry to lessen harmful effects in actual fact what is lessened, according to the Commission, "is the discomfort of the commercial target which is the audience."[27] Industry spokesmen argued that negative effects are lessened with compliance to a network violence code that prevents scenes involving too much blood and gore. According to the Commission, "Consistent delivery of products that are exciting or relaxing, often manipulatively so, is behind perceptions of television as addictive, a result that serves a number of distinctive commercial purposes."[28]

Identification with a dramatic character is one form of emotional response to a television drama. Vicarious pleasure is provided, based on viewer perceptions of characteristics shared with a character such as humanity, age, gender and appearance. It is also provided by viewer perceptions of characteristics that are not always shared, but admired, such as experience, ability, lifestyle and success. Because different human beings have different appetites for identification, successful television drama pulls the audience in by offering a number of possibilities for identification, usually in the form of both antisocial and prosocial characters with attractive attributes.

News conventions are similarly geared to dramatic but not always informational potential. Our eyes, minds and bodies are manipulated by newspaper headlines, layout and illustrations, and the corresponding production values of television and radio news just as they are in television and film drama. Thus news can have the same kinds of perverse effects on individuals and the social fabric as the entertainment media can.

The Commission pointed out that, "Desensitization to violence is one important category of cumulative effect. Long-term acquisition of norms is another."[29] The extent to which both our emotional and cognitive responses to stimuli are manipulated for profit was further explained:

> Even if television producers didn't test programs on just such a physiological basis—and they do—their intuitive skills in emotional and physiological manipulation are highly developed. As is suggested by the high incidence of gratuitous violence and action, television producers go to considerable lengths to deliver an exciting product. That is, a commercial consideration into which concerns about social effects must not intrude. Commercial broadcasters rarely claim a responsiveness to social concerns unless they coincide with commercial interest.[30]

Effects of Media Violence

The Commission reported on impressive evidence that media violence consistently increases aggression in a significant although minor portion of the audience, especially in children. However, it also found that much of the research it reviewed had been colored by misleading characterizations, false dichotomies and the artificial shifting of the burden of proof. For example, very early the debate became cast as aggression versus catharsis in terms of the effects of media violence. As a result, said the Commission, the catharsis theory had "plagued the media violence issue as a pernicious myth."

> Frequently ill-defined, if at all, it is based on a notion of expulsion of aggressive tendencies through vicarious identification with an aggressor in a film or television presentation. In this form, it is a hybrid of the Aristotelian concept of catharsis based on expulsion of *tragic* feelings through vicarious identification and the Freudian notion of substituting one (nondestructive) aggressive activity for another that could be harmful. The central place of

those separate Aristotelian and Freudian notions in our popular culture have made the hybrid intuitively plausible.[31]

On the whole, the experimental and related evidence was found to be overwhelmingly against the notion of catharsis, particularly in the sense of expulsion of aggression through vicarious identification. As to the reason why the "myth" remained so popular, the Commission speculated that "most people are reluctant to admit that things they enjoy could have adverse effects, or it may be a research failure to identify and isolate effects that help to confuse the issue, such as distraction, diversion and relaxation."[32]

The Commission found that in the research that had already been done a preoccupation with aggression versus catharsis had interfered with recognition of the diverse range of effects that media violence could be having. In the process, it had become convenient for some members of the media industries to insist that the matter had not been conclusively proven and that there was no reason for concern. It said:

> This rhetorical artifice exploited the methodological constraints of social science research in a complex area. Whereas it would be unethical for experimental researchers to attempt to elicit real rapes, murders and aggravated assaults in the laboratory, experimental surrogates were ridiculed as showing no real indication of violence in society.

Survey and correlational research that statistically linked real violence with media exposure could be explained away or rendered dubious because there could be—and are—so many other factors at work. But this is purely a negativistic and rhetorical argument. Wherever any phenomenon is caused or influenced by a whole range of complex factors, any one influence can be explained away because it is overwhelmed by the combination of all the other influences. Taken to absurdity, nothing is caused by anything.[33]

Another weakness perceived in the research was the failure to come to grips with various complexities such as the multimedia perspective. That means recognition of the fact that most people experience multimedia exposure and the effects as a composite. The Commission also concluded that repetitious effects needed to receive more attention and that this was often difficult for researchers because of time constraints. Two distinct kinds of repetitious effects were identified. The first included desensitization to violence with the added component of cumulative effect and long-term acquisition of norms. The second was short-term rather than cumulative and can be perpetuated because of repeated evocation.

An example is aggression based on arousal. Another is the eliciting of hostilities from news reports of crime. In fact, there was found to be much "complex trickery" in the research on short-term versus long-term effects. The Commission said:

> Much research has focused on whether or not effects of media violence, such as aggression, persist from the short into the medium and longer term.

This characterization would seem to imply that long-term effects are always short-term effects first; frequently the short-term and long-term effects can be quite different. The same characterization has been used to imply that short-term effects that fail to persist are unimportant, or can be explained away. On this line of reasoning, we would not be concerned with single murders, but only with repeated murders by the same person across a number of years.[34]

On the whole, the Commission found evidence of the existence of a number of categories of effects from media violence:

...violence-related expectations; aggression; replication of media models and criminal techniques; fear and anxiety; victimization; sensitization and defensiveness; desensitization and tolerance; distorted images of reality; entertainment, arousal and relaxation; spread of conflict and confrontation; agenda setting and dissemination of information; use of violence for media manipulation for the sake of publicity.[35]

"It was instructive," the Commission said, "that *all* of these effects can result from both news and entertainment media."[36] Nor, it continued, "does the complexity end there. Each category of effect in turn embraces distinctive subcategories. Effects interact. Demographic, social and personality variables intervene."[37]

The Interwoven Pattern

In short, the Commission's research showed that media violence was creating individually small but cumulatively significant effects on viewers, some of which were harmful. Where the social impact of the media is concerned, social and cultural patterns both shape and are shaped by media content, it said. In other words, the media operate in subtle and powerful ways through society's instruments of acculturation and socialization:

The structure of these various processes of media-society interaction reinforces the likelihood of pervasive media effects on the social fabric, including its fringes. An alternative approach is to focus on the individual, and on individual differences with respect to media interactions and effects. There is very considerable variety in the patterns of interaction and effects between individuals and mass media content.[38]

These observations resonate with those of scholars in cultural studies who define social instruments of acculturation and socialization in terms of a hegemonic process.[39] Specific examples discussed by the Commission included the dynamics of family life, peer pressures in adolescence, and the influence of athletics in modern society. The impact of television and how it interfaces with athletic pastimes was highlighted. Children, it pointed out, are influenced by their parents' viewing habits, reactions to television content, and attitudes toward the use of television generally. Ways in which athletics are covered on television become incorporated into family viewing habits with subsequent attitudinal trends. These, in turn, become normalized in society as a whole.

Increasingly, it is the sports with potentially troublesome imitative possibilities such as wrestling, boxing, football and hockey that receive the most attention:

> Athletics are a key part of developmental socialization in most societies. What many societies do not have is the extensive mass media involvement in this important socialization area...Football and hockey, and, to a lesser extent, boxing, are also the sports that young people, especially males, prefer to watch. It is certain they are receiving a heavy normative diet of the importance of winning and aggression, sometimes substituting violent tactics for skill and sportsmanship. It is less certain that they are receiving a substantial diet of prosocial content, which can have a powerful, positive effect.[40]

The Commission pointed out that athletics and the media presentation of athletics are intimately interwoven with peer-group processes and that these are often further reinforced through fictional programming. Frequently, peer processes amongst adolescents reinforce the influence of the media through films and popular music as well as television. Sometimes this influence shows up in extraordinarily rebellious tendencies toward parents and in social and dating patterns, particularly when heroes and role models, athletic and otherwise, resort to violence as a form of conflict resolution.

From the standpoint of individual responses to media consumption, the Commission found that selective perception is important where the impact of content is concerned, both for children and adults. This is partly because visual media, in particular, present far more information than an individual can absorb, especially at a single viewing. One result is that viewers tend to see what they want to see, to discover evidence that reinforces the view of the world that they already hold. Similarly, the beliefs that people hold can play a role in the television programs which they select to view and why. It may be for activation or arousal or for relaxation and diversion:

> Personality, lifestyle and life circumstances, motives for viewing, demographic factors and personal relationship variables seem to occur in complex clusters in relation to media effects. The important generalizations are not at all about specific effects across the population as a whole. Rather, the conclusion is that virtually all are affected, but in many, many different ways. The population-at-risk includes everyone. The research shows it is a fraud to promote the idea that only the mentally disordered and deviant are affected. That being the case, the permutations and combinations, including the dangerous ones, are endless.[41]

Industry and Policy

The Commission described the entire television industry in North America as being dominated by oligopolies, television advertisers, advertising agencies, networks and major production houses bonded together in a commercial straitjacket. In Canada, it said that the television industry was so tied to the American system that, if it were not for government regulation, it would disappear as a separate entity and that even with regulation the battle was being lost. Furthermore, American film and television industries automatically considered Canada to be part of the U.S. domestic market. In Canada, American programs and films attracted larger audiences and revenue. Trends in content tended, as a result, to be reflected in Canadian production in the effort to compete.

The news industries were also, it said, governed by economic imperatives and their own long-standing conventions. One of the most tenaciously held is that the news industries always know best and that critics should be viewed with suspicion as paving the way for political control over freedom of the press. Yet, the Commission pointed out, the economics of mass communications have drastically curtailed the notion of a competitive informational marketplace to which anyone can contribute his or her ideas and opinions. It was obvious by the mid 1970s that the number of news organizations in Canada was being significantly reduced through takeovers, mergers and the inability to survive.

The Commission noted that while censorship continued to be feared, there was little indication of self-regulation on the part of industry. Responsiveness to real problems and concerns simply was not happening. Ultimately, it pointed out, it was not a case of whether or not censorship should exist but of what kind and by whom it should be practiced. "Media content," said the Commission, "is already subjected to elaborate selection and explicit censorship by the media industries themselves, but any form of government involvement is characterized as evil."[42]

A major industry cop-out, it observed, was to advocate parental control as an approach to media violence effects:

> It is politically sly to distract attention by suggesting that the media would not wish to usurp the parents' role which, in large part they have already done, and to ignore the accumulated research evidence of a need for media content control at source. It is a fallacy that parents know best in relation to their children and television. Even if they wished to, it is extremely difficult for parents to equip themselves with the relevant information. In any case, parents confront insurmountable obstacles in attempting to control their children's media exposure, or the effects of the media on them.[43]

The LaMarsh Commission Conclusions

The Commission's conclusions, like those of many of its predecessors, were that the overwhelming weight of evidence indicates potential harm to society. While the total crime rate may increase or decrease marginally year by year, it said, violent crime had been consistently on the rise, and, though media violence is only one of many contributing factors, it was the largest single variable most amenable to rectification.

Certainly, media violence is not the sole cause of crime. However, it is one of the few that have been measured, even though the measurements may differ. Many people are becoming more indifferent to violence being perpetrated against others, as well as fearful of their own safety both at home and in the streets, parks and neighborhoods.[44]

While there seemed to be an increased awareness and conviction in many parts of society that media violence was a social menace and as such ought to be dealt with, the Commission said, entertainment television spokesmen entered no defense on either moral or ethical grounds. They argued instead, that competitively, to continue to make profits, they had no choice. They seemed to place profit above responsibility. Spokesmen for news and other print media argued that their job was to report news and public affairs, violent and nonviolent, or that in the case of books particularly, artistic freedom justified any seeming excesses. The Commission said:

Furthermore, the belief lingers that, in a democratic country, anyone can establish a newspaper or newsmagazine and contribute his own ideas and opinions to a competitive informational marketplace. However, in practice, the economics of mass communications have drastically curtailed such opportunities, and have steadily reduced the number of news organizations in Canada. The few that do survive wield enormous power in shaping our understanding of the world. Nevertheless, there is only weak recognition of any societal role or accountability for the news media that is not defined entirely by news people themselves.[45]

A constantly increasing flow of violence on U.S. networks and Canadian private networks and stations was observed although it noted that the publicly-owned Canadian Broadcasting Corporation (CBC) had a better record. This general trend, said the Commission, was a result of placing profit above social responsibility and stressed that any other industry proven to be, or even suspected of, putting profits ahead of the public good is challenged by governments or by the public and brought to account. This simply was not happening in the communications industry.

Another observation made was that, once television appropriated much of the entertainment market, a kind of escalation of violence occurred in which the main media components such as films, radio, and comic books fed on one another to keep the cycle going. At the same time, television had developed a special status in the media industry. It was in the home for all ages to watch. Therefore it had written its own rules and enforced them through network standards offices that determine what is aired.

The LaMarsh Commission Recommendations
Essentially, the conviction behind the Commission's recommendations was that the weight of both scientific research and public attitudes represented a widely based call for sweeping changes throughout the entire communications industry.

Also, that it was necessary for industry to become more responsible as well as responsive to the long-term public interest.

It's approach was considered to be one in which "the Canadian tradition of freedom of expression and creativity in the Communications industry," would be reinforced but at the same time "a wider freedom of choice for the public" was demanded:[46]

> Freedom with accountability is the hallmark of democracy. Freedom with responsibility should not be an impossible goal. We believe from our two years of work that true media responsibility and accountability can lead to a higher level of freedom for all, the public as well as the media masters, although, so far, only the public appears to accept that idea 100 percent.[47]

The Commission concluded that to achieve these goals it was necessary for its recommendations to go far beyond the product to the way in which it is actually produced. Furthermore, this was necessary, not only in media for entertainment purposes but in the practice of journalism as well.

Within the total set of 87 recommendations the Commission first called for a massive overhaul of the entire communications industry in the country. In the interim, before such a massive undertaking could be accomplished, it envisaged the CRTC assuming a more active role in monitoring the television industry's adherence to self-imposed codes on violence as a condition for their license renewals. Second, it recommended a number of legislative changes and financial incentives for better programming. Third, it spelled out potential initiatives to raise public awareness, provide better education on media, scholarly research on the impact and effects of the mass media, and more parental involvement.

A New System

The Commission adopted the position that, by diminishing the exploitation of violence, the communications industry would more accurately reflect the quality of life to which most Canadians aspire. It also identified at the outset the chronic problem which has beset the Canadian component of the communications industry at large:

> The public perceives television to be the major area of concern. This is so partly because Canada's broadcasting system—closely modeled on that of the United States in programming style—has chosen in content as well to be, at best, imitative of the U.S. system and, at worst, identical. Especially on private television, many time slots are filled with U.S. programs, often violent. They can be bought much more cheaply than the best programs that can be produced in Canada. The way of least resistance has been to allow them to dominate Canadian private television and, to a lesser extent, the publicly owned CBC. By abdicating responsibility for so much of each program day, our broadcasting networks, CBC as well as private, have failed to provide the kind of service that fosters Canadian cultural values on a national scale.[48]

Because of this failure the Commission called for a general inquiry into the future of Canadian Broadcasting and pointed to emerging models in Europe. In these models it was observed that government financial assistance was given to films of merit produced primarily for domestic audiences. Those who chose to produce films "of little merit, usually exploiting sex and/or violence and horror" were left to find their own financing.[49]

A new, radically altered national television system, more sensitive to the needs of the public with a reduction of depicted violence should, it said, involve placing all Canadian television programming under public control.[50] For U.S. and other imported programs it also advocated stricter control over violent content. For both cultural and identity purposes, the Commission called for a multichannel system with provincial and regional input including public representation and a full range of programs in both official languages with programs other than news produced by and purchased from independent producers.

Relevant subsidies should, it said, be gradually phased out so that annual user fees and advertising revenues would finance the system:

The cost would be shifted from the taxpayer to the individual user at an acceptable rate that would provide a vastly diversified, more Canadian service in which antisocial content, including violence, would have to meet stringent standards of relevance to plot or story lines, or not be shown.[51]

All television delivery systems should, the Commission said, be combined under a corporation of mixed public and private ownership, for distribution purposes, with 25 percent of the company's board of directors representing the CBC.[52] Furthermore, the programming arm of such a new television structure should be completely independent and answerable only to Parliament.[53]

In order to decentralize control in such a system and make it more responsive to real social imperatives it recommended regional councils of volunteer listeners and viewers for each official language made up of nominees from interested groups. Each regional council, in turn, would be represented on the national system's board of directors.[54] If the federal government failed to act, it recommended that the province of Ontario formulate a new regional autonomy and negotiate with other provinces for the purpose of establishing a system of coordinated provincial networks.[55]

In the view of the Commission, required CRTC monitoring of program content for violence and other antisocial acts, as part of its procedure for issuing or renewing licences for use of the publicly owned airwaves, was perfectly logical:

The CRTC already exercises total control over engineering matters, but only limited control over content. Can technical and engineering problems really be held to be of greater public importance than the material transmitted, when available knowledge indicates that some material is damaging to the public good? For example, if a television station regularly screens 40 murders a month in entertainment prime time, let the CRTC require it to justify such programming in terms of the public interest in which its license was issued.[56]

It also said the CRTC should:

> ...rigorously enforce adherence by cable-television licensees to their obligations to provide community access to their program channels to those who wish access; and to provide facilities and production staff to assist members of the public who wish to present their own programs on such channels.[57]

Legislation

The Commission recommended that the framework for a new system of communications management be covered in a new Broadcasting Act in which the primary purpose of Canadian television would be redefined as an independent service in the "enlightened public interest" with an aim to provide a better balance in all program categories.[58] A national Freedom of Expression Act embedded in the Constitution that would define the limits of free expression was also recommended with definitions that would include:

> ...libel, obscenity, breach of the Official Secrets Act, matters affecting the defense of Canada, treason, sedition, or promulgating information that leads to incitement of crime or violence.[59]

Such an act would take precedence over existing provincial and federal statutes.

To ensure adequate protection for both the public and the communications industry, the Commission recommended the institution of a national media council headed by a media ombudsman. This person would receive and act upon complaints regarding contravention of the Freedom of Expression Act and protect freedom of expression from attack. It envisaged such a council being set up on the basis of procedural recommendations stemming from a national conference of organizations concerned with the quality of Canadian life.

Especially, said the Commission, "those that do not feel the mass media are properly filling their real or implied mandate to contribute constructively to the Canadian social environment."[60] The council and its head would be mandated to write and enforce a code of ethics. It would also be funded by, and be responsible to, Parliament. The ombudsman, it said, should be an outstanding Canadian, ideally with a judicial background but, in any event, someone with a reputation for fairness and responsiveness. The Council would be expected to publish its judgements as a form of accumulating jurisprudence on media practices and would be "...empowered to receive complaints about all media, including films, song lyrics on records and as broadcast by radio, comic books, and media coverage of live theatre and concerts."[61]

The complaints procedure, the Commission said, should be cost-free to the complainant and set up on a nation-wide basis. In the event that the federal government failed to act on this matter, it recommended that the provinces take steps to appoint statutory provincial press councils and media ombudsmen.

It also recommended an industry-wide ban on advertising in all television programs for children as was already the case on the CBC and TVOntario[62] and the use of existing technology such as blocking devices,[63] to help parents achieve more effective guidance and control over what their children watch. The latter should, the Commission said, be required by law to be standard on all Canadian television sets sold after a certain date.

Financial Incentives

The Commission found that financial aid to the film industry in Canada was badly uncoordinated. Furthermore,

> As far as can be learned, artistic merit takes a distant second place in Canada to the simple question: will it sell? This to-hell-with-quality bent of the Canadian Film Development Corporation has resulted in the production of some commercially successful trash, some not commercially successful, but only rarely and almost by accident has it brought about a product of real merit in Canadian or any other terms.[64]

The Commission also recommended the establishment of an organization responsible to Parliament for policy and budget that would incorporate existing film institutions such as the National Film Board (NFB) and existing archives and libraries.[65] Recommendations 35 and 36 were particularly significant from the standpoint of government assistance for the production of prosocial media entertainment:

> The Commission recommends a strong policy in Film Canada of financing worthwhile films—not including those that exploit violence, horror, and sex—from the idea level through to final editing, including grants for script-writing, travel and research, toward making usable products for both cinemas and television. This financing would be by way of a flexible, selective system including grants, loans and guarantees, and assistance in the promotion, distribution and exhibition of the film product. The Commission recommends that the wholly controlled production arm of Film Canada (the National Film Board) leave adult feature films to private production companies that are bound to flourish under such a liberalized support policy, and concentrate on documentaries, shorts, children's films and animation, for both cinema use and television.[66]

To serve both Canadian official languages and the adaptation of foreign films, it recommended that such an entity include a dubbing and subtitling post-production facility as well as a distribution facility to offset the control of distribution in Canada of self-interested subsidiaries of U.S. film production houses.[67] These, themselves, it was observed, were controlled by U.S. conglomerates.

Research, Education, and Public Awareness

At the university level, the Commission recommended more research on the nature and effects of mass media, including journalism, in Canadian culture and that this scholarship take place in all provinces.[68] Within departments of education it encouraged the provision of professional development opportunities for journalists such as those available to teachers.[69]

Also, it said that journalists in both print and other media such as radio and television should familiarize themselves with current social science research on the impact of the media. Such familiarity should include what is known about the potential impact on social behavior from the depiction of violence, and measures should be taken to guard against "promulgating material injurious to the physical or mental health of the public."[70] This would include, said the Commission

> ...consideration of the impact of print or broadcast news on violent events in which the media are used by the perpetrators of violence to further their own ends. Regular non-crisis liaison between media and police forces for information purposes and possible action might obviate situations where police feel that media activities exacerbate already difficult situations. Police forces, on their part, should designate high-level officers to supply accurate information during and after such action.[71]

For children, news reports or summaries specifically directed to their needs were recommended.[72]

Public and high school courses on mass media, to promote media literacy at all school levels—public and highschool, university and extension—were recommended:

> Our intent is not that these be professionally oriented courses, but that they be designed to promote better understanding of individual media biases, political and commercial, and to enhance public ability to digest the media diet—for instance, to do so without accepting as truth everything they see, hear or read.[73]

Noting that TVOntario excelled in nonviolent programming, the Commission recommended that the Ontario government expand its services to become province-wide to include outlying production facilities so that input from all communities, particularly the Far North, could be more readily incorporated.[74]

Regarding sports violence and its effects on viewers of all ages, such as in televised hockey games, a policy of covering a violent incident on-air only as it happened was recommended,

> ...but that in situations seen by the director as being excessively violent, on-air shots be selected that do not cover the violence directly, using the delay before a normal replay to decide how much of the actuality should be shown.[75]

On the subject of classification the Commission recommended that, through the Ontario Institute for Studies in Education, the Ontario Government set up a panel which would include a group of expert consultants such as child psychologists, juvenile court judges, teachers, parents and other representative groups concerned with the quality of family life. Such a panel would devise a classification system,

> ...to determine the suitability of television programs for children's viewing and set up an advisory system to assist parents and other viewers...voice-over, subtitled warnings before some explicit scenes, or flashing symbols or lights used throughout some adult programs shown when children might be watching...an on-screen host who introduces and explains material that may prove offensive or harmful. The Commissioners envision standardization of such advisories so that they could also be published by use of a simple code: perhaps classified 4-V for most violent, graded down to 1-V for minimum violence.[76]

Such a system, it said, should be adopted by the CRTC which in turn should require implementation by all licensees through regular monitoring.[77]

At the same time, it also recommended that adult film cuts through the existing government supported Ontario Film Review Board[78] be abolished and that classification categories be developed on the basis of appropriateness for different age levels of children and youth. The Commission recommended that a small professional group be assisted by rotating panels of interested volunteers from throughout the province and, as necessary, be assisted by expert consultants. On the whole, however, it preferred that a national classification system be developed. This could be done:

> ...either by a Canadian classification office or by consultation between classification officers from province to province, with a view to providing a national standard that also would apply to films shown on television and on Canadian airlines.[79]

In Ontario the Commission recommended that films be classified on the basis of their themes:

> ...especially in regard to antisocial content. One category, open to anyone, should present sex only within the terms of a loving relationship; violence only when demonstrably in the service of maintaining law and order; with right and wrong clearly defined and the broadly practiced social mores unchallenged. A second category, open to anyone above age 12, should allow social themes beyond the normal comprehension of children, but should portray sex outside the context of loving relationships only as a secondary theme. In this category, explicit sex should be seen only in the confines of loving interaction; violence should never be preferred as a problem-solving choice; clear definitions of right and wrong should be offered.

> The third category, for those 18 and over, should be specifically adult in concept, counting on the ability of adults to distinguish between right and wrong, perhaps challenging social, sexual and violence mores, but never in a gratuitous, excessive way unrelated to the needs of the film. In this category

there would be no restriction of admissions for anyone 18 or over. All film classifying would be subject to an appeal procedure by the producer or distributor.[80]

In order to facilitate the protection of children, said the Commission, enforcement of the spirit of classification should occur through regular checks on movie audiences in theatres.[81] Classification should also be required in all promotional material. Similarly, television scheduling of films in prime time should reflect the Film Classification Board's age code.[82] In addition, in-flight movies for airlines needed to be screened to insure their suitability for children as passengers[83] and finally, the Commission said that the Ontario government should require screening of textbooks for schools for content that does psychological violence or provides violent role models for children.[84]

It said all levels of government had a responsibility to promote public understanding of the findings of scientific research regarding the effects of media content and should aim to make the public more critical and selective in its media consumption.[85] It envisaged, for example, the inclusion of promotional material in federal government mailings of Family Allowances and pensions, and in similar provincial and municipal mailings. Because of the seriousness of the subject, the Commission recommended that,

> ...a government-supported mass media publicity and advertising campaign be established, similar to those already conducted for such issues as the status of women, construction safety, alcohol abuse, and tobacco addiction.[86]

The Role of Parents

The Commission recognized that it is a deeply sought goal of most parents to influence the moral as well as physical development of their children, but that this has become increasingly difficult:

> ...this need is deepened by the eroded influence of the church and school on today's youngsters. The Commissioners also understand that it is impracticable for parents to monitor every moment of their children's media intake. Media spokesmen who insist that parents are totally responsible for what their children see or hear are simply avoiding their own role in today's unsatisfactory media diet.

The recommendations recognized, however, that parents have some part to play and that many are eager to do so. They were a response to the cries for help heard from people and were meant to assist them in exercising their responsibility.[87]

They stressed the need for parents to take an active role in regulating their children's viewing habits and to acquaint themselves with the choices their children were making:

> Research makes it clear that parents can lessen the potentially harmful impact of the media, especially television, by pointing out those themes, ideas or actions that violate the family's own standards. Parents should:

- Wherever possible, treat television as a shared activity in which the adult provides guidance and safety (in much the same way responsible mothers and fathers insist on accompanying their small children through dangerous traffic).

- At the very least, make sure they know what their children are watching by sampling programs seen regularly by the child (sitcoms, action and police dramas, sporting events).

- Discuss selections with the children so they understand parental approval or disapproval of a program's content.

- Understand and be guided by advisory or classification systems as these are instituted.

- Give serious attention to the number of hours and overall quality of their children's television consumption. The purpose of parental supervision of television is to guarantee each child a balanced life and the development of a wholesome value system incorporating reading, playing and creativity, as well as the ingestion of television.[88]

The Commission also said parents should insist that cinemas adhere to the law governing admission of children to view films classified as restricted or requiring adult accompaniment.[89] Finally, the Commission recommended that all relevant supporting material be deposited within a degree-granting institution in Ontario with an aim to serve the community, scholars and the media themselves.[90]

Essentially, it perceived its work as only a beginning in the process of providing public education on the effects of the media and their possible harm. The Commission said that its report offered an opportunity for members of the public to make up their own minds about what they wanted from the media and how they could get what they wanted.

The Commission made its recommendations on the basis of a wide and diverse range of responses. It said:

Perhaps it was natural that the people—the public—seemed to have the firmest ideas of what was harmful and what was not. They seemed to realize instinctively, at least to their own satisfaction, that a steady diet of violence in the so-called action programs on television, explicitly violent films, graphic details of murders and shootings and rapes and beatings in the news could not possibly make them better human beings or cause anything but harm to the ethical structure to which they aspire in their lives and those of their children.

Scientists in psychology, sociology and other social disciplines are generally more cautious in that they tend to present their findings as indications rather than hard facts; but the scientific trend toward a general belief in the harmful effects of depicted violence runs in the same direction as the more simplistic judgments of the public at large.[91]

Frequently, the Commission noted, the debate involved accusations of overreaction and unwarranted concern regarding the subject of violence within the communications industry with the controversy continually reinforced by the media themselves:

> Among both scientists and laymen, there are those who oppose the prevailing currents—individuals who argue that they've been watching or reading or hearing violence all their lives without ever going out and committing rape or murder or even pushing somebody at a bus stop; and there are scientists who argue that so many factors bear on public behavior (joblessness, economic deprivation, stress, oppression by other non-media conditions), that to assign major blame to the media is insupportable.

> Keeping up a running commentary on both conditions are the masters of the media themselves. Those who publish newspapers and magazines habitually invoke their traditional roles of holding up a mirror to life in which citizens may see themselves, and a window through which the public may see the world. What they choose for their mirror-window is characteristically more violent than the true real-life mix, but they parry any suggested change for the public good with the old saw that such action would be merely shooting the messenger.[92]

Claims were frequently made by members of the industry that, for the most part, television audience ratings and film box-office returns indicated that people were getting what they wanted. Nevertheless, the Commission said that at least some defensiveness on the part of those in the entertainment industries was called into question by the fact that, from time to time, with great fanfare, announcements would be made involving initiatives to de-emphasize violence in future programming.[93]

The Commission's inquiry and analysis of the data it collected, both on the basis of previous studies conducted and 28 additional ones they initiated to fill in perceived gaps in the existing literature, was a substantial addition to the existing body of knowledge on the issue of media violence, particularly in Canada.

In retrospect, it has been argued that some of their recommendations were extraordinarily ambitious if not somewhat unrealistic but that many continue to reflect a keen sense of future needs and directions in the communications industry. Some of its recommendations have been implemented but most have been ignored. Some are now dated and do not address the latest manifestations of communications technology such as the Internet.

Nevertheless, there was a sincere effort to investigate the issue as thoroughly and responsibly as possible followed by recommendations made in the best and broadest public interest. Consequently, the Commission's findings are every bit as relevant today as they were when they were first released more than two decades ago. ·

Notes

1. Ontario, 1976, p.1.
2. Ontario, 1977, Vol., p.4.
3. For full text of definitions see the Preface in Ontario, 1977.
4. This and subsequent quotations from Bill Davis are derived from a personal interview for this study on December 15, 1992.
5. This and subsequent quotations from Ken Marchant that are not specifically indicated as being derived from text were derived from a personal interview on September 8, 1993.
6. This and subsequent quotations from Roy McMurtry were derived from a personal interview on December 19, 1992.
7. This and subsequent quotations from Lucien Beaulieu which do not include a specific reference to text were derived from a personal interview on November 26, 1992.
8. This and subsequent quotations from Scott Young were derived from a personal interview on September 1, 1993.
9. This and subsequent quotations from Sheila Kieran that do not include a specific reference to text were derived from a personal interview on August 30, 1993.
10. Ontario, 1977, Vol. 1, p.4.
11. Ontario, 1977, Vol. 1, p. 374.
12. Ontario, 1977, Vol. 1, p.8.
13. Ontario, 1977, Vol. 1, p.8.
14. Ontario, 1977, Vol. 1, p.9.
15. Ontario, 1977, Vol. 1, p.10.
16. Ontario, 1977, Vol. 1, p. 7-8.
17. Ontario, 1977, Vol. 1, p.2.
18. Ontario, 1977, Vol. 1, p.2.
19. Sauvageau et al., 1992, p. 4-5.
20. For a detailed synopsis of the 28 studies undertaken by the LaMarsh Commission and a description of additional participants see Appendix A.
21. Ontario, 1977, Vol. 1, p.22.
22. Ontario, 1977, Vol. 1, p.23.
23. Ontario, 1077, Vol. 1, p.33.
24. Ontario, 1977, Vol. 1, p. 23.
25. Ontario, 1977, Vol. 1, p. 28.
26. Ontario, 1977, Vol. 1, p.24.
27. Ontario, 1977, Vol. 1, p.24.
28. Ontario, 1977, Vol. 1, p.24.
29. Ontario, 1977, Vol. 1, p. 26.
30. Ontario, 1977, Vol. 1, p. 23-4.
31. Ontario, 1977, Vol. 1, p. 25.
32. Ontario, 1977, Vol. 1, p. 25.
33. Ontario, 1977, Vol. 1, p. 25-6.
34. Ontario, 1977, Vol. 1, p.26.
35. Ontario, 1977, Vol. 1, p. 26.
36. Ontario, 1977, Vol. 1, p. 26.
37. Ontario, 1977, Vol. 1, p. 26.
38. Ontario, 1977, Vol. 1, p. 28.
39. Angus & Jhally, 1989; Barthes, 1973; Ellul, 1987; Gramsci, 1971; Nelson, 1988.
40. Ontario, 1977, Vol. 1, p. 28.
41. Ontario, 1977, Vol. 1, p. 28.
42. Ontario, 1977, Vol. 1, p. 29.
43. Ontario, 1977, Vol. 1, p. 30.

44. Ontario, 1977, Vol. 1, p. 50.

45. Ontario, 1977, Vol. 1, p.29.

46. Ontario, 1977, Vol. 1, p. 54.

47. Ontario, 1977, Vol. 1, p. 54.

48. Ontario, 1977, Vol. 1, Rec. No. 1, p. 55.

49. Ontario, 1977, Vol. 1, Rec. No. 24, p. 59.

50. Ontario, 1977, Vol. 1, Rec. No. 3, p. 55.

51. Ontario, 1977, Vol. 1, Rec. No. 4, p. 56.

52. Ontario, 1977, Vol. 1, Rec. No. 5, p. 56.

53. Ontario, 1977, Vol. 1, Rec. No. 6, p. 56.

54. Ontario, 1977, Vol. 1, Rec. No. 9, p. 56.

55. Ontario, 1977, Vol. 1, Rec. No. 14, p. 57.

56. Ontario, 1977, Vol. 1, Rec. No. 12, p. 57.

57. Ontario, 1977, Vol. 1, Rec. No. 23, p. 28.

58. Ontario, 1977, Vol. 1, Rec. No. 10, p. 56.

59. Ontario, 1977, Vol. 1, Rec. No. 44, p. 61.

60. Ontario, 1977, Vol. 1, Rec. No. 47, p. 61.

61. Ontario, 1977, Vol. 1, Rec. No. 55, p. 62.

62. Ontario, 1977, Vol. 1, Rec. No. 18, p. 57.

63. Ontario, 1977, Vol. 1, Rec. No. 19, p. 58.

64. Ontario, 1977, Vol. 1, Rec. No. 24, p. 58.

65. Ontario, 1977, Vol. 1, Rec. Nos. 24, 25, 26, p. 58-9.

66. Ontario, 1977, Vol. 1, Rec. Nos. 35 & 36. p. 60.

67. Ontario, 1977, Vol. 1, Rec. No. 37, p. 60.

68. Ontario, 1977, Vol. 1, Rec. No. 59, p. 62.

69. Ontario, 1977, Vol. 1, Rec. No. 60, 61, p. 62.

70. Ontario, 1977, Vol. 1, Rec. No. 62, p. 62.

71. Ontario, 1977, Vol. 1, Rec. No. 62, p. 62.

72. Ontario, 1977, Vol. 1, Rec. No. 64.

73. Ontario, 1977, Vol. 1, Rec. No. 65, p. 63.

74. Ontario, 1977, Vol. 1, Rec. No. 67, p. 68.

75. Ontario, 1977, Vol. 1, Rec. No. 66, p. 63.

76. Ontario, 1977, Vol. 1, Rec. No. 16, p. 57.

77. Ontario, 1977, Vol. 1, Rec. No. 17, p. 57.

78. This board's name has since been changed to the Ontario Film Review Board (OFRB).

79. Ontario, 1977, Vol. 1, Rec. No. 70, p. 64.

80. Ontario, 1977, Vol. 1, Rec. 71, p. 64.

81. Ontario, 1977, Vol. 1, Rec. No. 72, p. 64.

82. Ontario, 1977, Vol. 1, Rec. 73, p. 64.

83. Ontario, 1977, Vol. 1, Rec. No. 77, p. 64.

84. Ontario, 1977, Vol. 1, Rec. No. 76, p. 64.

85. Ontario, 1977, Vol. 1, Rec. No. 80, p. 64.

86. Ontario, 1977, Vol. 1, Rec. No. 81, p. 65.

87. Ontario, 1977, Vol. 1, Rec. No. 65, p. 65.

88. Ontario, 1977, Vol. 1, Rec. No. 83, p. 65.

89. Ontario, 1977, Vol. 1, Rec. No. 85, p. 65.

90. Ontario, 1977, Vol. 1, Rec. No. 87, p. 66.

91. Ontario, 1977, Vol. 1, p. 3.

92. Ontario, 1977, Vol. 1, p. 3.

93. Ontario, 1977, Vol. 1, p. 3.

Chapter 4

DEVELOPMENTS SINCE THE LAMARSH COMMISSION

WHERE THEY HAVE OCCURRED at all, public initiatives in response to various recommendations from the LaMarsh Report have been sporadic. Comments about the impact of the LaMarsh Report, from those closely involved in the initiation of the Commission and its work, have predominantly been ones of disappointment. According to Bill Davis the censorship issue is still a thorny one. Only at this critical juncture in our human history, as a result of more technology, the problems have been compounded. "Consequently," he said, "the Commission's findings are as relevant now as they were when they were first published in 1977."

Roy McMurtry also expressed disappointment in the lack of social pressure for change and said,

> The Report should have created a greater level of public concern in the same way that concern has risen over senseless death on highways from alcohol abuse...on the whole, governments in the western world have been frightened to death of being accused of being censors and have tended to bury their heads in the sand on this issue.

He referred to violence among young people, partly due to the numbing effect of violence as entertainment and partly to the way in which authority figures such as policemen are undermined. "Youth," he said, "has been desensitized and the violence they have been encouraged to act out has led to real tragedy. Often they are surprised over the consequences of their actions which demonstrates a kind of reality distortion."

The Commission defined censorship as "interference from government in the creative expression of thoughts, words, and pictures in a free marketplace of ideas." However, the Commission rejected the idea that violence in the media should be either protected or encouraged as a form of creative expression.

Unfortunately, since the LaMarsh Report has entered the public domain for discussion, it has not generated much meaningful debate on distinctions between reasonable limits as these might apply to a balance between freedom of expression and public safety through responsible regulation. Any attempts that the Commission made in differentiating between freedom of expression and freedom of enterprise for media industries have been largely ignored. In general, when they are referred to at all, research findings are taken out of context, described as inconclusive, and combined with the argument that the media are being unfairly blamed.

Artistic merit remains sacrosanct and social costs are of secondary importance. Whenever they are acknowledged at all, the perceived solution is still more 'education' and parental supervision of children. The notion that education should include reexamining the meaning of censorship, itself, is usually brushed off as the intolerant concern of right wing religious fundamentalists. *Any* restriction on media production is still regarded as censorship. "The slippery slope" argument frequently surfaces on the basis that if one restriction is imposed we run the risk of "opening the door for gestapo-like book burning scenes." The slippery slope on the other side of the mountain toward unimpeded cultural degradation and erosion of moral infrastructure is ignored.

These prevailing attitudes continue to be reinforced on a regular basis in the mainstream press, along with occasional reports on harmful effects, but whenever the focus involves analysis the only solution ever seriously considered is the responsibility of parents in monitoring their children's media habits. Another popular argument is that the nature of the current information-based economy makes it impossible to do anything at all.

This running commentary creates the illusion of balance in mainstream coverage on the issue of media violence while carefully derailing the possibility of public consensus on the need to get on with policy and implementation of recommendations from the LaMarsh and subsequent Reports. In the process, the way is paved for "business as usual." Since the highschool shootings in Littleton, Colorado and Taber, Alberta, one rare departure from this norm appeared in *The Toronto Star*. On June 6, 1999, Greg Quill wrote an article on "Driving up the cost of violence." In this case, coverage focused on how civil courts and insurance rates are now poised to do what legislators and educators haven't been able to change in popular culture.

Looking back over the passage of time, former LaMarsh Commissioner Lucien Beaulieu has commented on the continuing tendency in the media to report on media violence as something that parents should exercise more vigilance over in their children's viewing habits. He said, "How can we possibly say, well that's the responsibility of parents? What chance do they have given the odds that they are up against?" Indeed, the public mood, fostered by Conservative governments in the country bent on introducing boot camps for young offenders has now embraced a new tactic: suing the parents for their children's misdemeanors.[1]

The LaMarsh Commission Report, in his view, remains of value, despite the fact that it was released almost twenty years ago.

If society at large, the communications industry and government at all levels, are really serious about addressing the problem another Report should not be required. What is needed is a more realistic and intensive approach. Besides, it should not necessarily be up to anyone to demonstrate harmful effects. It should be required of the industry to demonstrate that *they* do not stimulate and produce harmful effects from their productions. Frankly, I find it incredible that so little has been done since the Report was released; perhaps it was ahead of its time but it was a good analysis of the subject and a tremendously important piece of work when it was released. It remains so.

On the whole, there have been some indications that Beaulieu's position is becoming more popular. In the July, 1996, issue of *Vanity Fair* it was reported that America's most successful lawyer turned novelist, John Grisham, was holding Oliver Stone accountable for a series of copycat killings which included a friend of his. Stone's film, *Natural Born Killers*. Grisham suggested legal remedy in which films are regarded as "something created and brought to market, not too dissimilar from breast implants."[2] If a problem occurs with the design and injury ensues from a defect, says Grisham, then its manufacturers should be held responsible.

The author of the article, Michael Shnayerson, pointed out that, as a mass-market filmmaker, Stone communicates with a large, often poorly educated audience that may take his screen violence literally and not see a "moral order turned upside down." He concluded that "Stone knows an artist has to stand against outside censorship of any kind. He just doesn't yet see that artists have to be accountable too."[3] Stone, in turn, argued that Grisham himself has become a very rich man as a result of a body of work which utilizes violent crime as a foundation for mass entertainment, pointing to his book, *A Time to Kill*, which was turned into a major motion picture.

While both artists could, no doubt, benefit from reflection on appropriate boundaries for self-censorship practiced by artists for centuries as an intrinsic component of their work, there have been subsequent initiatives consistent with Grisham's proposal. In March, 1999, a landmark decision from the Louisiana Supreme Court permitted a lawsuit to proceed against Oliver Stone and Time Warner Inc. for crimes attributed to the film *Natural Born Killers* paving the way for others like it. Several weeks later, the parents of children who were victims of a highschool shooting in Kentucky, in 1997, launched a $130 million product liability case against 25 media companies including Time Warner and the makers of the film *The Basketball Diaries*, which included teenage idol Leonardo DiCaprio as the perpetrator of a highschool shooting spree.

Jack Thompson, the lawyer acting for the parents, argues that the First Amendment protection for freedom of speech does not apply in this case because there is no government involved here. He said, "This is a civil dispute between private entities who want to fight it out in court" and compares the lawsuit to others filed against car companies for allegedly making defective vehicles.[4] In response to arguments that these kinds of cases have not stood up in court in the past, he refers to focus groups routinely used by companies to determine plot twists and emotional responses as evidence useful to his own case.

When Sheila Kieran was asked if she thought the work of the LaMarsh Commission has had much impact, she said unfortunately not.

> Whenever I hear of other government reports being released, as soon as I discover that the LaMarsh Report has not even been considered or acknowledged I tend to dismiss them as just smoke and mirrors with governments attempting to be seen as actually doing something useful. I am appalled at the extent to which the Commission's Report has been ignored.

Ken Marchant, in looking back over the recommendations, said one might disagree with the specifics but "they show a considerable degree of media sophistication and anticipated a number of things that have been done since, such as inquiries on the restructuring of the broadcast industry as well as specialty channels." He added, however, that some of the recommendations may have been too idealistic and utopian to begin with because of "extremely powerful forces whose commercial interests would be compromised if they showed less violence."

The LaMarsh Center

In terms of outcomes, the most obvious and immediate course of action was the establishment of the LaMarsh Research Center on Violence and Conflict Resolution, at York University in the Greater Toronto Area, known as the LaMarsh Center.[5] This was an outgrowth from recommendations in the Report that research into mass media effects in Canadian universities be expanded, and that the research begun by the Commission, its library, relevant supporting material, public briefs, and surveys, be deposited within a degree-granting Ontario institution with accessibility provided for the community, scholars, and the media.

In 1980, the LaMarsh Center was set up at York University with funding provided by the Ontario Government and the University itself. Both the provincial government and the University made a decision to contribute $100,000 each.[6] Since then the program has operated by using the annual interest which amounts to about $20,000. Over the years, assistance has also been provided by the Faculty of Arts, the Faculty of Graduate Studies and individual faculty members' research grants. From the beginning the initiative has been interdisciplinary.[7]

Although part of the initial purpose in setting up the program was to house the archival material collected by the Commission for further research purposes, according to former director Michael Smith, the Center had disposed of most of the material because of "lack of interest." In 1992, Ellis, one of the founding members who continues to assist with the direction of the LaMarsh Center, said that it was hoped that more research on the subject of popular culture "in general" would get underway soon. In the Center's annual reports for both 1991 and 1996 it was pointed out that the general objective always has been, and continues to be, to encourage, support, and facilitate the systematic development of theory and research on violence and conflict in a broadly defined way.

Wendy Josephson, a psychologist from the University of Winnipeg, became the first visiting fellow in 1988-9 and participated in a joint project with executive member and associate professor of psychology at York University, James Check. Together they revised a set of conflict tactic scales that were described as "a widely used measure of family violence."[8]

Information pamphlets on the Center boast that, on the basis of some 40 external research grants, contracts, and fellowships totaling more than $2 million, by 1996 its "core" members had produced over 200 books, book chapters, journal articles and reports "dealing wholly or partly with violence or conflict resolution." The education of graduate students continues to be emphasized as an important objective in the program. In 1994, Debra Pepler, Associate Professor in the Department of Psychology, replaced Desmond Ellis as director and by 1996 graduate students were being provided with office space, resources, and employment as research assistants on various LaMarsh projects. However, there was still very little evidence of serious attention, in a systematic way, to the work the LaMarsh Commission Report initiated.

Justification for the Center being upgraded to organized research unit status in 1991 was that scholarly interest in, and social concern about, violence and conflict had mushroomed in the preceding ten years, both nationally and internationally:

> At least five new journals on violence have appeared since 1986 (*Journal of Family Violence, Journal of Interpersonal Violence, Violence and Victims, International Review of Victimology,* and *Sexual Coercion and Assault*). None of these journals emanates from Canada, but Canadian scholars, including LaMarsh members, contribute to them. Several research units at other Canadian universities focus to some degree on violence (e.g., The Center for Criminological Research at the University of Alberta, University of Toronto's Center for Criminology), but LaMarsh has taken the lead in this field and is, in fact, the only research unit in Canada devoted entirely to the study of violence and conflict. Given the considerable number of requests for LaMarsh Reports, queries about research on violence, etc., it appears that LaMarsh is filling a need.[9]

When she was first appointed director of the Center, Pepler identified two primary objectives for her term. One was to communicate research efforts more consistently and broadly within the community. The other was to develop within the Center a more active focus on research both within and beyond the University itself. Two study groups were formed for this purpose: one on school violence and the other on alternative dispute resolution with plans underway for introduction of a third group to consider sports violence.[10]

Research activity at the Center, in general, was increased by the establishment of the Michael Smith Resource Center which was officially opened on April, 1996, with the goal of providing accessibility to resources for both university faculty and students as well as to personnel from the community. An additional initiative included the creation of a new category of External Associates. These associates are intended to be people in various fields outside the university but with a common interest in some aspect of violence or conflict resolution.

All associates of the LaMarsh Center receive notification of meetings, seminars, workshops, and symposia and have access to the Michael Smith Resource Center. The opportunity for interaction with York faculty and graduate students is also perceived to be one of the benefits. Up until June, 1999, there was still evidence of only one notice featuring a prominent researcher on the issue of media violence. American Lieutenant Colonel, David Grossman, a psychologist and author of the best seller *On Killing: The Psychological Cost of Learning to Kill in War and Society*, makes links between socializing strategies in military training and the effects of violence in the media. He was scheduled to speak at the Center on October 30, 1998, but for inexplicable reasons failed to appear.

On the whole, Kieran is disappointed that the original mandate of the Center to extend the work begun by the Commission has been largely ignored. When he was interviewed in 1993 and still director of the Center, Desmond Ellis said he has always held the opinion that the mass media have a minimal effect on the manifestation of violence in real life. The paper he wrote in 1975, he said, was still his definitive position on the subject.

In it he criticized the LaMarsh Commission's mandate which would, he explained, direct attention (and resources) away from theoretically interesting and more socially significant areas of enquiry. Television violence, in his view, was a much less urgent problem and not a cost effective approach to the allocation of scarce societal resources. The unfortunate irony, of course, is that Ellis was, despite his views, appointed as the Center's first director for the purposes of extending the work of the LaMarsh Commission.

In Canada, similarly persistent views of denial are frequently amplified through the mass media by psychologist Jonathan Freedman at the University of Toronto. In the early 1990s they were used primarily as a counterpoint for debate on the seriousness of harmful effects from media violence. More recently, they have become the authoritative, last word on the subject.[11] Freedman's and Ellis' tendencies to trivialize studies showing links between media violence and real life violence have also been reinforced by Thelma McCormack, past Chair of Women's Studies, Department of Sociology, York University, and herself an early advisor to the LaMarsh Commission.

This was particularly evident in the early months of 1999 when Canadians Concerned About Violence in Entertainment (C-CAVE) issued news releases objecting to both circulation of the ultra violent book *American Psycho* in Canada, and production of a film based on it in Toronto. In news coverage which followed, McCormack and others argued with me that the plot structure based on a wall street stock broker clad in designer suits who stalked and killed women by night in a myriad of gruesome ways was actually sophisticated satirical commentary on the lifestyles of the 1980s.

In a lecture series at the McLuhan Institute at the University of Toronto in 1994, McCormack presented a paper arguing that the Canadian Radio-television and Telecommunications Commission (CRTC) approved code on television violence, which came into effect in January of that year, violated the rights of children for freedom of expression. She also argued that violence in the community was actually declining as children watched less and less television, overlooking their seduction by more engaging and potentially even more harmful forces of popular culture such as computer and video games.[12]

Research on Pornography

Although the LaMarsh Commission Report did not include any specific recommendations on the topic of pornography, it began to dominate public concerns and subsequent reactions, including LaMarsh Center research, soon after its release, particularly as violence became increasingly intertwined with sexual imagery. An example of scholarly activity on the subject of pornography and sexual aggression as a social learning theory analysis was jointly undertaken by James Check and Neil Malamuth from the University of California in Los Angeles.[13]

The purpose was to reconsider research literature from the United States Commission Report on Pornography and Obscenity released in 1970 and compare some of the findings with the views of feminist writers on the subject. Check and Malamuth argued that feminists did not, in fact, hold views opposed to American researcher Bandura's social learning theory developed in 1977[14] as it applied to the themes of aggression and domination. One year earlier, Check undertook a study, on the basis of a LaMarsh Center grant, in collaboration with Nelson Heapy of Huron College, University of Western Ontario and Oleh Iwanyshyn of the Canadian Broadcasting Corporation (CBC). It was a survey of Canadian standards regarding sexual content in the media. In it, the controversial 1970 U.S. Commission's "clean bill of health" for nonviolent pornography was endorsed.[15]

When it was first released, one of the LaMarsh Center reports that received considerable attention within the schools and among community groups, including C-CAVE, was a study undertaken by Check and LaCrosse in 1989. It dealt with the need for curriculum development research in the area of human sexuality and personal relationships. It also stressed the serious problems facing Canadian society as a result of pornography, rape myths, sexual coercion, and other forms of violence, with clear warnings for parents and teachers.

In the 1980s, Check was frequently called upon to appear as an expert witness for the Crown on obscenity charges and he has arguably helped to strengthen legal opinion on demonstrably justifiable limits to the fundamental freedoms allowed for in the *Charter of Rights and Freedoms*. An example involves a judgement from the Alberta Queen's Bench in Regina v. Wagner:

> He [Check] contended that both sexually violent pornography and degrading and dehumanizing pornography convey the message that women enjoy abusive and antisocial behavior. Men who are repeatedly exposed to such films become more sexually aggressive in their relations with women and more tolerant of such behavior in others. That leads to increased callousness towards women on a personal level and less receptiveness to their legitimate

claims for equality and respect. Dr. Check buttressed his opinion by references to sociological studies, research, and experiments that produced findings in support of his point of view.

This court was convinced by his testimony that social harm does result from repeated exposure to obscene films. That being the case, the Crown demonstrably justified the need for S. 159 and the reasonable limitations it places on freedom of expression.[16]

In a paper presented at a conference on male sexuality held at Humber College in Toronto in 1987, Check discussed this decision and how it helped to establish a new definition of what was considered obscene under Section 159(8) of the Criminal Code by paving the way for "better distinctions" between definitions of pornography and erotica. He pointed out that in a number of subsequent court decisions the production and distribution of violent and nonviolent dehumanizing pornography, or both, had become illegal in Canada, whereas erotica had not. Previous cases, he said, had been decided primarily on the level of sexual explicitness of the materials in question.

New Initiatives Elsewhere

Despite the cloud of discredit surrounding the LaMarsh Report's conclusions and recommendations reflected in the establishment of the LaMarsh Center itself, the Report helped to stimulate academic interest on the topic of media violence elsewhere in North America. There have been several significant developments since then. First, an acceleration in the number of studies undertaken on the subject of media in general; second, a diversification of approaches and methodologies; and third, a convergence of data which offers more scope for interdisciplinary assessment of issues.

Another development, observed by Withey and Abeles in 1980, was a temporary shift of emphasis away from "media violence" to "pornography" on the part of television and film producers, which led to a proliferation of both sexually explicit and violent themes. In 1980, in her book *Take Back the Night*, Laura Lederer discussed estimates from the California Department of Justice that the pornography industry in the United States alone had risen to $4 billion. By 1992, Naomi Wolf referred to the $7 billion pornography industry as just one of many that "have arisen from the capital made out of unconscious anxieties, and are, in turn, able, through their influence on mass culture, to use, stimulate, and reinforce the hallucination in a rising economic spiral."[17]

New Methodologies and Old Responses

By the mid 1980s important strides were made on longitudinal studies involving both laboratory and field methodology: acknowledged by the LaMarsh Commission as a weakness in their own inquiry because of its limited time frame. Although field studies had in the past been criticized for being too diffuse and difficult for the introduction of adequate controls, it was becoming generally accepted that they help to overcome some of the limitations in the laboratory experiment because of the use of more naturalistic settings.

In 1986 the *Journal of Social Issues* devoted an entire volume to the subject of media violence effects. One article by Turner, Hesse, & Peterson-Lewis gave an overview of naturalistic studies on the long term effects of television violence. Reference was made to conclusions that the balance of findings indicated that television produces a long term increase in the aggressive behavior of boys but not of girls. Building upon observations made by the LaMarsh Commission, the quasi-experimental designs of Leonard Berkowitz reported on in 1986, and Phillips and Hensley in 1984, provided evidence that media publicity through the news about naturally occurring violence can produce short term effects by stimulating more violent crime. It was also pointed out by Phillips & Hensley that depictions of punished aggression seems to lead to decreases, while depictions of rewarded aggression leads to increases in violent crime.

Observations similar to those of the LaMarsh Commission were made and reported on, in England by William Belson in 1978, and in the United States in 1986, following a five year longitudinal study done by Dorothy and Jerome Singer. In all of these studies it was observed that a heavy diet of television violence is associated with decreased self restraint and increased aggressive behavior as well as with distorted perceptions that the world is a dangerous place.

Similarly, an increasing number of scholars from a broad range of disciplines had found that the actual effects of television on beliefs and behaviors depend upon a number of variables, such as the families' viewing habits.[18] Young children are more likely to be exposed to television violence if their parents choose this material for their own viewing.[19] In his own review of the literature in 1991, George Comstock found that 95 percent of what children watch, in the first place, is programming developed for adults. In other words, what is produced and distributed for adults is also available to, and watched by, children and teenagers. Comstock also found evidence of a growing preference for entertainment media over news media.[20]

Other observations have been, and continue to be made, that when the effects of media on children are being studied it is important to consider the effects of news programming as well as those of entertainment programming. In fact, many scholars, including those associated with cultural studies, tend to make observations about the increasingly blurred distinctions between news and entertainment. This has led to use of the jargonistic word "infotainment" to describe these trends, in which a kind of audience voyeurism is perceived to characterize many public affairs programs.[21]

The word "edutainment" has also been coined to described the extent to which new, interactive, computer technology is blurring the distinction between traditional forms of education and entertainment. In *The Toronto Star*, for example, it was reported by Nicolaas VanRijn in 1993 that encyclopedias, "come alive with film clips and sound bites."[22] Nevertheless, VanRijn emphasized, "Games is where this medium excels. Viacom's *Dracula* and its series *Sherlock Holmes, Consulting Detective*, Virgin's *7th Guest*, and Compu-Teach's *Destination Mars!* are examples of the very best."[23]

In a landmark longitudinal study spanning a period of over 20 years and reported on in 1987, American psychologists Leonard Eron and Rowell Huesmann examined third-grade children at three different stages. They started with 875 subjects, interviewing 735 of these in 1972. In 1984 they interviewed 295 of the original subjects, along with a number of spouses and children. One of their conclusions was that criminal behavior in their sample of adults was related to the amount of television viewed while these adults were children and, where the males were concerned, to their preference for television violence while they were children. The nature of these crimes ranged from murder and sexual assault to vandalism and traffic violations, frequently the result of drug and alcohol abuse.

The seriousness of criminal convictions by the age of thirty was shown to be significantly related to television violence viewing habits in boys at the age of eight years, even after social stress and I.Q. were partialled out of the data: that is, removed as influencing factors. They were also able to demonstrate that the effects of television violence depend partly upon moderating variables such as academic performance, family viewing habits, socioeconomic status, and family patterns of punishment.

Eron, Dorothy and Jerome Singer, and Zuckerman are among those who have stressed, based on research reported on in the 1980s, that interventions directed at mitigating the effects of media violence on delinquency and criminality should focus on the pre-adolescent years. According to Eron, interventions which combine both cognitive and behavioral approaches have the most promise. However, he said, "a major difficulty facing all intervention programs is the intractability of aggression itself. Aggression is a problem-solving behavior learned early in life, usually learned well and therefore quite resistant to change."[24] In the 1980s parallel longitudinal studies were being done in five countries: Australia, Finland, Israel, Poland and the United States.[25] The American Psychological Association Task Force, which reported on these and other studies, confirmed that the associations between viewing and aggression occurred in most populations studied.[26]

Despite the development of more sophisticated research methodology and accumulating evidence of harmful effects, the variety of findings in the investigations still tend to be picked up by decision makers and industry programmers and quoted according to which finding supports their own particular view.[27] The tendency for this practice to fuel controversy rather than to clarify the issues has not changed over the years. At the same time, more recent assessments of the literature have confirmed the LaMarsh Report findings that, frequently, psychologists have focused too narrowly on arousal responses to stimulation which may or may not have much bearing on violent behavior responses, especially when desensitization is taken into account. It has also been observed by others, like the LaMarsh Commission, that a preoccupation with methodological constraints, with insufficient attention paid to social and natural settings, continues to obscure objectives.[28]

Surveys and Polls

As pointed out by Denis Howitt in 1983, public inquiries, sometimes based solely on random, unscientific opinion surveys of the population at large, have tended to retard the development of a coherent body of knowledge on the subject of media violence. The widely circulated results of these studies contend that television violence has neither harmful nor beneficial effects, except perhaps on highly insecure and emotionally disturbed children. This view has won some uncritical acceptance from the public at large, although it had been observed long before the LaMarsh Report was published that the questionnaires in these polls seldom, if ever, directly examine the attitudes and social behavior of children.[29] These kind of results continue to confuse the debate because they are usually conducted by vested media interests in an attempt to demonstrate some measure of good corporate citizenship when public concerns mount and to discredit findings which hold them accountable.

In 1994 an example of this perennial tendency emerged in the press in London, England[30] after it was reported that 25 child psychologists, psychiatrists, and childcare experts backed findings presented at Nottingham University[31] which called for restrictions on the availability of violent videos for home viewing. It was immediately followed by a feature article on psychologist Ann Hagell who, together with co-author Tim Newbury, released survey results questioning the link between watching violent films or videos and violent or criminal behavior in young people.[32] The survey, conducted by polling 80 young offenders and 500 school children for their opinions, was commissioned by the British Board of Film Classification, the British Broadcasting Corporation, the Broadcasting Standards Council and the Independent Television Commission.

Albert Bandura has long been critical of this approach and in his early work hypothetically compared it to one in which a survey might be taken by a doctor polling parents about their opinions concerning a particular medication for the treatment of a childhood disease. The implication is, of course, that while parents are in many cases the proper authorities on what is best for their children, when it comes to specific, medically based diagnosis and treatment of disease they lack the necessary expertise.

American journalist, Cynthia Crossen, has pointed out that public-opinion polls "will dance to anybody's tune." Although they purport to be on a quest for truth, many, she has written, "are essentially vehicles for promoting products."[33] In response to this trend, Crossen reported in 1991 that the Council of American Survey Research Organizations had issued a code of standards, covering such topics as responsibility to the public. A further complication was noted as an outgrowth from lean budgets for research in colleges and universities.

While no one comes right out and asks for a certain finding in exchange for money, the sub-text, according to Paul Light, Associate Dean, Hubert Humphrey Institute, University of Minnesota, is that if researchers produce the right finding, more work—and funding—will come their way. "Once you're on that treadmill," he said, "It's hard to get off. In addition, many universities, which often get a cut of the fee, don't monitor the outside work done under their imprimatur."[34]

Psychiatric Approaches

In the past, clinical psychiatrists who have relied on case studies have come under scrutiny on the point of methodological limitations. In 1955, as a psychologist, Seymour Feshbach thought that most psychiatrists' findings were based on observations from clinical experience and therefore of limited value in determining cause and effect. Psychiatrists, in turn, have always tended to argue that all contributing factors are causal factors and all causal factors are contributing factors.

Since then, Brandon Centerwall's epidemiologic study completed in 1989, has been widely quoted in the general debate on media violence. It was one of the first studies to look at the statistical relationships between exposure to television violence and its nationwide impact. Centerwall studied homicide rates within the white population of South Africa, where television was not introduced until 1975, and homicide rates among the white population of the United States and Canada from 1945 to 1974.[35]

The research showed that increases in homicide rates occurred first in younger age groups, when those who had been young children at the time of the introduction of television entered their late teens. The increases then occurred successively in older age groupings as those members of the first television generation aged. The following is a partial summary of his findings:

> Following an intervention in South Africa to prevent the introduction of television technology, white homicide rates remained stable. In two control populations, Canadian and U.S. white homicide rates doubled following the introduction of television...An array of other factors—age distribution, urbanization, economic conditions, alcohol consumption, capital punishment, civil unrest, and firearms availability—were examined to determine whether they could explain the findings.

> None were found to be explanatory...the most parsimonious interpretation of the data is that they are consistent with the introduction of television causing a subsequent doubling of homicide rates. The 10- to 15-year lag between the introduction of television and changes in homicide rate...imply that the behavioral effects of exposure to television are primarily exerted upon children. Given that homicide is an adult activity, the initial generation of children exposed to television would have to age 10-15 years before they could be expected to influence rates of homicide.[36]

Centerwall also observed that the South African murder rate doubled in the 10 years after the introduction of television in 1975. He concluded in his study that television is a factor in approximately 10,000 homicides each year in the United States and that as many as half of all violent crimes are related to the impact of television on American and Canadian societies. Sadly, it is no longer possible to conclude that homicide is an adult activity given the growing number of murders committed by children and young adolescents in the 1990s.

Sociological and Other Related Approaches

At times, sociologists and their close cousins, communications scholars, have tended to dismiss the validity of effects when the context has not been considered. They see television more as a reinforcing agent than a direct causal or creative factor in the formation of attitudes and behavior patterns. However, for several decades now, George Gerbner has helped to clarify the importance of both "effects" and their "context." In his early work, within the context of "the hidden Curriculum," Gerbner discussed the "teacher image" in mass culture and related it to the ways in which private corporations have taken over many functions performed in the past by the parent, the church, and the school:

> The contention that the existence or meaning of an action or communication should not be assessed until its "effects" are established is tantamount to the assertion that the structure of a culture should not be investigated; only its tactics are to be subjected to "scientific" inquiry. Far from being scientific this in itself is a symbolic tactic attempting to define what is "scientifically" reasonable and respectable in a way that serves only the most dominant, pervasive, and taken-for-granted social interests.[37]

We are only vaguely aware, says Gerbner, of the fact that decisive policy-making is going on at the same time that attitudes and behavior patterns are being shaped. Cultural politics are as much a part of the fabric of modern life as economic, welfare, or military politics. Like Otto Larsen in 1968 and the LaMarsh Commission in 1977, before which he appeared, Gerbner emphasizes that abstract conceptions of "censorship" obscure the realities of direction, constraints, and controls in any mass production. Formal aesthetic categories derived from other times and places ignore social functions, relationships, and power, which lie at the heart of the cultural policy process.[38]

On the subject of cultural indicators, Gerbner has identified three areas of analysis: institutional process, message system, and cultivation. Like Noam Chomsky, he has argued that all media are managed and that selective suppression is part of the process.[39] An additional, more recent complication can be observed in the case of news programming, wherein manipulation of the media is legitimized by the demand for brevity and the need to cover an increasing number of important items in as short a time as possible. Derek DeKerchhove, from the McLuhan Center at the University of Toronto, sees these trends opening up the way for a whole series of new genres of what he has called "reality fraud":

> The feedback effect from press to TV and back, creates an impression which quickly turns into an emotion and feeds an opinion...As McLuhan quipped, "When information moves at electric speed, the worlds of trends and rumors become the 'real' world."[40]

Since Gerbner, Gross and Melody edited their text, *Communications Technology and Social Policy: Understanding the New "Cultural Revolution"* in 1973, what they said has been repeated by a number of media scholars including Herbert Schiller in 1989, Herman and Chomsky in 1988, Jerry Mander in 1978 and again in 1991, and Joyce Nelson in both 1988 and 1989. Here is an excerpt from Gerbner's analysis at that time:

> Perhaps more than at any other time in our history, information and control over communications can be directly associated with economic and political power. The new technologies provide a potential not only for changing the structure of present power relationships but also for substantially expanding the aggregate power of those in control of communications and information systems. Yet we have not learned to discipline technology. We have accepted the beneficial and detrimental consequences of its apparently deterministic process of development with little more than an abiding faith in an ideology that defines technological advance and equates the latter with human betterment.[41]

Also in 1973, Bill Melody examined the technological determinism that supports both the institutional arrangements that are found in the United States telecommunications and broadcasting industries and the direction of government regulatory policies. He noted the absence of policy planning and advocacy of public interest positions, and suggested a reevaluation of regulatory objectives and activities. These would, he explained, require examination of industry's structures and the justification of concentrations of economic power as a major part of continuing regulatory responsibility. This is, of course, what has been attempted by many of the inquiries over the years including the LaMarsh Report, but with few if any results so far.

The Concept of Ideological Child Abuse

Since its first box office film hit in 1990, the concept of ideological child abuse has frequently been linked with the record-breaking marketing sensation and glorification of the martial arts, "Teenage Mutant Ninja Turtles." According to Gerbner, "With 133 acts of mayhem per hour, they were the most violent films ever marketed to children and perhaps also the most appalling to adults who have the stamina, and stomach, to view them."[42] The first film was also rated by the International Coalition Against Violent Entertainment (ICAVE) as the most violent film produced that year.[43]

By mid 1991, worldwide retail sales from turtle paraphernalia such as T-shirts, toothbrushes, cookies, and bed-sheets reached a record $1 billion. When it was released for distribution, the film was classified as "Restricted" in several countries around the world including England and West Germany. In North America, however, distributors of the first film as well as its sequel enjoyed a parental guidance rating, from both industry in the United States and provincial government supported film review boards in Canada, enabling them to capitalize on the widest possible viewing audience.

One of the problems perceived with this kind of cartoon format for films and television programs for children, is that while scenes of blood and gore are minimal, the reliance and even celebration of violence as a conflict resolution skill is paramount. Another problem is that the absence of blood and gore means that the consequences of violence are glossed over. The LaMarsh Report associated this kind of programming with the "removal of audience discomfort" along with explicit scenes of blood and gore.

When the first turtle film was released, many kindergarten schools throughout North America quickly made it clear that the turtles were not welcome in their classrooms. In some cases, this policy was extended to include a later variation of the ninja turtle theme which manifested itself as the *Mighty Morphin Power Rangers*. On November 1, 1994, because of parental complaints—in a rare demonstration of responsible industry initiative—the Canadian Broadcast Standards Council ruled that the *Power Rangers* children's show was too violent for Canadian television.[44] Although the Youth Television Network, carried on cable, removed the show at once, Global Television, the Canadian broadcaster which, as a member of the industry-based Canadian Association of Broadcasters is directly subject to any of the Council's rulings, continued to carry the program with only minor modifications for several more months.[45]

With supporting documentation and quotations from Gerbner, Comstock and other major researchers, National Coalition on Television Violence (NCTV) newsletters and bulletins, circulated up until the early 1990s, frequently pointed out that a significant and growing portion of the current economy is based on ideological child abuse. According to Joseph Strayhorn, a University of Pittsburg psychiatrist, a director of NCTV and the author of many publications on child development: "It is nothing short of tragic, that despite the massive evidence showing harmful effects from fantasy violence on normal children, it continues to be produced and sold, blocking progress toward a nonviolent world."[46]

As a child psychiatrist and a researcher, as well as founding member of NCTV and ICAVE, Thomas Radecki has pointed out that never in the history of humankind has there been such aggressive marketing of violence to the nation's youngest people. It is now "virtually certain that the extreme violence of modern film entertainment is having a harmful effect on hundreds of millions of people around the world."[47]

Radecki's observations were reinforced by Eugene Provenzo from the Department of Education at the University of Miami when he reported on "the bad news" at a conference on electronic child abuse held in Toronto in 1993. At the time, he stressed that, with the arrival of new technologies involving "virtual reality" and interactive television, the problem has become even more critical. These warnings continue to be issued by George Gerbner along with findings he releases periodically through his on-going cultural indicators project at Temple University in Philadelphia.

In 1990, Radecki reported that horror and violent science fiction films had increased markedly since 1970 with a 600 percent increase in box office ticket sales by 1980. There was, in fact, a much larger increase in actual consumer habits because of the introduction of pay-cable television and video cassette recorders during the 1980s. Crime dramas in television programming rose from zero hours in 1955 to 27 hours per week in 1985. In children's programming, the number of hours of cartoons with exciting war themes increased from one half hour in 1982 to 27 hours per week in 1985.

Violence had grown rapidly in the previous 15-20 years in other areas of entertainment as well. In the best selling sex magazines, violent pictorials increased by approximately 115 percent between 1973 and 1983. With the advent of music videos considerably more violence was interjected into rock and rap visual images than was contained in the actual lyrics themselves. In addition, an intensely violent, hate-filled heavy metal subculture had appeared that never existed previously in rock or any other form of music entertainment.

Sports violence had increased with violent penalties occurring 350 percent more often in Canadian hockey in the 1970s than had been the case in the 1930s. There was also an observed increase in the tendency to focus on violent action in network broadcasts of professional hockey and football. By 1990, professional boxing had become the fourth most popular televised sport, despite a large number of studies showing sizeable amounts of brain damage in participants as well as harmful effects in viewers. Professional wrestling had become extremely popular, despite evidence of increases in anger in normal college students after viewing such programming. Martial arts, especially that associated with deadly weapons, had soared in popularity with a new emphasis on anger and revenge violence found in many martial arts magazines.

On the subject of war toys Radecki reported that, between 1982 and 1985, the sales of war toys had soared by 600 percent. Violent fantasy role-playing games such as *Dungeons and Dragons* had become commonplace, in themselves involving a $100 million industry. Approximately 50 such games were on the market. At that time there were already 125 reports in the media linking a heavy involvement in violent role-playing games to suicides or murders in real-life. Similarly there was a marked increase in the proportion of bestseller books with violent themes. In the first half of the century only 15 percent of bestsellers had themes of violence, by 1990 over 70 percent of bestsellers featured themes of intense violence.[48]

Commenting on the implications of these increases in violent entertainment, Radecki pointed out that:

Historians have attributed times of war as being times when violence has been glamorized, dating back to the year 1200 in Europe (Gurr, 1979). Epidemics of violence have had increases by as much as 300 percent, but these have always passed as peace was restored. Gurr has attributed the current world pandemic of violence, the first in world history, to fantasies of war being proliferated in television and film entertainment.[49]

He explained that violent entertainment is not a new phenomenon or concern. What is new, is the consistent emphasis on violent entertainment escalating with new technological innovations that go far beyond the crime novel. As a result the intensity of violence depicted has also increased.

In a study done by Radecki in 1988, covering 1500 films from 61 countries, indications were that in 1,000 of them, 72 percent contained some harmfully violent elements with Hong Kong, the United States and Mexico showing the highest number.[50] In 1991, Miriam Miedzian discussed similar trends, pointing out that homicide rates had gone up by 85 percent between 1960 and 1987. She compared these figures with studies on file from United States Senate Subcommittees on Juvenile Delinquency in 1954, 1961, and 1963, which indicated that the quantity of violent programs increased by as much as 300 percent between 1954 and 1961.

Hegemony and the Mass Media

In the last two decades attempts to examine and define the constitutive function of mass media in society have been reflected in widespread references to their "hegemonic" role. The concept of hegemony, as used by Antonio Gramsci over a quarter of a century ago, has contributed to an understanding of the process by which political consensus can be achieved without coercion in societies where there is structured inequality and rank differences in power.[51] According to Gramsci, it is the process by which subordinated classes are manoeuvred into consenting to their own domination. Several interlocking ideologies are usually involved, reflecting different societal positions. The overarching, predominant ideology, however, serves to absorb and pacify the attitudes and belief systems of subordinated groups.

A major theoretical construct within the predominating ideology is that class differences can be contained by social consensus rather than coercion.[52] What emerges instead, it is argued, is a mind-set that accepts structured inequality between social classes as an accidental by-product of the larger political system. This mind-set or *collective outlook* is widely perceived to be primarily orchestrated in contemporary society by mass media. The code of signs through advertising images and other forms of media, which emerges, reinforces the process as a kind of attitudinal cement. At the same time, there is a constant struggle among competing interests within popular culture, between marginalized groups and the dominant groups which aim to hold and exert power.[53]

In this context, many of Marshall McLuhan's theories have been evoked, among them his observations that "all technologies are extensions of our central nervous systems to increase power and speed" and that, "disintegration and reprieve alike are the consequence of ever faster movement of information by couriers on excellent roads."[54] These observations have helped to draw attention to a diminishing capacity for objectivity on the part of *everyone* involved in mass media, producers and consumers alike, at the same time that the growing volume and complexity of information in modern society makes it more difficult for an individual to become well informed on a variety of critical issues.

This circumstance precipitates an increasing reliance on "expertise" for opinions and advice of one kind or another. All of these factors make the possibilities for public manipulation through propaganda campaigns enormous because they create a climate of potential receptivity to propaganda on the basis that it always works best when the populace lacks adequate information to make informed choices.[55] People with awareness of these trends help to clarify the debate on "censorship." It sheds light on how the concept is exploited by dominant interests by the deliberate selection of certain kinds of information and the exclusion of others on any number of social issues, including media violence.

Cultural Studies

Related to the theory of hegemony and the mass media is the postmodernist contribution to textual analysis. This approach to the study of mass media is crucial because it has provided the bed rock for the study of media literacy in public schools. Though it began with the decoding and deconstruction of language and meaning with emphasis on the "signs, the signified and the signifier," the approach has been expanded to include visual text or images. One of the most widely read theorists in this area is John Fiske.[56] Along with his associates he has drawn upon the theories of feminism, Marxism, semiotics, post-structuralism and ethnography to probe the multifaceted way that television functions in late capitalist societies in order to serve dominant interests.

Both Fiske and Hartley have pointed to the sociology of mass communications as the predecessor for this academic interest:

> We speak here of an academic tradition because, although many of the early theories about television's effect on its audience have been modified, extended or discredited, it remains the case that later research has built upon and not entirely supplanted the assumptions inherent in the early work. For this reason, it is necessary to be aware of the most important of those underlying assumptions. There are at least three, which can best be thought of under the following headings: (1) individualism; (2) abstraction; and (3) functionalism.[57]

They argue that "individualism" is the assumption that tends to overlook the extent to which a person's response is culturally determined; hence the habit has sprung up of overemphasizing the television viewer as an individual with certain psychological needs. "Abstraction," on the other hand is explained as the tendency to assume that an individual's psychological needs are much the same regardless of social and cultural factors, whereas "functionalism" is based on the assumption that television is used by its viewers to satisfy psychological needs in more or less conscious and active ways.

They have postulated that, in the field of mass communication, earlier stimulus-response assumptions have been incorporated into the "uses and gratifications" theory. These assumptions involve five basic needs, all derived ultimately from the individual psyche. They include cognitive needs involving the acquisition of information, knowledge and understanding; affective needs involving emotional and aesthetic experiences such as love, friendship and the desire to see beautiful things; personal integrative needs such as the need for self-confidence, stability, status and reassurance; social integrative needs such as the need for strengthening contacts with family, friends and others; and finally, tension-release needs such as the need for escape and diversion.[58]

Fiske and Hartley have integrated these needs into three categories on the basis of established sociological theory concerning media effects: the need to understand one's social world, the need to act meaningfully and effectively in that world, and the need for fantasy-escape from daily problems and tensions. This approach has yielded new insights into the inter-textual relations of television within itself, with other media, and within social conversations that the medium spawns, depending upon the socially situated position of viewers.

Through their identification of an ideological code of patriarchy, along with an encoded ideology of capitalism, Fiske and Hartley have pointed out how the textual oppositions between hero or heroine and villain or villainess, winner and loser, and the violence by which this opposition is commonly dramatized, are metaphors for power relationships in society and how such discourses have become institutionalized because they are accepted by both industry and consumers.

By harnessing the new technologies, television producers have shattered existing boundaries between various forms of media. As a result, television produces reality more than it reflects it and becomes a frame or bearer of ideology which makes form synonymous with content. In this context, the fallacy of transparency needs to be exposed as an oversimplified approach to the analysis of the media. Said Fiske:

> ...television is seen either as a transparent window on the world or as a mirror reflecting our own reality back to us...the human or cultural agency in the process is masked: this means that the finished representation is naturalized, that it is made to appear the result of natural rather than cultural processes, it is taken away from the realm of history and culture and moved toward universal truth.[59]

On the whole, according to Fiske, the power of audiences as producers in the cultural economy has become considerable as meanings circulate within our commonly held belief systems without any real distinction between producers and consumers. The social experience of the subordinate can, in itself, become the origin of resistance, with various forms of resistance based on the sense people make of their experiences, particularly as audiences become more productive, discriminating, and televisually literate. Sometimes these meanings can serve the interests of the dominant class and sometimes they can serve those of the subordinate class.

Deanne Bogdan has also explored some of these inherent and inevitable contradictions, essential to a pluralist society. She says that "the aesthetic deployment of language and images for rhetorical effect invokes the dynamics of surrender, resistance, and complicity in the reader's negotiation of the relationship between convention and reality."[60] According to her, the continuum or chain reaction from author, to text, to respondent, is placed at one end of the pendulum of learning experience with the critical analytical antidote to seduction as the response or the "gap" which results to prevent this seduction at the other end:

> Reading as seduction summons up a view of the aesthetically educated response which would seem to be going in two directions at once. The first, moving through the felt effects of the aesthetic experience, undergone as though it were real, invites the reader's compliance with the seduction into the event; the second, moving away from it toward critical consciousness of the construction of the event, demands some resistance to the event.[61]

These modes of knowing, built on the foundations of Northrop Frye's analysis of direct and natural responses, have, said Bogdan, become commonly held tenets in English studies. She has extended this theory from the experience of reading and applied it to other media responses as well, arguing that if literary art, or indeed any kind of art, can influence society for good purposes, it can also do so for ill purposes and that this fundamental reality poses some important implications for the problem of adequately defining censorship.

Fiske, Hartley, Solomon and others who have focused on textual analysis, like Gerbner, Herman and Chomsky, Masterman, and Schiller who have discussed the larger social and political implications, observe the dynamics in contemporary mass media production and consumption as a component of the never-ending process of hegemony.[62] Despite these ongoing tensions, however, Fiske, like Schiller, has commented on the severe threat now posed to the usefulness and practicality of cultural commodities as the technologies of reproduction increasingly become the agents of popular power. The resulting power struggle can be observed in the growing emphasis from dominant interests on their rights to ownership of intellectual property as copyright legislation proliferates in corporate attempts to maintain control on all aspects of the new information-based economy.

Another trend has been observed in the shift of capitalist economics from production to marketing, which has increased the cultural value of commodities. As a result, "lifestyle," along with commodities themselves, is now being marketed and youth are increasingly being targeted for this combination. According to Ken Masterman, at Nottingham University in England, for media educators, the key questions of the 1990s and beyond "are going to relate to the extent to which market-driven media can actually deliver democratic values."[63]

On the whole, most textual analysts have tended to distance themselves from the debate on cause and effect by explaining that television does not cause identifiable effects on individuals but instead works to promote and circulate certain meanings of the world which serve some social interests better than others. There is no doubt that Fiske and other postmodernists have contributed to the comprehension of complex cultural processes that underlie television's meanings and pleasures if only because their work has had such a profound impact on the development of media literacy curriculum in high schools. What remains problematic is the inclination toward a neutral, impartial, values-free approach to the text regardless of its content, particularly on the subject of media violence. In the final analysis this manifestation is simply another round of hegemonic diffusion of attempts to address the deeper, underlying problem of moral confusion over the subject of violence in the media and its impact on society as a whole.

Gerbner has always been critical of textual analysis involving "powerful" audiences "resisting" cultivation, producing their own popular culture, uses and gratifications. Such analysis, he says, focuses on transformations of meaning and differences in perception and response but ignores or minimizes the commonalities television cultivates which are decisive in matters of public policy.[64] Perhaps the most compelling evidence to support Gerbner's point is the growing emphasis on media spectacles that dominate the news media. Examples include the Bobbit case (a trial in which the female member of a young couple by marriage snipped the penis off her husband which was subsequently re-attached successfully), the Tonya Harding case (in which a professional athlete colluded in the maiming of her competitor), and the arrest of football hero, O.J. Simpson (convicted of wife assault and accused of murdering his estranged wife and her companion). More recent examples include endless coverage of President Clinton's sex scandals and the barrage of voyeurist television footage of the high school shooting massacre in Littleton, Colorado in 1999, which reverberated with the threat of copycat crimes in high schools throughout North America for weeks. The spectacle itself has become the message.[65]

Other trends can be observed in communications technology, now dominated more than ever by corporate preoccupations with profit and "survival." In 1993, Antonia Zerbisias, media reporter for *The Toronto Star*, commented on the threat of direct broadcast satellite services which loomed over the future of the cable industry and broadcast networks. Interactive television in the home, she pointed out, was integral to the survival of the cable industry through "digital video compression," meaning more channels put into space now available for one channel only.

At stake is dominance of a business that, by the year 2000, is estimated to grow to $3.5 trillion world-wide. That's six times Canada's gross domestic product...What this all means is that basic cable will soon be pretty much like 1976 service—at 1996 prices. So, when cable companies and others talk of a glorious future where TVs will be used to teach and inform in ways we have yet to imagine, there will be entire groups of Canadians who will be excluded simply because they won't be able to afford it. And then what? Do better-off citizens subsidize lower-income groups' cable bills just so we're all on an equal democratic footing?[66]

Obviously, these trends present a somewhat different dimension to the postmodernist concept of the audience and producer symbiosis that Fiske and others have advanced.

Media Literacy Courses in the Schools

By 1975 media education had become the object of considerable attention in various parts of Canada, particularly in Ontario. TVOntario was one of the first public broadcasters to apply itself to the development of suitable resource material. Belief in the need for critical viewing skills which could be taught in schools prompted the development of the "Utilization Unit" in 1982 through what was then known as the Ontario Educational Communications Authority. Soon after, curriculum applications of critical viewing skills bearing the TVOntario logo began to find their way into Ontario classrooms.[67]

Several years earlier, in 1978, Toronto English teacher and high school principal Barry Duncan founded the Association of Media Literacy (AML). According to Duncan, there is no doubt that the LaMarsh Report, which called for the development of media literacy courses, added impetus to the development of media literacy in Ontario schools; but it was not officially introduced into the curriculum, beginning at the grade eleven level, until 1989. In 1998, in the midst of ruthless cuts to social programs and education budgets, the Harris Government moved to eliminate media literacy courses in Ontario schools, although Ryerson Polytechnical Institute professor, Donald Gilles, reported in a paper presented at the 1999 annual Canadian Communications Association Conference at the University of Sherbrooke in Quebec, that the program had, in fact, been salvaged.

In 1989, the Ontario Ministry of Education, together with the Ontario Teachers' Federation (OTF), developed their resource guide on media literacy to help teachers deal with mass media and popular culture.[68] Media literacy skills, they said, should be part of any school program from kindergarten to grade 12, with young people encouraged to understand a world profoundly influenced by the mass media. These skills should permeate the entire curriculum and be integrated into courses as diverse as social sciences and mathematics. Counting acts of violence as a potential mathematics exercise was one example discussed in an AML workshop for teachers on the subject of media literacy held at the Ontario Institute for Studies in Education in January, 1993.

The table of contents in the OTF Resource Guide covers a broad range of topics under the rubric of mass media such as television, film, radio, popular music and rock video, photography, print, and cross-media studies, with subtopics, such as advertising, sexuality in the media, violence in the media, Canadian identity and ownership, and reporting the news. The following observation appears in the introduction:

> The fact that the media have remained outside the school curriculum at the same time as they have come to dominate so many aspects of our society, and, indeed, our individual consciousness, is a tribute to their power to influence us on levels of which we are unaware. It is not surprising, then, that we have come to study the media; it is only surprising that it has taken us so long to start.[69]

The centrality of the media in our lives, manifested in a number of ways, is emphasized along with the need for shared responsibility between parents and educators. For many people, the total number of hours per week spent as media consumers is exceeded only by the time spent sleeping. By the time students finish highschool, it is estimated that students will have spent an average of 11,000 hours in school, compared to more than 15,000 hours watching television and 10,500 listening to popular music. They will also have seen several hundred films, over 100,000 acts of violence and been exposed to countless advertisements.

A critical approach to the role of media in society is encouraged, both for students who are inclined toward an unwarranted, blind faith in the integrity of media images and representations, as well as for students with an undifferentiated scepticism about the insidious nature of the media. Through widespread media literacy, it is argued, students will be able to make rational decisions and become effective agents of change.

The predominant aim, however, is to increase students' understanding and enjoyment of how the media work, how they produce meaning, how they are organized, and how they construct reality. In other words, the major emphasis is on enabling students to develop skills to create media products. It is expected that, by acquiring these skills, students "will then be in a position to control their relationship with the media."[70] Unfortunately, evidence following the 1999 Columbine highschool massacre that the perpetrators of the crime were thoroughly familiar with the worlds of celluloid and cyberspace, had searched the Internet for clues on how to execute it and created their own web site with plans for building bombs, has rendered this assumption naive.[71]

The teacher is referred to as both facilitator and co-learner. For elementary school children, decoding advertisements is described as one potential exercise in media literacy:

> They could also talk about what they would put in commercials for children if they were making them. Older children could begin to analyze the techniques and appeals of commercials, planning and story-boarding some of their own. They could also explore the relationship between commercials and programming, perhaps examining the link between children's cartoon characters and the sales of related products such as dolls or clothing. As they progress through the educational system, they may move on, for example, to more detailed examinations of commercials; studies of the effects of economic considerations on programming, content, and techniques; or research into issues such as the effects of ownership and control of media.[72]

It is acknowledged that it may be difficult to find socially redeeming values in many rock videos or programs with high audience ratings but that these are often the programs that students are most eager to discuss rather than "Masterpiece Theatre or CBC drama." The teacher is cautioned not to impose "a set of elitist values on the class";[73] the fundamental premise of "values education" being that the teacher should encourage students to develop values and tastes that are "relevant to their own immediate cultural context."[74]

The limitation to this line of reasoning is that if violent "action-packed" films are a part of the students' cultural context then that is where the teacher should start, with a nonjudgemental position on the nature of the material. This kind of popular culture, by corollary, then becomes a *normal* part of youth culture and merely adds to the problem by reinforcing the systemic aspect to a more broadly based culture of violence. It does nothing to address the wider problem of youth violence that has become such a critical problem in North America in recent years.

As director for the Center on Education and Cultural Studies at Miami University in Ohio, Peter McLaren has argued that, within the context of media literacy programs, liberal attempts to curtail violence are temporary at best:

> They are usually humanist endeavors that give students more personal and interpretive room in the classroom. Teachers that invite students to share in gently breaking down the monolithic meanings of official knowledge—by employing popular culture in their lessons, rap music, and so on—are better able to enlist the consent of students because they are, in effect, telling students that being cynical and street smart is "where it's at."[75]

Cognitive development can take place under both favorable and unfavorable conditions, often during attempts to resist domination and oppression. Rather than applying simple reforms to classroom practices with the introduction of surface themes and skills involving the media, teachers need to create spaces for students to learn how to genuinely understand and contest the structures of oppression that inform them. This is a necessary first step in transforming the culture of violence that shapes the direction of youth desire in so many aspects of North American society today.

Unfortunately, these are not the philosophical underpinnings for media literacy instruction in most schools. Despite their acknowledgment that potentially harmful effects of violence in the mass media reach consumers of all ages, Canadian media literacy teachers are encouraged to refer to the literature on the subject as "still being interpreted" and the findings as inconclusive.[76] In this context, consider the following OTF rationale:

> Students with media-literacy skills can begin to uncover the way in which the mass media make violence appealing, often linking it with power and pleasure in a way that makes it seem natural. Through this exploration, students are encouraged to raise questions about the culture of violence. In this regard, they need to question those representations in which conflict is resolved primarily by means of violence.[77]

If a teacher adds to this broad range of interpretive possibilities the reminder that research findings are "inconclusive," then leaves students to "make up their own minds" about whether this is good or bad, the likelihood that violence will automatically be rejected as a conflict resolution strategy is a leap in faith.

On the whole, what these varying positions within the OTF guide demonstrate is the wide margin of lattitude for individual interpretation concerning guidelines on teaching media literacy for teachers, on the basis of personal preference. While the Harris Government's threats to eliminate media literacy courses entirely can hardly be condoned, this is one area in which some standardization of teaching methods would be helpful.

AML Leadership

Throughout North America, the AML, now under the umbrella of the Canadian Association of Media Education Organizations (CAMEO) based in Toronto—the major component of the *Jesuit Communications Project*—has played a leading role in the development of resource materials on media literacy for teachers.[78] Symposia on media literacy are held periodically and regular newsletters are published. From time to time, projects are undertaken with funding from members of the media industries. Unfortunately, this practice has significantly compromised critical analysis of media text, particularly in ways advocated by Maclaren.[79]

One example occurred in October, 1993, when the AML, in cooperation with Youth Television Network (YTV) produced a classroom kit of resource material for media literacy teaching purposes. It included a newsletter, lesson plans, a videotape entitled YTV Outreach Reel and was distributed within the education community, free of charge. A copy was also sent to the author. Everyone was encouraged to duplicate and distribute the kit to colleagues for classroom use as it had been cleared for any potential copyright infringements.

In it, four lesson plans were developed with the help of a number of secondary school teachers in Ontario and Quebec. These included an outline for analyzing the Newsmagazine Format: TV v. Print, a "behind the scenes" look at making YTV news, guidance for "do-it-yourself" TV editorials, and images of youth in the news in ways that responded to the LaMarsh Commission call for more youth relevant approaches to news programming.

While there was much of value in it, the problem with this education kit was the misleading and inaccurate information on research findings about the potential harmful effects of media violence. It was not consistent with what, for example, Keith Spicer, then chair of the CRTC, and prominent researchers such as Edward Donnerstein from the University of California were saying. Namely, that the debate on research is over. It is now on policy.

Production of the video component followed the C.M. Hincks Institute Conference in February 1993, one of three international symposiums co-ordinated by Spicer when he was still chair of the CRTC, and in which Barry Duncan participated as a panelist on behalf of the AML. It was at this particular symposium that, in his keynote address, Donnerstein stated that 99 percent of researchers now agree that there are harmful effects on viewers from violence in the media. Where there is less agreement, said Donnerstein, is on how much harm is being done and to whom. At the American Psychological

Association Conference held in Toronto, in August of that year, Leonard Eron repeated that the debate on research showing harmful effects is over; it is now on policy. These kind of definitive positions are also readily available to anyone who wishes to access them on the American Medical Association web site.[80] Nevertheless, on John Punjente's web site, which outlines the work and mission of the Jesuit Communications Project, Jonathan Freedman at the University of Toronto, who consistently argues that there is no evidence of harmful effects, is the only psychologist quoted at all.[81]

In other words, growing consensus within the research community throughout North America, as well as within the public at large, that exposure to media violence has no harmful effects continues to be ignored in Canada by leading advocates of media literacy within the educational community itself. By collaborating in the production of resource material for teaching purposes in schools that promotes the notion of no "hard" evidence of harmful effects, industry is let off the hook and history is allowed to repeat itself. Television producers pose as benign partners in facilitating resource materials for teaching purposes in the classroom while undermining the credibility of research findings that might point toward the need for greater responsibility and accountability in industry *choices* for what gets produced and distributed in the first place.

The tendency within the educational community, itself, to trivialize research findings on the seriousness of media violence and its harmful effects also surfaced in a book by Duncan and three other leading media literacy teachers in Ontario, published in 1996. The section on media violence, similarly, emphasized that there is no conclusive evidence showing harmful effects. In this case, a reprint from a 1984 issue of *TV Guide* written by Mike Oppenheim actually called for not less but more "realistic" violence on television.[82]

Unfortunately these teaching methods place the predominant onus of responsibility for appropriate responses on the shoulders of the most vulnerable and least powerful members of society, youth itself, with *educators* being manoeuvred into collaboration with industry in perpetuating the problem of a violent culture. While discretionary viewing is certainly a laudable and necessary goal for both teachers and students, it exaggerates what media literacy, as one of many strategies for dealing with the problem of media violence is able to accomplish in a market driven economy where large media conglomerates have control over the stories that enter the social and cultural domain.

The reality of this diminishing influence on the part of teachers was underscored in 1996 by the controversy over the introduction of the Youth News Network into Canadian classrooms. Parent groups, teachers unions and CAMEO, among others, have fought a losing battle in their opposition to the commercial 12-minute newscast promoted by YNN president Roderick MacDonald. It was finally successfully introduced into a highschool in Peel County in Ontario in 1999 as a pilot project in exchange for free donated communications technology.

Students are 'required' to watch this newscast in order for schools to qualify for free equipment that they could then use for more pedagogically sound reasons. MacDonald, who insists he has never found any evidence that advertising has a harmful effect on children, has been quietly approaching provincial education ministry officials across the country for several years. In 1996, one school board outside Montreal even signed up for its own pilot without the participation of the Quebec Education Ministry.[83] The one in Peel county, however, is the first to actually get off the ground.

Also in 1996, it was estimated that 40 percent of American students were watching a daily commercial newscast, sponsored predominantly by companies selling soft drinks, sports equipment, candy and acne medicine on the similar Channel One service. Some were even rumored to be receiving detentions for refusing to watch the newscast, replete with commercials, from principals afraid of losing their donated equipment.[84]

Emphasis from John Punjente, president of CAMEO, that there are commercial free alternatives to YNN has, in the end, not made much difference.[85] In Canada, these have included a weekly half hour commercial free news program for youth offered by YTV, complete with print and Internet study supplements and a 15 minute daily news program produced for teens by Turner Multi Media, offered by CNN Newsroom and distributed in Canada by Calgary Television. The latter is provided to schools with no commercials and considered by Pungente to be more popular in the United States than Channel One. In addition, CBC Newsworld has offered a daily 15 minute news broadcast aimed specifically at youth. Punjente also points out that cable launched in classrooms in September, 1995, by Canadian cable and speciality channels already allows students to watch an extensive array of commercial-free, copyright-cleared programs in the classroom.

On the whole, it is clear that, on a number of levels, despite the LaMarsh Commission, the establishment of the LaMarsh Center, and additional evidence of harmful effects from new studies undertaken in a variety of disciplines that both directly and indirectly built on the work the Commission had started, progress in Canada in addressing the issue of violence in the communications industry has been extremely modest.

For a while there was some evidence of response to recommendations for more education on how media work within the industries themselves, particularly through the development of media literacy resource material in co-operation with educators and the introduction of cable into schools, but in general, market forces invading the classroom have accelerated. As Heather-Jane Robertson, director of professional development for the Canadian Teachers Federation and author of the book, *No More Teachers, No More Books—The Commercialization of Canada's Schools*, published in 1997, points out, public schools are being drawn more and more into the orbit of serving corporate sponsors.

Notes

1. Sheppard, R., 1996a, July 3, *The Globe and Mail*, p. A13.

2. Shnayerson, M., 1966, July, *Vanity Fair*, p.100.

3. Shnayerson, M., 1966, p. 144.

4. Puente, 1999, April 13, *USA Today*, p.3A.

5. Although the *LaMarsh Research Programme on Violence and Conflict Resolution* was not officially renamed *The LaMarsh Centre for Research and Conflict Resolution* until after 1991, from its inception it was referred to as a centre.

6. LaMarsh Centre Annual Report, 1991.

7. LaMarsh Centre Annual Report, 1991, p.1; Lamarsh Centre, 1996, p.1.

8. LaMarsh Centre Annual Report, 1991, p.1.

9. LaMarsh Centre Annual Report, 1991, p.19.

10. LaMarsh Centre Report, 1996, p.3.

11. CFRB Radio, 1993, Jan. 26, Ian Hawtin Live; Fischer, 1993, Nov. 6, *The Edmonton Journal*, p.E2; CFTO Television, 1994, Nov. 8, Canada A.M. with Valerie Pringle; Freedman, 1994, Nov. 7, *The Globe and Mail*, p.A13.

12. Although I had been invited to participate in the seminar I was not given an opportunity to debate McCormack's points.

13. Check and Malamuth, 1986.

14. Bandura, 1973.

15. Check et al., 1985, p. 3.

16. 1985, p. 336.

17. Wolf, 1992, p. 17. Other aspects described in *The Beauty Myth* as conscious market manipulation hurtful to women include the $33-billion-a-year diet industry, the $20-billion cosmetic industry, and the $300-million cosmetic surgery industry.

18. Levinger, G., 1986, *Journal of Social Sciences* 43 (3).

19. Huesmann & Malamuth, 1986, *Journal of Social Sciences* 42 (3) 1-7.

20. 1991, Preface.

21. Duncan, 1988; Giroux, 1989.

22. 1993, December 12. CD-ROM: Computer's next frontier? *The Sunday Star*, p. A1.

23. 1993, December 12. CD-ROM: Computer's next frontier? *The Sunday Star*, p. A1.

24. Eron, 1986, p. 155.

25. Turner et al., 1986.

26. Huston et al., 1992.

27. Rogers Community Television, 1994a&b; Withey & Abeles, 1980; Youth News Network, 1994, March, The YTV Newsletter, Toronto.

28. Huston et al., 1992.

29. Bandura, 1961, 1963, 1973; Larsen et al., 1968; Wertham, 1968.

30. Weale, 1994, April 13, *The Times*, (Great Britain)p.6.

31. Newton, 1994, Violence and the Protection of Children, Great Britain.

32. Moir, 1994, April 13, *The Guardian*, p.7.

33. 1991, Dec. 7, *The Globe and Mail*, p. D5.

34. Crossen, 1991, Dec. 7, *The Globe and Mail*, p.D5.

35. To avoid using figures distorted by racial conflict, Centerwall compared only the white homicide rates on the basis that most victims of racial violence were black.

36. 1989, p. 15.

37. 1973, p.269.

38. Gerbner, 1973, 1980, 1991a.

39. Herman and Chomsky, 1988.

40. 1990, December, *Edges: New Planetary Patterns*, p.15.

41. Gerbner, 1973, Preface.

42. 1991b, p. 1.
43. NCTV, 1990c.
44. Lacey, 1994a, Nov. 2, *The Globe and Mail*, p.C2.
45. Lacey, 1994b, Nov. 9, *The Globe and Mail*, p.C2.
46. NCTV, 1990c, April 9, News release, Champaign, IL, p.2.
47. I-CAVE, December 1989-January 1990, p. 13.
48. Radecki, 1990, p. 6-7. TV and other forms of violent entertainment. A cause of 50% of real-life violence. Champaign, IL. ICAVE.
49. Radecki, 1990, p.6-7.
50. I-CAVE, December 1989-January 1990.
51. 1971.
52. Ellul, 1987; Gramsci, 1971; Sullivan, 1982.
53. Angus & Jhally, 1988; Fiske, 1987; Herman & Chomsky, 1988; Sullivan, 1987; Solomon, 1988.
54. 1964.
55. Ellul, 1987; Herman & Chomsky, 1988.
56. Fiske & Hartley, 1978, reprinted four times; reprinted 1985; Fiske, 1987. 9. 1987, p. 71.
57. 1985. p. 72-73.
58. 1987. p. 21.
59. 1992b, p.1.
60. 1992b, p. 1.
61. Fiske, 1987; Fiske and Hartley, 1985; Solomon, 1988; Gerbner, 1991a; Herman and Chomsky, 1988; Masterman (in Pungente & Duncan, 1994); Schiller, 1989 a & b.
62. Pungente & Duncan, 1994, p. 16.
63. Pungente & Duncan, 1994, p. 16.
64. 1994, p.E3.
65. 1993, p. D5.
66. Zerbisias, 1993, June 26, *The Toronto Star*. Morrison has frequently argued that the CRTC ignores its consumer-protection mandate, in this instance by paving the way for higher cable bills for millions of Canadians.
67. OTF & Ontario Ministry of Education, 1989.
68. OTF & Ontario Ministry of Education, 1989, p. 5.
69. OTF & Ontario Ministry of Education, 1989.
70. OTF & Ontario Ministry of Education, 1989, p. 12.
71. Cribb, 1999.
72. OTF & Ontario Ministry of Education, 1989.
73. OTF & Ontario Ministry of Education, 1989.
74. McLaren, 1993, p.11.
75. Dyson, 1995.
76. OTF & Ontario Ministry of Education, 1989.
77. Duncan, 1993. Spring letter to members, *Mediacy*, 15 (2) p.1.
78. Duncan, 1993.
79. http://interact.uoregon.edu/JCP.medialit/JCP/index/html, 1999.
80. http://www.ama-assn.org/
81. http://interact.uoregon.edu/JCP.medialit/JCP/index.html, 1999.
82. Duncan et al., 1996.
83. Krueger, 1996, Feb. 2, *The Globe and Mail*, p. A14.
84. Krueger, 1996, p. A14.
85. Personal Communication, Jan. 9, 1996.

Chapter 5

THE ASCENDANCY OF PORNOGRAPHY

BY THE END OF 1977 the issue of television violence was no longer under active discussion in broadcasting circles. Competition for ratings became the major focus instead. Attention of critics was drawn to a new development: the steady, calculated infusion of sexually suggestive themes, references, and language in television programming. Observations on the part of both researchers and commentators within the mainstream media indicated steady departure from existing standards of decorum in network codes, with themes of illegitimacy, abortion, incest, homosexuality, rape, and extra marital affairs becoming increasingly dominant.

A familiar refrain, first voiced by the American based National Broadcasting Corporation in 1977, could be heard throughout the industry, namely, that the industry did not want to be a trend-setter and that it actually lagged behind the sexual revolution but felt certain that the trend toward sex-oriented programming would continue. As American researchers Withey and Abeles put it in 1980, "a self-fulfilling prophecy because those who did the predicting also made the decisions."[1]

Another Subject of Controversy

In their criticism of research methodology on the subject of pornography, Withey and Abeles discuss the 1970 *Report of the Commission on Obscenity and Pornography*, set up at the time in response to growing public concern over the widespread availability of media with explicit sexual depictions. The Commission had given pornography a clean bill of health stating that on the basis of available data, "it was not possible to conclude that erotic material is a significant cause of crime."[2] The contrast between this conclusion and that of the U.S. Surgeon General's Report on television violence in 1978 became a matter of controversy. Withey and Abeles were among those who argued that what was true for violence in television programming would also hold true for sexually explicit material, and that a more systematic approach to the total context in which these materials were used, and their use encouraged, had to be taken into account. In their discussion of the 1970 Report, they drew attention to dissenting

Commissioner Winfrey Link's claim that valid studies on the subject of pornography done previously had been suppressed due to vested interests on the part of some members appointed to the Commission.[3]

The Report was also disclaimed by subsequent studies on the topic, including the U.S. *Final Report of the Attorney General's Commission on Pornography* released in 1986. Also known as the Meese Commission, the latter was not, however, without its own discreditors. They included Edward Donnerstein, one of the key witnesses for the Meese Commission, a psychologist and major American researcher on both violence and sexual explicitness in the media.

Along with colleagues, Penrod and Linz, Donnerstein reported in a book published in 1987, following the Meese Commission, that "individuals exposed to certain types of materials respond with blunted sensitivity to violence against women, calloused attitudes about rape, and sexual arousal to rape depictions and laboratory simulations of aggression against women."[4] They said their aim was to go beyond the Commission's findings but apart from the usual arguments associated with limitations to laboratory research there were few conclusions that might lead to constructive corrective action beyond a call for more research itself.

The book was fraught with contradictions with little new discussion offered apart from a criticism of the Meese Commission recommendations, particularly the call for an expansion of existing obscenity statues and stricter enforcement of these laws. This has since become an observable pattern to Donnerstein's position when he has spoken on the subject. Examples in Canada include the Symposium on Pornography and Media Violence held at OISE, February, 1984; Humber College Conference on Male Sexuality, February, 1987; C.M. Hincks Institute Conference on the Impact of Television Violence on Children, 1993; and the APA Annual Conference in Toronto, August, 1993.

American feminist and scholar, Gloria Cowan, has pinpointed some reasons for contradictions among pornography researchers in general. In a paper presented at the annual meeting of the Scientific Society for the Study of Sex in San Diego, California in 1992, she spoke on three issues: the lack of attention paid to degrading and dehumanizing pornography and the imprecise selection of materials in research studies; the distortion of findings by researchers; and the inconsistencies in statements made. She said:

> During the Minneapolis hearing on pornography in 1983, and in response to a question asked by Catherine Mackinnon about the long term effects of x-rated material without violence, Donnerstein replied: "You get increases in sex stereotypes and pretty much exactly the same things in terms of the attitudes that you get with the violent material. The only difference is the immediate increase in aggression. That is really where the differences occur."

In contrast, in his testimony to the joint select committee on video material in Australia in 1985, Donnerstein stated that "sexually explicit material has no effects on behavior, attitudes or any effects. Take away the violent element, no effects."[5]

Another shortcoming in the work done on pornography, said Cowan, is that, too often, researchers are overly committed to their own versions of what they perceive to be the appropriate focus and tend to concentrate too heavily on discrediting the findings of other researchers.

In the studies that James Check released through the LaMarsh Center in the 1980s, on attitudes and behavior regarding pornography, sexual coercion, and violence among adolescents and young adults, he found that young people aged 12 to 17 years tend to be the primary consumers of pornography with reliance on it as a form of sex education; that 37 percent expressed an interest in watching sexually violent scenes such as rape, torture, and bondage; and that adults tended to express very little interest in such scenes.[6]

Check, Zillmann, and Bryant are among those who have contributed some of the best known studies on degrading or dehumanizing material that affects attitudinal and emotional responses, however, these tend to be dismissed by researchers who believe it is only the violence that is important. Also, Check's position on his own findings, like Donnerstein's has tended to be inconsistent.[7] A key reason for inconsistencies and denial on the part of pornography researchers, almost certainly, is the political or ideological distaste for recommendations with wide ranging legal solutions.

Fraser Committee Ignores Research Findings
This tenacious resistance to evidence of harmful effects was implicit in the conclusions on pornography and prostitution reached in the report released in Canada in 1985 by a special committee set up by the Federal Government to study these issues. Known as The Fraser Report, it was fraught with ambiguities and claims of inconclusive evidence to the point where it was ultimately rejected by the very government who had set up the Committee in the first place.

In the process of gathering their evidence, the Committee deliberately ignored the findings released at the second major *Symposium on Pornography and Media Violence* held in North America at the Ontario Institute for Studies in Education (OISE) in February, 1984.[8] The Symposium was specifically timed to coincide with its scheduled hearings in Toronto. Committee members were present and, later, provided with transcripts. The Committee's response of total denial was evident to everyone, including members of Canadians Concerned About Violence In Entertainment (C-CAVE), who co-sponsored and attended the conference and later read the Report.

Participants at the conference included over 30 prominent American and Canadian researchers, writers, community activists, educators, health care workers, members of the media, and municipal politicians. Among those present were Donnerstein, Zillmann, Bryant, Malamuth, Check, Singer, Huesmann, Eron, and U.S. Surgeon General C. Everett Koop. In his remarks, Koop emphasized that violence throughout North America had reached epidemic proportions and that media violence, pornographic and otherwise, was a major causal factor.[9] Still, several months later, the Fraser Report would cite no conclusive evidence of harmful effects.[10]

As an antidote to this myopic response from the Fraser Commission, C-CAVE board member and OISE doctoral candidate, David Scott, assisted in the publication of a resource book in Washington, D.C. entitled *Pornography: Its Effects on the Family, Community and Culture*.[11] The book included a discussion of pornography, its effects, the victimizers, the victims, television violence research, the role of organized crime, the effects on community and culture, and some strategies for change. It was later criticized by Donnerstein and others, both for the manner in which the research was discussed and for the emphasis on the need for public education and policy rather than more research.[12]

Industry Orchestrated Opposition to New Legislation

C-CAVE's objections to the conclusions in the Fraser Report were amplified by the Canadian public at large. More action was demanded and another, follow-up study was done by the Ministry of Justice.[13] A series of bills to amend the Criminal Code on definitions of pornography were then introduced in the House of Commons, all of them dying on the order paper at one time or another until May, 1993, when a new child pornography bill was introduced, and subsequently implemented.

Reasons for the delay of almost ten years for this particular initiative are various. One of them was the result of well-funded and well orchestrated propaganda campaigns from pornographic media interests opposed to any interference with their corporate activity. An example manifested itself in 1986 in the form of a "leaked" memo from Argyle Communications Inc., at the time the Toronto affiliate of Gray and Company, a large Washington, D.C. based public relations agency. In Canada, it was distributed by the Metro Residents Action Committee on Violence Toward Women and Children (METRAC).

The memo included an outline of a campaign underway for the purpose of discrediting the U.S. Meese Commission Report, but it was, in fact, the brainchild of the Toronto based operation. One of the agency's strategies read as follows:

> A way must be found to discredit the organizations and individuals who have begun to disrupt the legitimate business activities of publishers. This can be accomplished by creation of a broad coalition of individuals and organizations opposed to the Commission's findings and recommendations...these new groups would include academics, civil libertarians, religious leaders, civic and community leaders, politicians, columnists, commentators and entertainers. It might be called "Americans for the Right to Read" or "The First Amendment Coalition."[14]

Soon after, evidence that these strategies were being implemented began to surface in the public debate on the subject of pornography. A series of public meetings was held throughout Toronto, mainly in public libraries, without panel representation in defense of the bill. There was also a visible shift in the balance of coverage on the issue of pornography that had hitherto appeared in mainstream newspapers.

In my own analysis of 93 articles which appeared in *The Toronto Star* over a period of 15 months from the time the bill was first introduced into the House of Commons on May 4, 1987, until it was declared virtually defeated on July 14, 1988, and eventually died on the order paper when a federal election was called several months later, only six could be described as reflecting the position of the Justice Department where the bill had first been drafted.[15]

In 1987, Toronto feminist and legal scholar Reva Landau published a brief involving an analysis and detailed critique of the relevant bill on behalf of an action group she helped form called Committee Against Pornography. On the basis of her research, Landau registered a twelve page protest to the Ontario Press Council accusing *The Toronto Star* of inaccurate, misleading and biased reporting in connection with the bill. The newspaper's response was that the bill was a complex one that had been interpreted in "different ways by different people" but that their columns reflected the views of a major segment of the cultural community.[16] Precisely who they meant by "the cultural community" was unclear. Were they referring to the artistic community, the movie distributors who have always contributed so much to their advertising revenue, or both?

This experience on the part of Landau and other Canadians concerned about the proliferation of pornography in the country serves to demonstrate how biased in favor of the press existing press councils can be. Another example surfaced in 1998 following C-CAVE volunteer Valerie Smith's complaint about coverage in *The Toronto Star* in July, 1997, of the shock rock band *Marilyn Manson*. Concerns she expressed in press releases and through media interviews with reporters focused on the names of serial killers adopted by the band and the violent, anti-Semitic, racist and misogynist messages in their music lyrics, dress and performances. These were described in front-page coverage in *The Toronto Star* as a "tempest in a T-shirt."[17]

The complaint was dismissed "with reservations" only because, in the Council's view, the story should have been described as "analysis but not opinion." At the hearing, the reporter in question persuaded the Council that he had merely attempted "to elevate the level of debate by placing the controversy over the band [which led to cancellation of a concert in Calgary] in a broader context than the 'he-said-she-said' type of story."

Both of these examples underscore the continuing need for impartial media councils and an ombudsman acting solely in the public interest, as recommended by the LaMarsh Report and more recently in a "People's Communication Charter" approved at the International Founding Convention for the Cultural Environment Movement in St. Louis, Missouri in 1996.[18]

They also illustrate the extraordinary degree to which the cultural industries will mount well funded public relations campaigns to protect their business interests, despite public concern about perceived excesses. These social realities make meaningful change especially difficult for underfunded and overworked volunteer organizations attempting to act in the public interest with only marginal interest and support from relevant government departments; underscoring reasons why progress in addressing media violence, pornographic and otherwise, is so slow.

Similar ways in which institutionalized violence is maintained and protected by public relations expertise have been argued by Joyce Nelson in her book *Sultans of Sleaze* published in 1989.[19] They also help to illuminate the potential for eruption of real life violence from frustration and anger about the possibility of change at all. One example is already manifesting itself in the rising evidence of diminishing faith in public institutions within the public at large.

More Federal Initiatives

In 1993, the Canadian Government's Standing Committee on Culture and Communications made a number of recommendations. One was that the Federal Minister of Justice, in collaboration with his provincial counterparts, study the matter of extremely violent forms of entertainment, such as slasher and snuff films, to determine the criminal legislative measures needed to control them and to design such legislation to conform to the *Canadian Charter of Rights and Freedoms*.[20]

Others were that the Minister of Justice introduce legislation to control extremely violent forms of entertainment, such as slasher and snuff films, and amend the *Criminal Code* accordingly; that the Minister of Finance review and, if necessary, revise the *Customs Tariff* to ensure that it complemented the necessary amendments to the *Criminal Code*.[21]

The only action resulting from this Report was passage in July, 1993, of the child pornography bill which made the production, distribution, and possession of child pornography a criminal offence in Canada, punishable by up to five years in prison for simple possession of the illicit material. As a result, any film magazine or video that shows explicit sexual activity involving people under 18, or adults pretending to be under the age of 18, can be considered child pornography.

Opposition to the new legislation began to surface in the media immediately, in ways that were reminiscent of previous bills on pornography, with calls to have it revoked. The usual objections surfaced. There were criticisms that the bill was passed with "undue haste," was badly flawed because it was too broad, allowing for too much "misadventure" on the part of police forces and border guards, that the burden of proof rests with the accused, that merit can only be assessed after the fact and that "artists," whose defense is unsuccessful, risk going to jail.[22] Although there was some news coverage on the fact that the bill had many supporters as well as detractors, most of it focused on objections raised within the arts community.

Renewed Public Debate over Definitions

The first artist to be charged under the new legislation was Eli Langer who had five oil paintings and 35 pencil drawings seized from the Mercer Union Art Gallery in Toronto on December 15, 1993. Among the materials seized were some of the following examples as they were described by the press:

> ...a drawing depicting a bound and gagged boy being sodomized, and an oil painting of a young girl with what Lander describes as "body fluid" dripping from her lips. Other drawings depict sex between children.[23]

In his defense, Langer argued that he did not use models, that his work was the product of his imagination, and that it involved a serious "exploration of the phenomenon of sexual intimacy between adults and children."[24] Other descriptions of his work seized included references to drawings of children performing oral and anal sex, a naked little girl sitting on the lap of a naked old man and a little girl sitting across the neck of a man who is lying on his back and has an erection.[25]

At the time, the possibilities of Langer's work being exempted on the basis of artistic merit led Canadian journalist, Bronwyn Drainie, to reflect on the difficulties of defining art simply on the basis of something hanging in a legitimate "art gallery."

> Let's suppose that before mounting this show, the artist took his paintings and drawings to a photo lab that specializes in doing transparencies for artists. Transparencies are what artists and their agents send to curators and gallery owners in other cities to stimulate interest in their work.

> Now let's suppose that the photo lab owner is an unscrupulous fellow who sees the commercial potential of Langer's work. Under the counter he sells a duplicate set of negatives to one of the large pornography distribution firms in the United States who prints thousands of postcards from Langer's images. When you come across one of Langer's drawings covered in greasy thumb-prints and possibly other substances at the back of a porn shop in Philadelphia, is it still art?[26]

Other journalists commented as well with reviews of debate on the topic over the previous two decades.[27] Proponents of the bill argued that if, as a society, we are serious about addressing the problem of child sexual abuse, than we need clear statements that children are not to be used for the sexual gratification of adults.[28] Lawyers among them argued that exemption in the Code for artistic merit should be removed entirely.

By the time the trial involving Langer's work began, there was evidence that his defense was well organized, well funded, and broadly supported. Witnesses testifying on his behalf, apart from University of Toronto psychologist Jonathan Freedman, artists, art critics, art therapists, and female university-based lecturers on sexuality and pornography in popular culture, included prominent media personalities.

Once again, as it did in 1987-88 when bill C-54 was tabled in the House of Commons, *The Toronto Star* contributed generous coverage for the opposition with dire predictions that "Michelangelo's renaissance masterpiece, the statue David, could be banned in Canada under the federal government's sweeping anti-child pornography law."[29]

Coverage in *The Globe and Mail*, was more balanced and included references to expert witness testimony on behalf of the Crown and evidence involving an issue of the NAMBLA *Bulletin*, a periodical for a group called the North American Men and Boys Love Association, which advocates sex between adult males and young boys. The *Bulletin* contained an article on the Langer case that included reproductions of the artist's sketches.[30]

On April 20, 1995, the Ontario Court ruled that the paintings and drawings seized by police should be returned to Langer because the seizures violated his constitutional right to free speech on the basis of demonstrated artistic merit. Judge McCombs, the presiding judge, also ruled, however, that the legislation was valid and that the protection of children takes precedence over the right to free speech.[31]

Although the charges against Langer were dropped and his art work was returned, the child pornography legislation itself had survived. In October, 1995, Langer's challenge against these laws in the form of an appeal to the Supreme court was also denied,[32] but by 1999 it was again in jeopardy following a decision from Justice Duncan Shaw of the B.C. Supreme Court when he dismissed two charges of possession of child pornography against John Robin Sharpe of Vancouver on the basis that possession of child pornography "is not a reasonable limit on freedom of expression guaranteed by the Charter of Rights and Freedoms."[33]

Nevertheless, in the appeal which followed, lawyers acting on behalf of Sharpe quickly dropped their objections to possession of "graphic" depictions of children but continued to argue for exemptions for computer simulations and drawings. This time, the Federal Government stepped in with intervenor status to protect its legislation. On June 30 the Appeal Court ruled 2-1 in favor of Sharpe that the law contravenes the Charter of Rights and Freedoms and the case is now before the Supreme Court of Canada. Although the opposition is urging the government to invoke the notwithstanding clause of the Constitution so that the pornography law will stand no matter what the courts rule, Federal Minister of Justice Ann McLellan stated that it is premature to do so before the Supreme Court makes its ruling.[34]

The Impact of New Legislation on Child Pornography

Although in the spring of 1993 both Mr. Blais and federal MP, Otto Jelinek, supported a proposal to broaden the legal definition of obscenity to include undue exploitation of crime, horror, cruelty, and violence that is degrading and dehumanizing, even if it contains no sexual element, this component was not included in the new legislation. Nevertheless, since it has come into effect, the police have been able to lay a number of additional charges related to child pornography.

By October of 1993, five people were arrested in what was described as the largest seizure of child pornography in Canadian history. In *The Toronto Star* it was reported that, "Thousands of videotapes, many made in Metro, were seized following a six-month probe by members of the Project P joint-forces operation of Metro police and the Ontario Provincial Police."[35] The new legislation also had an impact on one of the nation's largest commercial computer bulletin boards. The Mississauga based CRS Online immediately made a decision to discontinue its adult conference and told its 10,000 members that all relevant files and CD-ROMS had been destroyed. Because there had been evidence that stories about minors and young children being forced into sexual acts by adults was surfacing in the material, they said they were no longer prepared to take the required legal risks. According to general manager David Chaloner, the company "also felt that it was inconsistent with the future direction of CRS to continue providing access to adult material."[36]

Chaloner did not see the decision to exclude sexually explicit material as censorship but rather as good business sense because parents were beginning to take their business less seriously when they learned about, and in many cases objected to, the pornographic content.[37] A similar decision was made at the University of Waterloo after six years of resistance.[38] Five electronic bulletin boards that dealt with violent sex and pornography were banned from its campus.

By the end of 1996 the proliferation of pornography on the Internet had penetrated the innermost sanctum of the Canadian Federal Government itself, prompting Defense Minister Doug Young to order an internal investigation into the alleged use of military computers to access and store child pornography.[39]

The second charge of its kind, in a little over one month, it resulted in the arrest of a high-level civilian scientist working on secret projects within the Department of National Defense after police discovered large caches of child pornography. In a myriad of ways, the Internet is quickly becoming what police in a number of countries have defined as a prime source of hard-core child pornography. This has prompted calls for Internet providers to develop codes of conduct and responsibility for what they host.[40]

More Manifestations of the Problem

Pornography as a form of media violence continues to proliferate and new legislation on child pornography emerging in various jurisdictions around the world only addresses a small portion of it. In Canada, one manifestation of the problem left unaddressed by amendments to the Criminal Code in 1993 was the marketing of serial killer board games such as those distributed by Diamond Distributors, a U.S. company with branch offices in Burnaby, B.C. and Edmonton, AB.

According to B.C. reporter James Risdon, who first discovered the problem in 1992, "Packaged in its own plastic body bag, Serial Killer Games comes complete with an illustrated game board, a bag of 25 babies, four serial killer figures, crime and outcome cards, and instructions."[41] These games have also inspired a similar genre of violent entertainment called *True Crime Trading Cards*, produced by *Eclipse Books* in California. According to one account, they "outline the killer's criminal history and carry a water color likeness. When the killer is unknown, cards sometimes depict the victim."[42] In many instances the killer's history includes an addiction to pornography.

In 1994, the Canadian Government's Standing Committee on Justice and Legal Affairs drafted amendments to the Criminal Code on these crime cards and board games that would have legalized the commercial use and sale of crime cards and board games to anyone over the age of 18 years. C-CAVE and citizen's groups represented by parents whose children had been murdered by serial killers argued against them on the basis that such amendments would normalize this kind of entertainment by putting the Government's stamp of approval on its legal sale to anyone at all.[43]

Describing these cards in a newsletter published by Canadians Against Violence Everywhere Advocating Its Termination (CAVEAT) in 1993, Debbie Mahaffy, whose daughter Leslie had been murdered by Paul Bernardo, posed this question: "What's next? Gang rape cards?" Despite several years of petitioning by Mahaffy and others these cards still remain eligible for entry into Canada and available to anyone of any age because they are not considered illegal either under Obscenity Clause 163(8) of the Criminal Code or any other provision.

In July of 1993, other limitations to the new amendments in the criminal code on pornography and media violence surfaced in Ontario government debates at Queen's Park on interactive video games. Public protest over this new genre of violent entertainment revolved around CD-ROM discs marketed by Sega entitled *Night Trap*. The game featured actual images of women rather than cartoon-like characters.

Company Vice-President, Jeff McCarthy, described the trend toward more realistic video games portraying more sex and violence as the generation of children reared on video games got older.[44] Opposition critics argued that voluntary controls by the industry were not sufficient while the Attorney General of the day, Marion Boyd, argued that drafting legislation to control video games was a difficult process requiring federal-provincial cooperation to overcome jurisdictional limits.[45] While this was being explored she recommended consumer boycotts which, in her view, were the most powerful and effective way to address the problem anyway.

Once again, history was repeating itself as government authorities evaded an opportunity to address the issue of media violence in order to avoid accusations of censorship. News coverage, such as a review of *Night Trap* in *The Wall Street Journal*, in which it was stated that the game, with the sound and feel of a B-grade slasher film, provided a glimpse of where video games may be headed in the future, seducing more and more young people of all ages around the world into amusing themselves with ever increasing variations of violent imagery, had no impact.[46]

Boyd's approach was the same as that of California Attorney General Dan Lungren, who was also calling upon video game manufacturers and retailers to "voluntarily" remove from the market games which contained graphic, gratuitous violence. He, too, carefully emphasized that he was not proposing "censorship or mandatory government action" but appealing instead to industry to exercise their "sense of corporate and personal responsibility."[47]

In public statements made on behalf of Sega, Jeff McCarthy pointed out that the company was doing its "best to inform consumers and parents."[48] Rating stickers on games sold, it was reported, like movie ratings, would advise parents in three categories: GA for general audience, MA-13 for mature audiences and MA-17 for adults only. Few observers, however, have ever believed that ratings and warning labels are very helpful for a variety of reasons among them the fact that anyone at all who uses this game as a form of entertainment is at risk. Also, it is generally acknowledged among researchers that once a product is out on the market, children of all ages usually end up with access to it in one way or another.

By the end of the year it was announced that *Night Trap* would no longer be distributed in Canada, however, insignificant variations continue to be released into the Canadian market. Clearly, trends in the technology, itself, underscore the growing urgency for government action as virtual reality games now offer enhanced opportunities to participate in the experience of actually *killing* someone.[49]

The urgency and seriousness of problems posed by new interactive technology were stressed by Eugene Provenzo in 1993 when he attended a conference on electronic child abuse organized in Toronto by the Institute for the Prevention of Child Abuse. As a toy designer, social scientist, and educator, he warned parents about the potent impact and increasing dangers of ever more graphic depictions and diversified forms of violence on the market as the technologies converge.

The extent to which pornography, sex, and violence as entertainment, and violence in real life have converged, with the boundaries between the two becoming increasingly blurred, was, for the author, further underscored during a forum on violence in the media at Stephen Leacock Highschool in Scarborough in 1993.

Because Canadian serial killer, Paul Bernardo, had grown up in Scarborough, the social impact of the crimes with which he was charged and subsequently convicted, among them the murder of Leslie Mahaffy and Kristin French, was felt particularly strongly in that community. Television host, Paris Black's reference to the fact that Bernardo, when he was first put in jail, received thousands of letters from young female fans was—it was generally agreed—a demonstration of what U.S. Surgeon General Koop meant when he said a decade earlier that violence in society, exacerbated by violence in the media, has become an extremely serious mental health problem throughout North America.[50]

Exploiting the Threat of Censorship for Profit
During the summer of 1993, intense public interest, both inside Canada and beyond its borders, was focused on the charges faced by Karla Homolka, the 23-year-old in St. Catharines, ON, who was sentenced to 12 years in prison for manslaughter in the deaths of teenagers Leslie Mahaffy and Kristin French. A press ban was imposed on publication of the evidence because Paul Bernardo, her estranged husband, still faced two charges of first-degree murder in connection with the deaths.

The presiding judge closed the courtroom to the general public and prohibited the media from publishing or broadcasting any details about the circumstances of the deaths. Judge Kovacs stated that Bernardo's right to a fair trial on the murder charges had to take precedence over freedom of expression. This decision precipitated an avalanche of media attention and debate in ways that offered the public an exceptional opportunity to observe the expression of *institutionalized* violence in the media when the overriding consideration is profit.

Although the need for protection of the families and communities traumatized by the murders was not stipulated as a factor for imposition of the ban, it was soon apparent that the ban would have that side-effect. When Debbie Mahaffy was interviewed for *Maclean's Magazine* her comments underscored the potential for justification of the ban on humanitarian grounds alone.

> My emotion coming out of court was one of despair. It was like my daughter had just died again. Then to meet a couple of reporters who were genuinely moved, for a fleeting moment, my grief was magnified.

> I don't want to comment on the sentence she [Karla Homolka] received. But I will say that sitting through all the evidence was a very emotionally difficult and draining experience...In some ways, I'm glad that there will be some time before the...trial comes up. Every month helps me to cope with all the pain. Every extra month will help my son cope...I want it to end. I don't ever want to see another image of that body bag again. I don't want to see those men carrying my daughter from the lake...It aches to be constantly reminded.[51]

Despite the evident, humanitarian component as a side-effect to the press ban imposed by Judge Kovacs, the day after the Homolka trial was concluded, representatives for *The Globe and Mail, The Toronto Sun* and the *Canadian Broadcasting Corporation* announced that they planned an appeal. John Cruickshank, then managing editor of *The Globe and Mail* explained that "the overall issue the court will be asked to decide is whether the 'enormous public interest' in the proceedings can be reconciled with the valid interest of ensuring a fair trial for Ms. Homolka's estranged husband, Paul Bernardo, on two charges of first-degree murder."[52] For Cruickshank, the need for the victim's families to be spared unnecessary additional pain and suffering on the basis of Debbie Mahaffy's own frequently reported preference for a ban on publication of the circumstances of the deaths of her daughter and Kristin French, was a nonissue.

A number of lawyers commented on the validity of the ban, among them Nancy Toran-Harbin, executive director of the Family Abuse Crisis Exchange (FACE), former board member of C-CAVE, and former co-chair of the Coalition for Responsible Television (CRTV). She argued that the impact of communications technology on the public court is increasingly in danger of transforming it into a "tabloid court." Said Toran-Harbin:

> During the past ten years there has been a burgeoning recognition within the justice system of a pressing need to address the short and long term impact of violent crime upon victims of violence. It is now accepted that damage is not confined to the primary victim, but rather extends to a group of secondary victims comprised of the victim's family and intimate circle. In addition, it is now being recognized that a larger constellation of individuals can, to a significant degree, be detrimentally affected, namely, the peers, friends and acquaintances of the victims and their families.[53]

The public, she pointed out, was already fully aware of many horrifying aspects relating to the case and wondered what possible principle of justice would be served through publicizing additional minute details about, for example, the last words uttered by "two terrorized children?" Said Toran-Harbin:

> In the most active area of free speech and press litigation under the Charter, our courts have ruled in the most powerful terms that the public, including the press, has a constitutional right to attend court proceedings, as well as a constitutional right to freely report to others what has transpired there, subject only to narrow limits. If we accept the premise that it is desirable for the justice system to treat victims of crime with at least the equivalent regard and humanity as is in the law guaranteed to the accused, it is appropriate to explore methods which aim toward such attainment.[54]

She drew attention to frequently reported instances where publicity surrounding the graphic details of brutal murders have served as blueprints for further crimes. A serial killer who is able to successfully conceal evidence, even temporarily, poses a significant ongoing threat to public safety. For this reason the justice system is required to interpret and determine a balance in the face of competing values and needs.

Others have pointed out that distinctions need to be drawn between public voyeurism and the public right to information, with more emphasis placed on determining what it is the public really needs to know. According to Toronto criminal lawyer Edward Greenspan:

> ...the public's essential right to know doesn't mean that they have the right to know everything...Consider the example of a victim in a sexual assault

case. We protect their identity, for good reason…some bans are legitimate. And most bans are temporary. The public's right to know is merely postponed—they have a right to know, but not necessarily immediately.[55]

From the time the ban was first imposed, there was speculation on precisely how it might be enforced. Legal options available to Attorney-General Marion Boyd, as chief law officer for the province, included the opportunity to lay criminal charges against both cable television outlets and stations that distributed shows violating the ban. A spokesman for Rogers Cablesystems, however, countered with the familiar argument, that the "company views itself only as the carrier of information, irrespective of its content."[56]

The complications that began to impede enforcement of the ban prompted Bob Rae, then Premier for Ontario, to accuse the U.S. media of showing disrespect for Ontario's judicial system by publishing details of the Karla Homolka trial that the Canadian media themselves were banned from reporting.[57] By that time, however, most coverage revolved around the ban's impact on basic rights to freedom of the press and the public right to know.

In *The Toronto Star* Osgoode Hall law professor, Alan Young, commented on the "foolishness" of the court decision but not necessarily of our laws in general. Young explained that Canadian judges have been able to shield courtroom testimony in a way that American judges cannot because of differences in the power relationship between the media and the two justice systems.[58]

Brian Greenspan, past president of the Criminal Lawyers Association, pointed out that the press ban on the Homolka trial was by no means the first time one has been imposed in Canada.[59] What was new, he said, was the reaction of the media. Like Young, he also commented on fundamental differences between the American and Canadian judicial systems, involving the questioning of witnesses. These, he said, tend to precipitate the requirement of a ban in Canadian court cases more often and he urged the Canadian public not to allow themselves to be "held hostage by the American media."

Nelson Thall, President of the Marshall McLuhan Centre on Global Communications in Toronto, added his own voice to the discussion. He pointed out that although the court had acted in good faith to protect Paul Bernardo's right to a fair trial, it had, through its ignorance of the ground rules of the new environment, taken actions which had resulted in the opposite effect from that which had been hoped for. Making reference to "our new mind-to-mind awareness," which makes us all part of the "new tribal crowd," he said Judge Kovacs had made an error in not excluding all electronic media and allowing only the press to cover the case.[60]

Sheila Kieran, as a former journalist and a director of the LaMarsh Commission, contributed her perspective to the debate over the ban:

Before the media in Canada and the United States implode in further self-righteous indignation, it might be useful to consider elements of the

Homolka ban that are not getting sufficient attention. The first, and most fundamental is the media's idea of themselves. They insist their job is to ensure you live in a free and open society, protected against dictators who can't wait to subvert justice and strangle your access to information.

Hardly. The first job of your newspaper or television station is to make money.[61]

As Kieran pointed out, one thing in particular the case demonstrated was the growing chasm between Canadians, their politicians and media editors/owners. It was an insult to suggest that people were too passive to defy a court order which, in fact, seemed to many people a difficult but reasonable compromise between an open society and the need to ensure a fair trial. The streets were not filled with hordes demanding to know immediately every appalling detail of how two lively young women were killed. Said Kieran:

> The media seem oblivious to the fact that, for each of the people who rushed across the border to wallow in the horrific details in U.S. newspapers, thousands were apparently content to live in a country where the presumption of innocence and the right to a fair trial are considered something more than mere obstacles to test the press's cunning and perseverance.[62]

Corporate Greed with Municipal Collusion

The controversy over this particular press ban was not by any means the final demonstration of the media industry's opportunism in the aftermath of the murders of the Mahaffy and French girls. One month after conclusion of the Bernardo trial Bret Easton Ellis, author of the hideously sadistic novel *American Psycho*, a book identified as a blueprint for Bernardo's behavior and crimes by the Crown Attorney's office during the trial, appeared in Toronto as part of Harbourfront's International Festival of Authors. Harbourfront is primarily funded by the Canadian taxpayer which means that the same public traumatized by the trial and mourning for the children Bernardo murdered was, in effect, paying to provide a forum and publicity for one of his favorite authors. This happened despite objections from across the country to distribution of the book in Canada when it was first published, and to the fact that it was ruled inadmissable by the Judge during pre-trial arguments in the Bernardo trial, on the basis that the contents were so vile and vicious that if read in whole or in part by the jury they would have a significant prejudicial effect.[63]

Ellis enjoyed extensive publicity while in Toronto, both from *The Toronto Star* and *The Globe and Mail*.[64] Further taxpaying support for the amplification of his ideas and notoriety was provided by a public broadcaster, as well, when TVOntario host Steve Paikin interviewed him during a main stage reading, followed by book autographing. When he was contacted and confronted with the possibility of his book's connection with the Bernardo case by a reporter from *The Toronto Sun* several months earlier he insisted he was not to blame, claiming that, "Maybe they would have gotten an idea how to murder someone but they were probably going to do it anyway."[65] The novel was found at Paul Bernardo's bedside and prosecutors alleged that he "read it as a bible."[66] Like Bernardo in real life in Toronto's financial district, the novel's main character, was a stylish, New York stockbroker who worked by day on Wall Street and stalked young women by night.

In fact, it was controversial in Canada long before its release in the winter of 1990-91 when Ellis's original publisher, New York's Simon & Schuster decided to cancel its contract with him despite the $300,000 advance he had already been paid. After Vintage Books, a branch of Random House, bought the rights and released it anyway, the Canadian Navy bought copies of *American Psycho* prompting Mary Clancy, M.P for Halifax and Liberal Opposition Critic for the Status of Women at the time, to call for the book's removal.[67] When this was done at the request of Mary Collins, then Associate Defense Minister, Clancy stated in a letter to *The Toronto Star* that Collins was not telling Canadian sailors what they could or could not read but merely refusing to sanction federal government funding of violent, sexist material, known to have a harmful effect.

Public objections from C-CAVE and other organizations in October, 1995, that, given the known influence of the book on the behavior of Paul Bernardo, we should not be funding, promoting or sanctioning it by giving its author a voice, were ignored. Said Valerie Smith,

> The public deserves an apology from Harbourfront officials. But, regardless of whether that is forthcoming, each and every federally elected politician in Canada will receive a copy of this release, information on the connection to the Bernardo case, and excerpts from *American Psycho*, so that when Harbourfront's funding comes up for consideration, politicians can make an informed decision.

Despite her efforts to inform all federally elected politicians on the matter, the issue faded into obscurity. Similarly, a C-CAVE intervention at Toronto City Hall when Harbourfront's funding came up for renewal several months later, made no difference. It was approved without relevant comment.

Decisions involving *American Psycho* have by no means been the only demonstration of questionable judgement on the part of Harbourfront officials. From February 2, to April 8, 1996, Harbourfront's Art Gallery, The Power Plant, hosted an exhibition entitled "The American Trip" in which it purported to offer "the latest on artists in the forefront of expression of outlaw activity." Print material accompanying the exhibition explained that the purpose was to "highlight disillusionment with the American Dream" and to challenge the boundaries of censorship "on the edge of what can or cannot be shown in galleries." Displays involved the theme of "teenage lust" experienced by outlaw artists drifting in and out of jail. Accompanying photographs focused on drugs, violence, rock and roll, and sex with references to the experiences of pre-adolescent children.

The exhibition also celebrated images of sex and death with themes of kids killing parents and the world of bike gangs with their dress codes and symbols. There was exploration of the psychopath and con man "transformed from outlaw to celebrity" with serial killers used as examples. These themes of sex, violence and racism were all mounted in an exhibition at public expense in order to "test the boundaries of censorship."

Mixed Public Responses

Following Bernardo's trial, in which he was convicted on a number of charges for life in prison, among them as a dangerous offender, strong opposition arose to further, graphic accounts of the murders and accompanying sexual assaults being readily available to the public in the form of videos produced by Bernardo and Homalka. It came both from the families themselves and members of the community at large.

As a compromise between the public's right to know and the community's right to protection from further trauma during the Bernardo trial Patrick Lesage, the presiding judge, ruled that, as evidence, details of the videos produced by Bernardo and Homalka recording the death and murder of the young girls could be heard by the entire court but seen only by the jury itself.

Later the families of the two schoolgirls killed by Bernardo, with the help of lawyer Tim Danson, sought to have a section of the Criminal Code amended to bar the news media and other members of the public from courtrooms in cases where evidence is recognized as pornographic. He argued for protection from invasion of common-law rights to privacy for victims. The families also wanted all but two of the video tapes, used as evidence in the trial, to be destroyed. These would remain in the hands of the Crown prosecutor in the event that Bernardo's appeal was successful.[68]

In 1998, the Ontario Court of Appeal dismissed the appeal. Instead, the presiding judge ruled that any order restricting access should be left to the discretion of the judge conducting the proceeding. In April, 1999, after the case had been heard by the Supreme Court of Canada, the families' plea was rejected again.

In the end, community compassion for the families traumatized by the French and Mahaffy murders was itself mixed. The library board within the City of St. Catharines, where the French family resides, voted to remove from its shelves all copies of the book, Lethal Marriage, by reporter Nick Pron of The Toronto Star. It is an account of the Bernardo trial considered by many to be graphic imagery and gratuitous pornography. The library board in the city of Burlington, where Mahaffy lives, however, was voted down 8-3 on the basis that the "fundamental right of free speech and freedom of expression should be upheld."[69] The house in St. Catherines, itself, where the murders were carried out was demolished with police, and government officials, both municipal and provincial, working together to iron out the details.[70]

During the Bernardo trial and immediately after, there were numerous examples of reporters, lawyers, judges, members of the victims' families and those providing support for them suffering from post traumatic stress disorders. Describing her own experiences Patricia Herdman, co-president of the Coalition for Responsible Television (CRTV) and a personal friend of Debbie Mahaffy, who sat through portions of the trial with her in 1995 said:

> From June through October...I could not concentrate. I experienced severe depression. I burst into tears while working at my client's office. My husband found me one night curled up in the fetal position in my office at home sobbing. I stayed like that for more than an hour. All that night, my body hurt. Breathing hurt. My mood swings were sudden and I was often short-tempered. As I described it to my family, I had a very, very "thin emotional buffer." It was easy to trigger me into deep sorrow.[71]

Herdman also "lost some memory" during the trial when one of the tapes of the murders produced by Bernardo and Homalka was played on June 2, 1995. Said Herdman, "Sometime in early October, I remembered the scream and that's all I have been able to recover from my memory of the tape."

On the whole, despite accumulating evidence of harmful effects and the proliferation of new forms of pornography from technological innovations, little has been done to reverse these trends. Minor amendments to the Criminal Code making the production, distribution, and possession of child pornography illegal, continue to be challenged as unconstitutional.

Meanwhile, tragic murders are being exploited with extraordinary callousness for profit-making purposes without any consideration for the impact on the survivors of victims. The observation made by the LaMarsh Report that profit tends to override social costs within the media industries remains a critical and growing problem.

In 1996, Allan Rock, as Minister of Justice and Attorney General of Canada, released a consultation paper dealing with the issue of undue exploitation of violence. The purpose was described as threefold: to disseminate information about the issue, to seek views from the general public on questions connected to the issue which included violence on "the information highway," and to gather information on current research and programs dealing with the effects of exposure to media violence.[72]

The paper was unfortunately fraught with contradictions and inconsistencies in terms of earlier positions adopted by Rock such as the one he took at the United Nations 9th Congress on Crime Prevention held in Cairo, Egypt in 1995. There the Minister stressed, in his opening remarks at a one day seminar on the role of media in crime prevention organized by the Canadian delegation, that none of the freedoms in our Constitutional Charter are absolute; that they are all subject to limitations which can be justified in a free and democratic society.[73] Yet, in the Consultation Paper which appeared a year later, the position adopted was that Charter protection applies to freedom of expression regardless of what form it takes. Recommendations from the previous Government's Standing Committee Report on Violence in the Media had been ignored entirely.

By 1999, it was reported that both the Governments of Ontario and Canada had provided generous funding for the pornographic movie, *Bubbles, Galore*, an award winner at the Cannes Film Festival that year. The Festival, itself, was chaired by controversial Canadian film producer, David Cronenberg, himself a frequent recipient of government grants.[74] In the weeks that followed, further coverage focused on generous public funds for a whole myriad of unsavory productions from the standpoint of the public interest and welfare. Underscoring Canada's leadership in the current global race to the bottom on standards, on May 12, in *The Globe and Mail*, Alison Vale pointed out that the Canadian film industry simply couldn't survive without sex and violence supported by tax dollars from the public purse.

Notes

1. Withey & Abeles, 1980, p. 130.
2. Donnerstein et al., 1987, p. 34.
3. 1980, p. 377.
4. 1987, p. 5.
5. Cowan, 1992, p. 2-3.
6. Check & LaCrosse, 1989.
7. Check et al., 1985; Check, 1986.
8. Epstein, 1984.
9. Dyson, 1995, 1988a; Epstein, 1984.
10. Fraser, 1985, p. 101.
11. 1985.
12. 1987.
13. Dyson, 1988a.
14. Johnson, 1986, p.4.
15. The six articles included: "Legal definition of pornography broken into six areas," May 5, 1987; "Porn curbs don't bear on normal sex critics told," May 6, 1987; "Pornography bill 'tough but fair'," May 23, 1987; "Pornography bill requires sober debate," May 23, 1987; "Forget press freedom stop smut merchants" January 10, 1988; "Fact vs fiction in new anti-pornography bill," February 26, 1988.
16. Landau, personal communication, January 25, 1988.
17. Ontario Press Council, 1998.
18. CEM Steering Committee, 1989, March 18, Temple University, Philadelphia.
19. Nelson, 1989.
20. 1993, p. 74.
21. 1993, p. 74.
22. Harris, 1993, June 30, *The Globe and Mail*, p. C1.
23. Exhibit busted, 1993, Dec 23-29, *Now Magazine*, p. 11.
24. Exhibit busted, 1993, p. 11.
25. Taylor, 1993, Dec. 23, *The Globe and Mail*, p. A7.
26. 1994, Jan. 7, *The Globe and Mail*, p. C1.
27. 1994, p. C1.
28. Fine, 1994, Feb. 26, *The Globe and Mail*, p. A1, A6.
29. Tyler, 1994a, Oct. 12-13, *The Toronto Star*, p. A4; 1994b, p. A4.
30. Claridge, 1994, Oct. 6, *The Globe and Mail*, p.C4.
31. Downey, 1995, April 21, *The Globe and Mail*, p.A6.

32. "Top court refuses," 1995, Oct. 14, *The Toronto Star*, p.A4.

33. Matas, 1999.

34. Armstrong, 1999, June 30, *The Globe and Mail*, p.A1.

35. Wilkes, 1993, Oct. 3, *The Toronto Star*, p.A11.

36. Lester, 1993, Oct. 5, *The Toronto Sun*, p.43.

37. Chernos, 1993, Dec. 1, *Toronto Computes!*, p.51-52.

38. Gooderham, 1994, Feb. 5, *The Globe and Mail*, p.A1.

39. Feschuk,S & H.Hess, 1996, Dec.10, *The Globe and Mail*, p.A1.

40. International Symposium on Hate on the Internet, Toronto, March, 1999; Heather,D. 1998.

41. Risdon, 1992, Aug. 16, Murder: The Boardgame, *The News*, Bunaby, B.C., p. 1.

42. Killer cards, 1993, March 1, *Hamilton Spectator*, p. B6.

43. Dyson, 1994c, Spring *C-CAVE News*, p.4-5.

44. Mackie, 1993, July 14, *The Globe and Mail*, p. A3.

45. Mackie, 1993, p. A3.

46. Mackie, 1993, p. A3.

47. Lungren, 1993, Nov. 16, News Release, CA Department of Justice.

48. Dawson & Harvey, 1993, July 14, *The Toronto Sun*, p.16.

49. Dawson & Harvey, 1993, p. 16.

50. Epstein, 1984. Producer, Video Symposium, Feb. 5, 1984, OISE and C-CAVE.

51. *Brady*, 1993, July 19, *Maclean's Magazine*, p. 17.

52. Claridge, 1993, July 7, *The Globe and Mail*, p. A4.

53. 1993, *Law Society of Upper Canada Gazette*, 27, p.111-112.

54. 1993, p.111-112.

55. Cheney, 1993, July 3, *The Toronto Star*, p.D1.

56. Tyler, 1993, July 15, *The Toronto Star*, p.A10.

57. Cheney, 1993, D1.

58. Tyler, 1993, p. A4.

59. CBC Radio, 1993b, Dec. 1, Radio Noon.

60. Thall, 1993, Dec. 8, *The Globe nd Mail*, p. A18.

61. Kieran, 1993, ec. 9, *The Toronto Star*, p.A27.

62. 1993, p.A27.

63. Personal communication, Smith, Oct. 15, 1995, Cairns, 1995, p.3. Sept. 1, *The Toronto Sun*.

64. Marchand, 1995, p.C1, Kirchhoff,1995, p.D1.

65. V. Smith, personal communication, Oct.15, 1995.

66. Cairins, 1995, p.3.

67. Cairns, 1995, p.3.

68. "Bernardo victims' kin," 1996, Feb. 6, *The Globe nd Mail*, p.A8.

69. Vincent, 1995, Nov. 17, *The Toronto Star*, p.A.15.

70. "Bernardo's house," 1995, Nov. 17, *The Toronto Star*, p.A.15.

71. Personal Communication, December 1, 1995.

72. Canada, 1996, Dept. of Justice, Ottawa, Undue Exploitaton of Violence.

73. Dyson, April 24, 1996, Response to Allan Rock's Consultation Paper on Undue Exploitation of Violence.

74. Fire, R. 1999.

Chapter 6

OTHER MODEST GAINS

SO FAR, RESPONSES TO THE LaMarsh Commission's recommendations for communications industry overhaul have been minimal at best. The closest example to implementation of its recommendation for a "freedom of expression" act appears, in very general terms, in the *Charter of Rights for Canadians*. Brought in by Prime Minister Pierre Trudeau in 1981, it was an attempt to define our basic liberties.

Only brief reference is made in the Charter to the subject of free expression in the section on fundamental freedoms. These include "the right to freedom of conscience and religion; freedom of thought, belief, opinion and expression, including freedom of the press and other media of communication." If anything, lawsuits such as those involving the possession of child pornography and media pressure for access into the court room under any circumstances, have resulted in the Charter being invoked much more often to serve industrial interests than to protect individual freedoms.

Responses to Recommendations for Industry Overhaul in Canada
In 1993, Trina McQueen, a former Canadian Broadcasting Association (CBC) executive, later with Discovery Channel Canada, replaced Laurier LaPierre as head of the industry-based Action Group on Violent Television (AGVOT) set up to address the issue of media violence several months earlier.[1] In a personal interview, she discussed ways in which the broadcasting system in Canada had been overhauled since 1977.

Following introduction of the first broadcasting act in the mid 1920s, there have been five restructuring exercises, she explained, and between 10 to 15 major studies of the broadcasting industry. The most recent reorganization up until then had occurred in 1991 with the introduction of a new Broadcasting Act. Although, it was widely heralded in the media as being long overdue and a necessary update to changing circumstances, an examination of this Act indicates nothing specific in it that addressed the subject of media violence.

It begins with the following explanation:

This Act shall be construed and applied in a manner that is consistent with the freedom of expression and journalistic, creative and programming independence enjoyed by broadcasting undertakings.[2]

Air waves and radio frequencies are acknowledged as public property to be used by licensed broadcasters in ways that ensure public service essential to the maintenance and enhancement of national identity and cultural sovereignty. However, restriction of counterproductive and harmful elements in popular culture such as violence, as they were defined in the LaMarsh Report, are not addressed from the standpoint of any clearly spelled out limitations or regulations for anyone in Canadian society. Instead, the emphasis is on "a high standard," with development of Canadian expression through a wide range of programming that reflects Canadian attitudes, opinions, ideas, values and artistic creativity.[3]

The needs and aspirations of all Canadians are defined within the context of "equal rights, linguistic duality and recognition of the multi-cultural and multi-racial nature of Canadian society." There is no reference at all to the rights and aspirations of Canadians to freedom from harmful effects in the public airwaves. Instead, the predominant emphasis is on conditions for broadcasting policy involving Canadian ownership and control with operation in both official languages serving to "safeguard, enrich and strengthen the cultural, political, social and economic fabric" of the country.[4]

The Act calls for contributions from Canadian independent production houses, better distribution of Canadian programming, conflict-of-interest disputes resolved in the public interest and responsiveness to the evolving "demands of the public."[5] For greater certainty, it is stressed that the Act applies to all broadcasting undertakings whether or not they are carried on for profit.

As an alternative to the LaMarsh Commission's recommendations for a national media council with regional representation, McQueen[6] explained that the Canadian Radio-television and Telecommunications Commission (CRTC) structure has changed to include regional commissioners.

The CRTC now has a complaints commission with very wide powers. The public doesn't take advantage of it enough and the CRTC is extremely conservative in exercising its mandate. The CRTC can order a wide variety of sanctions. It can and has required broadcasters not to air advertisements. It can order that a remedial program be produced and aired. It can call an offender to a public hearing on complaints and can impose stiffer requirements as conditions for licensure. It can also force an apology. For public complaints, at the present time, the first recourse is to contact the Canadian Broadcast Standards Council (CBSC), set up by the Canadian Association of Broadcasters (CAB). The second one is to approach the CRTC.

McQueen believes that violence in films, videos, and television programming needs to be addressed; that legislation defining obscenity is a necessity; and that government regulation requiring adherence to an appropriately developed classification system is needed. She said:

I believe in free speech but I also believe, in the words of one American Supreme Court judge who said, "freedom of speech does not include the right to shout fire in a crowded theatre"...some violence in films is the equivalent to this kind of speech. Violence in films and television can ignite social harm and cause less safety in the community. Therefore, as a society, we have to establish some limits to what is permissible.

In McQueen's view, the main catalyst for change is public pressure. It was not clear, however, just how much and what kind of public pressure she had in mind. Experience has demonstrated that mobilizing support within the CRTC on behalf of the public interest is a Herculean task that is becoming more difficult with each passing year.

By 1999, evidence of AGVOT commitment to addressing violence in the media had disappeared entirely, with McQueen's own specialty Channel under attack from critics for airing objectionable material. On November 8, 1998, Valerie Smith filed a complaint against the Channel with the Ministry of the Solicitor General and Correctional Services for Ontario. For a second season in a row, Discovery Channel was running the Canadian television series *Exhibit A: Secrets of Forensic Science*, with information provided for this series by the Chief Coroner's Office, despite the known dangers of rapists and murderers being provided with information on how to avoid apprehension and/or conviction.[7]

Updating the CRTC Mandate

In 1996, public notice was given for re-examination of the CRTC mandate on standardization of regulations for broadcast distributors involving cable and satellite systems. Most of the 54 page notice dealt with market share and technologies. In her submission, Patricia Herdman, co-chair of the Coalition for Responsible Television, pointed out content regulations should be the same throughout all technologies, especially with respect to guidelines on violence. This was necessary in order to avoid confusing consumers on how and where to voice their opinions.

She called for mandatory V-chip technology for all forms of distribution mechanisms, to help prevent children from accessing unsuitable products with half the gross annual revenues from sales of these directed into an independently run Canadian production fund specifically ear-marked for the development of quality, non-violent children's programming in both official languages; and for one percent of the licensing fees collected from both television and other forms of broadcast distribution licenses to be directed to the Coalition so that they could advocate effectively on behalf of the consumer. All of these requests were ignored.

Legislation for the Protection of Children

LaMarsh Report recommendations for inexpensive tuning and locking devices to be mandatory on all television sets sold in Canada have never been implemented. Before he departed as chair of the CRTC in 1996, Keith Spicer called for the V-chip as a key strategy for blocking out all gratuitous violence and for a while it was an extremely popular suggestion at workshops and conferences on the subject of television violence. Engineering professor Tim Collings at Simon Fraser University in British Columbia was crowned by Spicer as the great Canadian inventor about to empower parents with appropriate devices to control their children's viewing habits through, as he put it, "self-censorship...without clamping down on the creative freedoms of the television and movie industry."[8]

Collings' invention, announced at an international symposium on "The Canadian Example" co-sponsored by the CRTC in Paris, in 1994, was promoted by Spicer on an international basis. He used the rationale that "it protects the widest possible creative freedoms in the recording arts [by] rightfully [placing] the final viewing decision in the hands of the parent."[9]

Once again, the onus was on parents to address the problem while industry was, in fact, offered an opportunity to profit further from their own acknowledged excesses. In the United States, Congress called for all television sets sold in the country to be fitted with mandatory blocking devices beginning in 1998, but the deadline has since been stretched to 1999. In Canada, from the time this solution was first rediscovered it was anticipated that consumers would pay extra for the service involving blocking devices either by being charged directly on their cable bill or through the purchase of a decoder that Collings estimated would cost around $100.

Shaw Cable now makes a digital box available for a monthly charge of $10.95 with various options such as pay per view programming and parental control through the use of codes for specific programs and channels, but it is still a far cry from the lauded V-chip. Other technological quick fixes reportedly available to parents include electronic devices called "TV Allowance."[10] Designed to limit the amount of time a child can watch television: families can settle on a specific amount of viewing time with the number of hours of allotted viewing time fed into a machine that resembles a desktop calculator. When a child's viewing time is up, the set evidently turns off automatically until the new week begins.

When it was first announced, Collings acknowledged a drawback to his own invention in that parents do not always know in advance whether a show, even one listed as family fare, will contain unacceptable scenes or language. Nevertheless, parents who in many cases are already feeling overburdened would still be required to search through TV listings for programs or stations they did not want their children to see. He conceded that at first glance the system may sound complicated to use, but that the emphasis was on enough information for "intelligent" parenting.

Although few would disagree that market availability of these blocking devices for assisting parents is long overdue, the fact remains that industry, with the support of government officials, planned to profit further from the socially harmful cultural commodities they created in the first place. They are responsible for endangering children yet parents are being expected to assume the burden of additional costs to protect them. If parents are unable to measure up to the challenges of intelligent and increasingly expensive parenting because of the complexities involved in using the system—too bad.

On the whole, one of the best indications of intelligent, as well as cost effective parenting in response to the problem of violent content, can be seen in the trend toward cancellation of cable subscriptions entirely as families learn to get by with broadcast television alone. At the same time, this circumstance underscores a root component of violence in the media as a fundamental construct upon which the industry as a whole operates. Despite its widespread documentation in the literature on the subject, this observation has obviously not yet penetrated the general public consciousness or the minds of those who purport to act in the public interest.

Advertising Directed to Children

In response to the LaMarsh Commission's recommendation for an industry-wide ban on all children's advertisements, McQueen said the CBC has always had a policy not to include advertising directed toward children, but that such a policy could have the effect of stifling incentives to produce children's programming in the private sector. This conventional wisdom within broadcasting circles as a whole led, for a brief period in 1996, to discussion in favor of the reintroduction of advertising into children's programming for the CBC with support and encouragement from some child advocates such as the Alliance for Children and Television. On the whole, McQueen said she, herself, favored a system where the CBC would become completely public and not have to rely on advertising revenue at all, with private broadcasters free to do as they wished with a minimum of government regulation.

So far, legislation banning advertising directed toward children has been developed in only one Canadian province. The Quebec Consumer Protection Act survived a Charter challenge in a Supreme Court of Canada decision in April, 1989, setting a precedent on the whole issue of balancing rights to protection with freedom of expression. In this case (known as the Irwin Toy Case), the Court stated:

> The evidence sustains the reasonableness of the legislature's conclusion that a ban on commercial advertising directed to children was the minimal impairment of free expression consistent with the pressing and substantial goal of protecting children against manipulation through such advertising...the onus of justifying the limitation of a Charter right or freedom rested upon the party seeking to uphold the limitation.

> [I]n our opinion, a corporation cannot avail itself of the protection afforded by S.7 of the Charter: S.7 serves to underline the human element involved, only human beings can enjoy those rights.[11]

The Court interpreted the nature of the Broadcast Code for Advertising to Children, and how it functions as an instrument of CRTC (1984) policy, as follows:

> The Broadcast Code for Advertising to Children has been designed to complement the general principles for ethical advertising outlined in the Canadian Code of Advertising Standards which applies to all advertising.

> Both Codes are supplementary to all federal and provincial laws and regulations governing advertising, including those regulations and procedures established by the Canadian Radio-Television and Tele-Communications Commission, the Department of Consumer and Corporate Affairs and Health and Welfare, Canada.[12]

To determine whether or not an advertisement is directed at persons under 13 years of age, the Quebec Consumer Protection Act stipulates that the context of the presentation, such as the nature and intended purpose of the goods advertised, the manner of presentation, and the time and place it is shown must be taken into account. Program announcements, for example, would be exempt.

Generally, it was pointed out, federal regulation of advertising takes place through the CRTC whose regulations and procedures are deemed supplementary to all federal and provincial laws, and whose regulations governing advertising and the Code are not to be considered the only standard to be applied. The Supreme Court stated that federal and provincial legislation were designed to coexist and that compliance with one did not mean defiance of the other.

On the subject of violence as it relates to freedom of expression, in discussion of the Irwin Toy Case, the Court stated that, "While the guarantee of free expression protects all content of expression, certainly violence as a *form* of expression receives no such protection."[13] Action on the part of picketers, for example, would not be protected in cases that included threats of violence or acts of violence. The Court summarized its decision with the following conclusion:

> [T]he rule-making record establishes that the specific cognitive abilities of young children lead to their inability to fully understand child-oriented television advertising, even if they grasp some aspects of it. They place indiscriminate trust in the selling message. They do not correctly perceive persuasive bias in advertising, and their life experience is insufficient to help them counter-argue. Finally, the content, placement and various techniques used in child-oriented television commercials attract children and enhance the advertising and the product. As a result, children are not able to evaluate adequately child-oriented advertising.[14]

So far, there is no evidence that other provinces in Canada are contemplating legislation comparable to that developed in Quebec with respect to advertising directed toward children of any age. The customary route of calling for consumer boycotts and demanding industry restraint is still the only alternative ever considered. In 1993, for example, in Ontario, the North York Board of Health prompted by letters of protest from professional organizations throughout North America, which included the Infant Feeding Action Coalition (IFAC) in Canada, and members of the Society for Nutrition Education (SNE) in the United States, called on Canadian distributors to remove from the market baby bottles designed with Pepsi, Diet Pepsi and 7-Up advertising labels, and slogans, such as "Gotta Have It" and "You've Got the Right One Baby." These organizations also urged parents to boycott the products and "discourage children from buying them."[15]

Once again, the perceived onus was on parents to assume the burden of protecting their children from the harmful effects of commodities. Industries, themselves, which target children as consumers were excused from addressing the potential impact of the products they design, produce, and market. In the case of the aforementioned products sold for infant feeding purposes, where the well known strategy of brand name recognition was employed, there was no indication that anyone offended by the Pepsi-labeled milk bottles, or any other similar kinds of advertisements for that matter, considered addressing the larger, underlying problem involving the propriety of advertising directed toward young children in the first place.

Industry spokesperson, Ann Ward, was able to explain, unchallenged, that the educational pamphlet designed to accompany the bottles "instructs parents never to fill the bottles with soft drinks, sweetened gelatin or other liquids such as sugar water."[16] She added, as if to conclude the matter, that the bottles with the Pepsi logos were Munchkin's most popular product, drudging up the old argument that the company was only supplying what the consumer wanted. The concerns of nutrition experts that parents who used these bottles were put in a position where they automatically became advocates for pop and soft drinks in their children's dietary habits were ignored, in the end, by everyone.

Landmark Court Precedents

Although other provinces in Canada have not adopted legislation on advertising directed toward children similar to that developed in the province of Quebec, the Supreme Court of Canada decision in which this legislation was upheld did serve as a precedent for a widely publicized decision which followed in March, 1992. Regina vs. Butler, a case involving pornography, has frequently surfaced in public discussion on arguments favoring limits to freedom of expression in the interests of collective safety.

In this particular case, pornography merchants from Manitoba appealed to the highest Court in the country for protection of their right to market material which had been found to be obscene in the lower provincial court, under the Charter of Rights guarantee of freedom of expression. The appeal was rejected on the basis that the Charter does not protect violent forms of expression. The court's definition of obscenity at the time of the Butler decision, as set out in S.163(159)(8) of the Criminal Code, was: "Any publication a dominant characteristic of which is the undue exploitation of sex, or of sex and any one or more of the following subjects, namely, crime, horror, cruelty and violence."[17] Furthermore, the Court said, freedom of expression is intended to allow for the free exchange of thoughts, opinions, and beliefs, not a series of unconnected sexual adventures which in this case, "for the most part were unencumbered by any dialogue other than moans, sighs and groans."[18]

These two cases—Irwin Toy Case, 1989 and Regina v. Butler, 1992—illustrate that, within the legal community itself, different interpretations of what constitutes legitimate protection for freedom of expression and the right to protection from harmful effects co-exist. In the case of Regina v. Butler, the decision was unanimous; whereas the Quebec legislation banning advertising directed toward children 13 years and under was upheld only because 5 out of the 9 judges voted in its favor.[19]

To some extent, the legal aspects of the debate, itself, have blocked the development of limits to excesses in the production and distribution of cultural products defined as media violence. In his address to The Empire Club of Canada, following the Butler decision, the late John Sopinka, at the time a member of the Supreme Court of Canada, acknowledged that free speech is one of the most difficult areas of the law with which the courts have had to deal.

Like other legal authorities, he stressed that freedom of speech is not absolute and that in some circumstances it poses a threat to others that is so great it must be curbed.[20] Said Sopinka:

> The Charter has provided us with the means to ward off unwarranted attacks on free speech by the state. It may fine-tune the libel laws if it appears that they are too restrictive. With respect to demands for political correctness, we must still rely on the common sense of public opinion to stand up for the right to say things no matter how unpalatable they may seem.[21]

He added that we cannot turn to the courts for redress in every single instance. In a democratic society, public attitudes or "standards" will always provide vital arbitration on what can or cannot be said and these will, as they do now, influence court decisions. Sopinka's remarks illuminate the extent to which the legal process, like the media industry is, in fact, a component of society at large, often exhibiting similar reluctance in coming to terms with the harmful effects of popular culture.

By 1995, legal trends were beginning to indicate a tilt toward American constitutional decision-making in a number of Supreme Court of Canada decisions. In one of them, major sections of the Tobacco Products Control Act were struck down, allowing tobacco products in Canada to be advertised without restriction. In the process, said University of Toronto political scientist Peter Russell, the court was not producing the kind of jurisprudence the country expects in the interpretation of fundamental rights and freedoms. Advertising of a poisonous, toxic substance was, he added, hardly a fundamental right worthy of constitutional protection.[22] In response, Health Canada released a paper entitled "Tobacco Control: A Blueprint to Protect the Health of Canadians" laying out a comprehensive legislative plan to manage the risk posed to society by a hazardous product to which some 6.5 million Canadians are addicted.[23]

The new Tobacco Act, passed in 1997, stopped short of banning tobacco advertisements and sponsorship of sports and arts events entirely. Cigarette company ads at cultural and sporting events are now restricted to the bottom 10 percent of onsite ads and banned from bus panels, broadcast outlets, billboards and street kiosks. Initially, in an attempt to ward off the legislation, a $1 million campaign was launched by the cigarette manufacturers to try to stop Canadian children from smoking.[24] As in the case of violence on television, however, a fundamental point was once again overlooked—the more it is implied that either smoking or indulgence in violence as entertainment is "mature" or "glamorous" adult behavior the more adolescents will aspire to copy it.

In the United States, similar initiatives have been launched by health and community advocates for bans involving tobacco advertising. In 1996 it was reported in *The Wall Street Journal* that a federal appeals court upheld, for the second time, a ban in Baltimore, Maryland, on most cigarette billboard advertising in areas frequented by children. This was interpreted as a "boost" to the odds that similar but more sweeping cigarette advertising restrictions proposed by the Food and Drug Administration would survive court challenges.[25]

Still, despite the fact that it was noted by the appeals court that the Supreme Court has repeatedly recognized that children deserve special protection when considering government imposed limits to free speech such as restrictions on cable programming and indecent speech, it was also noted that, in recent years, the U.S. Supreme Court has grown increasingly hostile to government limits on commercial speech such as advertising. Nevertheless, there have been an increasing number of smoking liability cases coming before the courts in the United States.[26] In 1998, 46 states settled for a total of $206-billion payable over 25 years. The remaining four states reached settlements ranging from $4-billion to $15-billion. All of this has prompted at least two provincial governments in Canada, Ontario and British Colombia, to file similar lawsuits as essential components in their health care reform programs.[27]

Legal Trends on Violence in Popular Culture

Inevitably, within the legal community, court decisions in one jurisdiction influence those in others. Like the Canadian media, which is so dominated by trends in the United States, so is our legal system. There are, however, instances where the Canadian judiciary has adopted a more equality, harms-based approach in its interpretation of civil liberties. The Irwin Toy Case and the Butler decision, for example, contrast markedly with one California landmark decision, McCollum et al. v. CBS et al., reached on July 12, 1988.[28]

Similar cases brought before the courts in the United States over the years have had virtually no successful outcome on the part of the plaintiffs. It is for this reason that this particular California decision remains key. On October 26, 1984, John Daniel McCollum shot and killed himself at the age of 19 while lying on his bed listening to rock star Ozzy Osbourne's recorded song, *Suicide Solution*.

The plaintiffs filed suit against the defendants on the basis of theories of negligence, product liability, and intentional misconduct. The claim was that Osbourne was a well known "mad man" of rock-and-roll and had become a cult figure; also, that his songs and record album covers demonstrate a preoccupation with unusual, antisocial, and bizarre attitudes and beliefs "often emphasizing such things as satanic worship or emulation, the mocking of religious beliefs and death."[29]

The plaintiffs further alleged that all of the defendants, through their efforts with the media, press releases, and the promotion of Osbourne's records, had sought to cultivate this image and to profit from it; that Osbourne in his music sought to appeal to an audience which included troubled adolescents and young adults having a difficult time during a transitional period in their lives.[30]

The case was dismissed on the basis that the plaintiffs' pleading failed "to allege any basis for overcoming the bar of the First Amendment's guarantee of free speech and expression and...sufficient facts to show any intentional or negligent invasion of plaintiffs' rights."[31] Reference was made in the written decision to the "novel attempt" to seek post-publication damages for the general public dissemination of recorded music and lyrics and the overriding constitutional principle that material communicated by the public media, which in this case included artistic expressions such as music and lyrics, is generally to be accorded protection under the First Amendment of the Constitution of the United States.[32]

Dozens of precedents for this decision were cited, and while the lyrics from Osbourne's song, *Suicide Solution*, were described by the Court as "unintelligible," the Court nevertheless decided that:

> The life of the imagination and intellect is of comparable import to the presentation of the political process; the First Amendment reaches beyond protection of citizen participation in, and ultimate control over, governmental affairs and protects in addition the interest in free interchange of ideas and impressions for their own sake, for whatever benefit the individual may gain.[33]

It was, however, also pointed out that freedom of speech guaranteed by the First Amendment is not absolute and that there are, in fact, certain limitations such as libel, slander, misrepresentation, obscenity, perjury, false advertising, solicitation of crime, complicity by encouragement, conspiracy and the like.[34] Still, the Court concluded that it was appropriate to bring this particular action to a prompt end because unnecessarily protracted litigation would have a chilling effect upon the exercise of First Amendment rights and for that reason speedy resolution of cases involving free speech is desirable.[35]

This familiar disregard, on the part of the American Courts, of evidence showing harmful effects surfaced again in several court cases in 1996 when Internet indecency provisions were struck down in the federal Telecommunications Act enacted earlier that year.[36] An analysis of the courts' interpretation in these cases by American lawyer John Duffy revolved exclusively around the divergence between the rights of minors and adults.

This, he said, lay at the heart of the indecency doctrine and by corollary made V-chip technology to block out violence and other devices designed to "empower" parents superior solutions to prohibitions in technologies to children. He argued that, while it might be acceptable to "limit" children's First Amendment rights on the basis of ensuring them protection, such an alternative was not justifiable because of the subsequent assault on the First Amendment rights of "mature" adults.

In the wake of the Columbine highschool massacre in Littleton Colorado in April, 1999, there is some evidence that the tide of public opinion, and by corollary legal opinion, is beginning to turn. Even before that tragedy, two lawsuits were launched against producers and distributors of violence in popular culture within a few weeks of each other for similar, previous tragedies with the first paving the way for the second. The first was filed against Oliver Stone and Time Warner Inc. for crimes attributed to the ultra-violent film, *Natural Born Killers*, in the state of Louisiana. By allowing that case to stand the Supreme Court opened the door for a similar lawsuit for $130 million against 25 media companies including Time Warner and the makers of the DiCaprio film, *The Basketball Diaries*.[37]

Indeed, there are indications that Hollywood studios may soon have more to worry about than just bad box office returns. Regardless of whether they are won or lost, these cases have already sent shock waves throughout the industry. Shock rock musician, Marilyn Manson, implicated in the crimes at Columbine Highschool, canceled a nation wide tour one week later.[38] In Florida, workers for Disneyland unplugged or removed 30 violent video games from arcades and hotels, among them the carnage soaked titles "Quake" and "Doom," which were also implicated in the Columbine shootings and named in the Kentucky lawsuit.[39] On May 1, 1999, a jury in the state of Michigan added a further chill to the carefree atmosphere of business as usual by ordering producers of *The Jenny Jones Show* to pay more than $25 million to the family of a gay man who was slain after revealing during the taping of a show that he had a crush on a male guest.[40]

For the protection of profits, civil cases are easily and readily launched within the popular culture industries. In 1993, the plight of a California based group of musicians, who were treading through a minefield of lawsuits for copyright infringements, was discussed in Toronto's *Eye Magazine*. One of them was brought forward by a group of Irish rock stars called "U2" on the basis that the lyrics in their songs had been appropriated. This was happening at the same time that they, themselves, were being sued by their own label company for specific press releases included in a magazine about an earlier, related lawsuit:

> Copyright, copywrong: The continuing legal troubles of California sample swipers Negativland show up the music industry's hypocritical attitude to copyright law. If U2 does it to you, it's art. If you do it to U2, get a good lawyer…In this information age, culture is almost in the air we breath. The themes of the dominant corporate culture are in the media, in the products we buy, and like an infectious pop tune, inside our heads. Our role is to consume and be happy. But what if we take that pop tune and put it in our own art? We become outlaws.[41]

The point is that dominant interests within the popular culture industries are quick to resort to legal protection for their own self-serving ends and the public has been rather slow in catching onto the game. In the final analysis, challenging them on their own terms may end up serving the public interest in a way that previous strategies such as regulation and education alone have not. This particular case also helps to demonstrate how corporate interests in profit drive the popularity of specific kinds of popular culture far more than creativity ever does.

Ways in which protection for corporate freedom of expression dominates legal decisions in the United States and most other jurisdictions around the world are discussed by David Sheff in his book *Game Over: How NINTENDO Zapped an American Industry, Captured Your Dollars, and Enslaved Your Children*, published in 1993. Despite occasional reference to complaints and protests from parents, teachers, and health professionals, on the whole, the book is about the fierce competition between corporate high technology giants such as Atari, Sony, Phillips, Sega, and Nintendo for a share of the billion dollar youth market that communications technology has helped to create. Any references at all, to legal cases, involve copyright disputes among the giants themselves. Ethical considerations on the issue of advertising and marketing directed to children were ignored entirely, although the issue of violence accelerating along with competition was noted.

On the subject of war toys, Canadian Physicians for Global Survival (CPGS) have pointed out that Sweden and Norway have successful voluntary restriction on the sale of such toys, that Malta prohibits their import, that Greece bans television advertising of them, that Australia places some restriction on their imports, and that the European Parliament has recommended that its member states ban their advertising of war toys and reduce their sale.

In 1993, child psychiatrist and past president of the organization, Joanna Santa Barbara, developed a pamphlet for the provision of public education on the subject of war toys, outlining initiatives in other jurisdictions to offset harmful effects. She defined them as "any toy whose fantasized purpose is to kill, wound or disable." Although attention is frequently focused on these various initiatives in other countries to protect children from exploitation in an increasingly aggressive cultural commodities market by North American community-based groups, with the exception of the province of Quebec, they are still being ignored at policy making levels at both provincial and federal levels in Canada and in the United States.

This lack of initiative in North America is in direct contrast to what was called for at the *International Symposium on Television, Film and Violence: Constitutional Theory and the Direction of Research*, in Montreal, in November, 1992. At that time, American legal scholar Jerome Barron from the National Law Center at George Washington University spoke about the "scientific" debate, the "legal-political" debate and "ethical questioning of audio-visual violence." In his view a degree of social consensus had already been formed around issues of gratuitous violence and he urged the development of more concern, predicting that it would be less likely, in such a context, for freedom of expression to be invoked to legitimize gratuitous violence.[42]

So far, it is obvious that the degree of consensus about which Barron spoke is still minimal in American attitudes and behavior on the ethical dimension involving media violence. This was evident in a report released in 1996 documenting threats to children in cyberspace from the onslaught of interactive marketing practices. Kathryn Montgomery, president of the Washington, D.C. based Center for Media Education (CME) and principal co-author of the report issued a warning that the interactive nature of the Internet was giving marketers unprecedented powers to gather detailed information from children. Along with other education, consumer and health groups, the CME called upon the Federal Communications Commission (FCC) to develop comprehensive safeguards designed to protect children from exploitive and unfair advertising and marketing practices online.

Montgomery did not, however, question the propriety of advertising directed to children in the first place. She concluded a news release on the matter by saying, "Our goal is not to ban advertising and marketing to children in cyberspace. What we want are rules of the game that will place limits on manipulative and exploitive practices and ensure that children are treated fairly, truthfully and appropriately. It is critically important to develop safeguards now, before the most egregious marketing techniques become commonplace."[43] That such marketing techniques have already been commonplace for some time was somehow overlooked.

Converging Exploitation

On the whole, there is little evidence that legal and educational frameworks for the facilitation of greater public awareness of "ethical dimensions" are keeping pace with the rapid escalation of violence as entertainment anywhere in the world. Instead, evidence grows that the problem is becoming increasingly urgent as the different technologies converge. Consider the following example:

> From Boston to Berlin, from Paris to Perth, from Jakarta to Kjibouti, all the world's children are doing it: tearing off heads or ripping out hearts in Mortal Kombat, crashing race cars in SuperMario Karts, going to war in Battlesphere. Poor Marshall McLuhan. Can this world of blood and mayhem be his global village? It appears so. Not Mickey Mouse, not CNN, not even McDonald's or MTV is achieving the reach of the vidgame revolution insinuating itself into the souls of the young. Any town with electrical power—or at least a store selling Game Boys and batteries—can become an outpost of this burgeoning international phenomenon.[44]

In 1993, it was reported that the video game industry took in "$5.3 billion a year in the U.S. alone, about $400 million more than Americans spent on movies."[45] In the process, the emerging synergism within the entertainment industry as a whole was being enthusiastically applauded as various players competed for a portion of the gateway to the new information highway. Three years later Sega negotiated partnerships with Time Warner and Tele-Communications Inc. for the creation of a special Sega channel on existing cable-TV systems. The behemoth was also aligning itself with AT&T to enable Sega Genesis owners to compete over ordinary telephone lines with similarly equipped players anywhere in the world.[46]

These new games have brought the latest in technologically improved depictions of violence that now offer versions of heads rolling and spattered blood on the screen. When the game was first released for distribution, to counter complaints, Nintendo chose to delete the digitalized blood in its versions of Mortal Kombat; and Sega decided to use a warning label alerting parents that the game is not suitable for children under 13 years of age. But these labels seldom have much impact and can actually make the game more attractive to young people, particularly rebellious adolescents individuating from their parents.[47] Although warning labels for the guidance of parents who wish to monitor their children's television viewing or video game playing habits can be helpful in providing some measure of public education, it is delusionary at best for anyone to expect such measures alone to adequately address the problem of accessibility.

The tendency toward contradictory approaches from the industry in their treatment of the violent entertainment problem, since the arrival on the market of interactive video-games, has been evident in other ways as well. In 1993, when *Mortal Kombat* was first introduced into Canada for home video game use, news items focused on concerns about new heights of gratuitous violence in popular culture.[48] Paradoxically, these were, at times, interspersed with advertisements for the video itself.

On specialty channel MuchMusic, advertisements were actually followed by pubic service announcements aimed at cautioning young people about the dangers of drug and alcohol abuse.[49] One wonders if MuchMusic was encouraging young people to amuse themselves to death with video games instead. What these conflicting approaches to programming demonstrate is that there is no consistency in policy on how the harmful effects of violent entertainment on young people are being addressed by various aspects of the industry either on the part of television producers or program sponsors.

Compounding the problem, by 1996, there was evidence of a new, youthful enthusiasm in coverage of these video-games. In *The Toronto Star* William Burrill lightheartedly reported that the biggest news from Sega was the introduction by that fall of the "Net Link," a peripheral product that would, using a 32-bit Sega Saturn game console as a modem, allow one to surf the Internet with a television set as a monitor.[50] A new game called "virtual Fighter 2," with the added "punch" of being a sequel "to Sega's hottest beat-'em-up chop-socky-fighting game" was promised soon, explained Burrill, along with "five third-party fantasy sword 'n' sandal epics." As the acknowledged leaders in the "next gen" game wars Sega had by that time sold over 5 million genesis units worldwide.

Also in 1996, *Sega City Playdium*, an entertainment center featuring interactive video games, simulators and motion-based rides aimed at people of all ages "who had grown up with and love interactive technology"[51] opened in Mississauga, Ontario. Although there are rows and rows of games designated as mature themes with an occasional warning flashing across one of the promotional screens, there is no evidence of any kind of restrictions on who can actually play these games.

In 1998, construction began on three more arcades in Edmonton, Alberta, Burnaby, B.C., and downtown Toronto. The plan, according to Playdium Entertainment Corporation, is "to dominate the emerging market for high-tech thrill seekers" and "give consumers a chance to get accustomed to spending their entertainment dollars in the hybrid arcade/indoor theme parks."[52]

Notes

1. "McQueen sees," 1993, July 27, *The Globe and Mail*, p.C4.
2. Canada, 1991, p.3. Ottawa, Minister of supply and Services.
3. Canada, 1991, p.3.
4. Canada, 1991, p.3.
5. Canada, 1991, p.7.
6. This and subsequent quotations from Trina McQueen are derived from a personal interview for this study on May 21, 1993.
7. Trainor, 1992, Dec. 18, *Psychiatric News*, CPA..
8. Ainsworth, 1993, Sept. 20, *The Toronto Star*, p.A1.

9. CRTC, 1994, Oc. 7, "Canada and TV Violence: Cooperation and Consensus," Ottawa, Author.

10. Ainsworth, 1993, p.A1

11. Regina v. Irwin Toys 1989 in Law Society of Upper Canada, 1989, p. i.

12. LSUC, 1989, p.202.

13. LSUC, 1989, p.213.

14. LSUC, 1989, p.234.

15. Platiel, 1993, Oct. 8, *The Globe and Mail*, p.A3.

16. Platiel, 1993, p.A3.

17. Regina v. Butler, 1992, p.233. IS.C.R.452, Criminal Code, R.S.C., 1895, Chapter C-46.

18. Regina v. Butler, 1992, p.229.

19. LSUC, 1989; Regina v. Butler, 1992.

20. Sopinka, 1992, April 16, p.1.

21. Sopinka, 1992, April 16, p.9.

22. Vienneau, 1996, July 29, *The Toronto Star*, p.A10.

23. Sutherland et. al., 1996, July 29, *The Globe and Mail*, p. A15.

24. Harper, T., 1996, Oct. 22, *The Toronto Star*, p.A3.

25. Geyelin, M. 1996, November 11, *Wall Street Journal*.

26. McCall, W. 1999, March 31, *The Globe and Mail*, p.A19.

27. Coutts, J., 1999April 24, *The Globe and Mail*, p.A13.

28. McCollum, J., Lugenbuehl, G., Estate of John Daniel McCollum, Jack McCollum [Administrator] v. John "Ozzy" Osbourne, CBS Records, CBS Incorporated, Jet Records, Bob Daisley, Randy Rhoads, Essex Music International Limited, & Essex Music International Incorporated, 1988.
   According to Paul Zarins, International and Foreign Law Librarian at the Jacob Burns Law Library, George Washington University, Washington DC with whom I spoke in November of 1992, this case is indicative of trends in the USA.

29. McCollum et al. v. CBS et al., 1988, p.4.

30. McCollum et al. v. CBS et al., 1988, p.5.

31. McCollum et al. v. CBS et al., 1988, p.2.

32. McCollum et al. v. CBS et al., 1988, p.7.

33. McCollum et al. v. CBS et al., 1988, p.8.

34. McCollum et al. v. CBS et al., 1988, p.8.

35. McCollum et al. v. CBS et al., 1988, p. 16.

36. Duffy, J., 1996, *Children and Indecency*, Washington, D.C., CME, pp.1-10.

37. Puente, 1999, April 13, *USA Today*, p.A3.

38. Marilyn Manson, 1999, April 29, *The National Post*, p.A13.

39. Huffstutter, 1999, May 14, *Los Angeles Times*.

40. CNN. 1999, May 1.

41. Twomey, 1993, Oct. 14, *Eye Magazine*, p.14.

42. 1992, p.3-4.

43. Montgomery, 1996March 28, News Release, CME, Washington, D.C.

44. Jackson, 1993, Sept. 27, *Time Magazine*, p. 47.

45. Greenwald, 1993, Sept. 27, *Time Magazine*, p. 42.

46. Greenwald, 1993, p. 44.

47. Jenish, 1992, Dec. 7, *Maclean's Magazine*, p.40-44.

48. CBC Television, 1993c, Sept. 13, Evening News with Stu Patterson.

49. Citytv, 1993aSept. 14, *MuchMusic* Evening News.

50. 1996, July 16, p.H4.

51. Kerr, 1996, July 23, *The Globe and Mail*, p.C2.

52. Rowan and MacDonald, 1998, march 18, *The Globe and Mail*, p.B3.

Chapter 7

ANOTHER ROUND OF PUBLIC PROTEST

IN 1992, PUBLIC INDIGNATION over rising levels of violence in popular culture began to gather momentum throughout Canada. In November of that year, 14 year-old Virginie Larivière from the province of Quebec, whose sister had been brutally murdered presented Brian Mulroney, then Prime Minister, with a petition signed by over 1.3 million people. These signatures had been gathered from across the country, demanding that the government do something about violence on television. The petition was a clear indication of growing concern about real life violence in society and the conviction that violence in entertainment is a causal factor.

It was an initiative that reinforced Keith Spicer's decision to address the issue in his capacity as chair of the Canadian Radio-television and Telecommunications Commission (CRTC). Between 1990 and October, 1995, the Commission released into the public domain a series of fact sheets with specific initiatives pertaining to the issue of violence on television. These began with reference to the Montreal Polytechnique shootings in December, 1989, which, in turn, prompted two studies to examine both research and policy developments in other jurisdictions. A review of over 200 scientific studies was undertaken, most of them by this time well known among social scientists and communications scholars.[1] The fact sheets ended with an announcement of the June, 1995 deadline for submissions to the CRTC for the public hearings on television violence held later that year.[2]

The CRTC called upon the broadcasting industry to develop a stronger code on violence, the cable industry to develop its own antiviolence strategy, and provincial ministers responsible for regulating video stores and cinema theatres for cooperation in the development of criteria on warnings, classification and policies on rental to minors. Similar overtures were made to Canadian pay-TV and specialty services, leading executives and producers of American studios and networks, as well as government, industry, and consumer representatives in Western Europe.

Dialogue was established with representatives of the Canadian Teachers' Federation (CTF), the Canadian Home and School and Parent-Teachers Federation (CHSPTF), the Canadian Advertising Foundation (CAF), the Canadian

Broadcasting Corporation (CBC), the National Film Board of Canada (NFBC) and community advocacy groups, which included Canadians Concerned About Violence In Entertainment (C-CAVE).

The first of three international conferences in Canada on media violence was cosponsored by the CRTC and the Quebec Institute on Research and Culture, and held in Montreal in November, 1992. The second took place in Toronto at the C.M. Hincks Institute in February, 1993. At that time, Perrin Beatty, then the federal Minister of Communications, announced a 5 point strategy to deal with violence in children's television. Once again, the focus was on government shifting the onus of responsibility onto various segments of the television industry through the already familiar but predominantly unsuccessful practice of encouraging self-regulation.

The strategy involved a "strong" code of ethics to set the boundaries for drama and music videos; a public education campaign to include public service announcements and a number of media-literacy initiatives with campaigns orchestrated by the Canadian Association of Broadcasters (CAB), the Canadian Cable Television Association (CCTA), and the Government through the National Film Board (NFB), and Health and Welfare. Canada's major advertisers were to be encouraged not to place advertisements within violent television programs but to develop educational tools for parents and children and to sponsor public awareness campaigns instead. Collaboration with the United States in dealing with violent television programming was also part of Beatty's strategy along with an award program to recognize those whose contributions helped to make television less violent, or who had funded or promoted quality children's programming. This recognition was proposed in the form of the Virginie Larivière Television Award.[3]

A third international conference was held in Montreal, in April, 1993, organized by the Federal Department of Communications and the industry-based national action group (AGVOT) that evolved from the C.M. Hincks Institute conference held in Toronto, in February. Apart from Canadian participants, there were international delegates from broadcast standards councils in Australia, Belgium, France, New Zealand, and the United Kingdom, as well as one commissioner from the Council of Europe, and one from the European Community, all of whom had developed their own "Codes of Conduct." The emphasis was on "balancing responsibilities" with references to the rising demand for government intervention which was resulting in more "cooperation between government and industry."

Classification systems, viewer warnings, and specified programming periods were acknowledged as the most "common" measures adopted, always on a "strictly voluntary" basis because of the perceived dangers from censorship. Difficulties, however, faced by regulators in disciplining broadcasters who violated "voluntary standards," it was noted, were leading some countries to take more stringent action. Representatives from France, the United Kingdom and New Zealand spoke of legislation in their countries for the imposition of fines on private broadcasters in breach of the fundamental principles safeguarding children against violent programming. Disciplinary measures reportedly developed and imposed in other countries as well included the condition, suspension, and/or denial of broadcast licenses in Australia, Belgium and the United States.[4]

Canadian officials, however, concluded that the major emphasis should remain on encouraging the free flow of audiovisual products and harmonization of standards governing violence on television in a way that might result in "widespread agreement." It was unclear who would decide, either on behalf of government or industry, what would be suitable for children, adolescents, or adults, and how distinctions would be made. Instead the rhetoric spilled into broader issues arising from trans-frontier models to address violence on television. These were perceived to include among other things "conflict amongst existing national legislation and a range of diverse cultural and social values."[5] Care was called for in scheduling of program classifications, especially when there was a time difference between countries, and reference was made to the Commission of the European Community and the Council of Europe who had overcome these difficulties.

Concerns expressed previously at the 1993 C.M. Hincks Institute Conference, and by that time well supported in the literature on media violence,[6] that rating systems and warning labels are of nominal value in addressing the problem were ignored. Beatty still clung to the well worn mantra of how a uniform, national classification system for television programming, films, and videos would assist parents in making responsible viewing choices for their children.

He praised Astral Communications for developing viewer warnings for their pay-TV channels, involving a flashing white "V" in a red box which they promised would be shown before and during films containing violent scenes, congratulated members of the industry for the work they had already done on the development of a single agency for classification of films and videos in Canada and urged provincial governments to weigh it seriously, but avoided entirely the call made by Donnerstein at the C.M. Hincks Institute conference for input from educators and researchers in developing classification criteria and warning symbols.

Beatty also said that, as one of Canada's major advertisers, the federal government was determined to avoid booking government advertisements during programs containing scenes of gratuitous violence or explicit sex. He pointed out that in March, 1993, the Institute of Canadian Advertising had announced its support of his 5 point strategy for the purpose of addressing violence on television. Neither Beatty's initiatives nor the Institute's announced endorsement of his 5 point strategy, however, appeared to have had any impact on policy advisors developing the federal Progressive Conservative Party advertisements for the election campaign that same year.

When the party aired a television advertisement which showed a woman being sawed in half by a magician as an attack on the Reform party's deficit-cutting proposals it was the National Action Committee on the Status of Women who demanded that it be pulled on the basis that it promoted both violence and the objectification of women.[7] In the end, the governing political party was no more responsive to Beatty's strategy than the Canadian Broadcasting Corporation (CBC) when in September of 1993 it chose to air advertisements for, *Mortal Kombat*, along with news stories, reporting on the extraordinarily violent aspects of the new interactive video game.[8]

For a while there was room for cautious optimism that developing policy on the subject of television violence was indeed having some impact on decision-making within some aspects of the industry. For example, several weeks after the code was announced, C-CAVE was approached by a Toronto-based advertising agency with an invitation for collaboration, at their own expense, on public awareness campaigns aimed at halting the escalation of violence in society.[9] Ironically, the project was aborted because of technical complications related to C-CAVE's continuing inability to receive federal government endorsement as a registered charitable organization.[10]

Despite numerous applications to the Ministry of Revenue in Ottawa over a period of more than eleven years, submitted by lawyers on a pro bono basis, and on the most recent occasion, accompanied by a letter of support from the CRTC itself, receipt of this charitable number has consistently been denied. Its main advantage would be a greatly enhanced potential for fundraising activities but government officials remain unconvinced that C-CAVE serves the public interest by providing public education on the subject of media violence. Meanwhile, ineffective policies on the part of both industry and government continue to hegemonically diffuse opposition to media violence on the part of overworked and underfunded citizens by ensuring that they remain at the margins of policy making on the issue.

A New Code on Violence

The subject of uniform codes on violence within the Canadian industry is not a new one. The process began in 1983, when the Canadian Association of Broadcasters (CAB) undertook to consult with community groups and, in 1987, announced the development of a new Code. Because the CRTC, quite appropriately, was not prepared to approve this rather vague though 'newly developed' Code, in 1992, C-CAVE responded to an invitation from the CAB to review the 1987 draft and suggested revisions. By October, 1993, the CRTC announced that they were prepared to approve the revised Code from the CAB; that it would come into force on January 1, 1994; and that it would allow a reasonable period of time for broadcasters to adapt their practices to meet its requirements.[11]

Compliance with the Code was to become a condition both for obtaining and renewing licenses for all privately-owned television stations and networks. The Canadian Broadcast Standards Council (CBSC), established by the CAB, would administer the television violence Code and handle complaints from the public with the CRTC closely monitoring the process. The CRTC's position on implementation of the Code was enshrined in the belief, according to its former chairman, Keith Spicer, that "cooperative efforts by industry, the public and governments offer the most effective and 'civilized' ways of dealing with the violence issue. If, in the end of course, this approach was not working, he said, the CRTC would not rule out more coercive regulatory or legislative action.[12]

Key commitments made by private broadcasters included: an outright ban on the broadcast of gratuitous violence based on a clear definition of what constitutes gratuitous violence; a "watershed" hour of 9 p.m. before which programming containing scenes of violence suitable for adults would not be aired; and a special "sensitivity" in children's programming. Themes of violence against vulnerable groups such as women, visible minorities and animals were to be avoided and a national program classification system was to be developed and tested in cooperation with other segments of the broadcasting system and incorporated into the Code by September, 1994. This deadline was first extended by the CRTC for two years and then gradually abandoned entirely following Spicer's departure from the CRTC in 1996.[13]

Particular rules for children's programming include the stipulations that: animated programming not invite dangerous imitation; violence not be shown as a preferred way to solve problems; the consequences of violence be portrayed; and, in animated programs, violence not be the central theme.[14]

Notably absent from the Code, was any specific reference to, or restriction of, advertising directed toward children, with or without violent imagery. This, of course, paved the way for further inconsistencies in that programs considered too violent could still, nonetheless, be advertised.

The Canadian Broadcast Standards Council

It soon became apparent to community groups that the complaint procedure for viewers, which was to be administered by the industry-run Broadcast Standards Council, was too cumbersome, convoluted and difficult for the average person to use. These concerns, along with the impression that the process was heavily stacked in favor of the broadcaster, were expressed at a meeting for community organizations called by Keith Spicer in Hull in January, 1994. There was, for example, a "Complainant Waiver," that had to be signed before any action would be taken by a CBSC regional council; the second step in the process commenced only if someone was not satisfied with a local broadcaster's response to a complaint. Essentially what was implied was that the CBSC would not investigate a complaint if it had been directed to the CRTC as well. From the outset, the entire procedure appeared to have been designed to frustrate virtually any complainant into compliance.

Criticism continued for several years before the waiver was finally dropped, but by 1998 it was clear that the CRTC would not, under any circumstances, interfere with any aspect of the complaint process anyway. When CAB members, Western International Communications (WIC) and CHUM-Ltd., brought American radio shock jock Howard Stern onto their two radio stations, Q107-FM in Toronto and CHOM-Ltd., in Montreal, in September, 1997, precipitating thousands of complaints directed to both the CRTC and the CBSC, the CRTC merely turned the matter over to the CBSC entirely and has refused to get involved since, despite the fact that the Council has twice found these two radio stations to be in violation of their own broadcasting codes.[15]

In less than a year, over one dozen news releases and countless letters of protest went out to the CBSC, the CRTC, Sheila Copps, Minister of Heritage and local federal MPs from C-CAVE members, occasionally in collaboration with other organizations calling for enforcement of existing codes of ethics, among them MediaWatch, the U.S. based Cultural Environment Movement (CEM), Friends of Canadian Broadcasting (FCB), Science for Peace Canada, and various groups and individuals, all to no avail. Meanwhile Pat Cardinal, President of Q107-FM emphasized in a lecture he gave in Toronto at a public library in February, 1998, that the CAB Codes "are not set in stone." He explained that, given Stern's popularity, community standards were "shifting" and that the Codes should now be adjusted to reflect the new reality. In other words, his argument was that the way should now be *paved* for the growing popularity of misogynist, homophobic and racist radio programming among listeners between the ages of 12 and 35 that they, themselves, have purposely stimulated to drive up their ratings.

In June, 1998, when the issue of Stern was raised at the Congress for the Social Sciences and Humanities at the University of Ottawa, Ron Cohen, chair of the CBSC explained in one panel discussion that the Stern show had been "successfully contained" and not allowed to spread beyond Toronto and Montreal. Also that extra producers hired earlier in the year, for the purpose of dubbing out objectionable content, demonstrated adherence from the relevant stations to the industry's Codes of Conduct.

In August of that year Stern was taken off the air in Montreal and CHUM Ltd. made a decision not to bring him to late night television in Toronto on Citytv, partly in response to questioning from one CRTC commissioner during a license application hearing from the Conglomerate, for one of its specialty channels. Nevertheless, he remains on the air in Toronto, occasionally discussing tragedies such as those involving the displacement and massacre of Albanian refugees as a result of the war in Kosovo in 1999, with jocularity and flippant trivialization.

For a while, before Spicer stepped down from the CRTC, there was some indication that various regional divisions within the CBSC were becoming more responsive to public concerns. One example involved the decision from the Ontario Regional Council, who ruled on the children's show, *The Mighty Morphin Power Rangers* in 1994, in response to complaints from parents.[16] Rated as one of the most popular programs for young children in North American, it was deemed to be too violent for Canadian television for a number of reasons, among them the conclusion that the good messages were overwhelmed by violent, action-filled scenes; that there was no alternative strategy to violence for conflict resolution; that the theme invites imitation from children; that the *Power Rangers* always win, which is not the way life really is; and that violence was the central theme in the plot, not judiciously used to develop the plot and characters.[17]

Ironically, reaction from the two television stations in Canada who carried the program resulted in YTV pulling the show off the air immediately but with CAB member, Global Television, waiting for cooperation from American producers to "meet Canadian standards."[18] Unfortunately, at the time, the potential for this initiative to be built upon was undermined somewhat by media literacy advocates in Nova Scotia who said that, compared to public education, the decision would have little impact.[19] Children's story writer, Janet Nostbakken, also an advocate of media literacy as the most effective method in addressing the problem of media violence, was similarly critical of the decision and sympathized with Saban Enterprises, California based producers of the television program, for having been "unfairly singled out" in a cultural climate where there are so many other, similar excesses.[20]

These responses were inconsistent with those of the Federation of Women Teachers' Associations of Ontario (FWTO), which called for total cancellation of the show. Expressing approval for the YTV decision to pull the program the Federation emphasized that "if the industry's watchdog, the CBSC, was to have any credibility, we would have to see stations complying with its decisions."[21] Unfortunately, this particular, CBSC initiative remains a rare exception and departure from the industry norm.

In fact, from the time the code on violence was first approved by the CRTC there were numerous examples that adherence was not being taken seriously by the industry and, in turn, overlooked by the federal regulator. In Toronto, a decision made by Citytv to purchase a highly contentious as well as popular program aired on MTV in the U.S. for regular scheduling on their MuchMusic channel actually coincided with the CRTC's announced approval of the CAB code in 1993. Entitled *Beavis and Butt-head*, it was described in *Newsweek* as:

> ...two "animated miscreants"...at the low end of the food chain. Caught in the ungainly nadir of adolescence, they are not nice boys. They torture animals, they harass girls and sniff paint thinner. They like to burn things. They are the spiritual descendants of the semi-sentient teens from *Wayne's World* and *Bill and Ted's Excellent Adventure*, only dumber and meaner. The downward spiral of the living white male surely ends here: in a little pimple named Butt-head whose idea of an idea is, "Hey, Beavis, let's go over to Stuart's house and light one in his cat's butt."[22]

The show's creator, Mike Judge, a parent of a two-year-old, was described by Leland as being hauntingly similar to his character, Butt-head, who admitted that in his own youth "he and his friends used to set fires, just to see how many they could keep going at once and still be able to stomp them out." One 24-year-old fan of the show Leland interviewed explained that her generation was able to relate to the "lunatic fringe of teenagers who have fallen out of society and who live in a world of TV. It's kind of sick, but we like to laugh at them and say, 'I'm not a loser'."[23]

In California, opposition to the show was waged by a retired broadcasting executive following the discovery of a cat killed by a firecracker which he had traced to the show's thematic material. In addition, throughout the U.S. a number of copycat fires started by children as young as five years, including one in which a two-year-old child died, were being traced to the program.[24]

Neither the controversial reception the show was receiving in the United States, nor the CRTC approval of a new Code on Violence developed by the

CAB, deterred Citytv from their decision to purchase and air the series which began on November 10, 1993. Sexist language was pervasive and a commercial cut in the program of its premier episode promised that, "Beavis and Butt-head will be right back, practising antisocial behavior and bad manners."[25]

C-CAVE sent a letter to Citytv expressing concern after receiving a number of phone calls from members and journalists about this decision. A reply from Sarah Crawford, Communications Manager for the MuchMusic network, included the following excerpts:

> We know the show is controversial and we know that some adults don't think it's especially funny. But it's important to remember that many cartoon and comedy shows over the years have depicted a brand of humor that does not have cross-generational appeal...we believe *Beavis and Butt-head* is in sync with this younger generation and poses no greater threat to them than did "The Three Stooges."[26]

Crawford also said:

> We take great exception to your view that we are ignoring CBSC guidelines. In fact, the opposite is true. We take the guidelines seriously and select and schedule programming with thought and sensitivity, going as far as soliciting viewer feedback on many of our specific programs. While we have purchased the rights to the adult animated series *Beavis and Butt-head* we have held off airing it as a series until we have completed our study of the series as a whole and our review of each episode by our Internal Review Committee.[27]

Furthermore, pointed out Crawford, MuchMusic and Citytv as a matter of policy explore the issue of violence in society and the media in their shows.

She drew attention to an award winning television special produced in 1993 entitled *In Your Face: Violence in Music*,[28] pointing out that it was being made available to schools and interest groups free of charge and was being "applauded by them."[29] There was indeed, considerable attention focused on research findings showing harmful effects from media violence in a way that could be deemed useful for public education purposes. The irony was that, once again, the television industry was demonstrating a kind of schizoid attitude in their programming decisions, alternating between programming that drew attention to the problem with programming that helped to foster it, depending upon the kind that happened to serve their particular purposes at any given time. *Beavis and Butt-head* remained on the air until March, 1998, and was taken off the air only to be replaced, according to a report from John Allemang in *The Globe and Mail*, by CAB member, Global Television, with an even more aggressively obnoxious set of characters in a new program called *South Park*.[30]

One year after the CAB Code on Violence was approved by the CRTC, the Coalition for Responsible Television (CRTV) reviewed concerns received from parents and educators and reported that young children continued to be targeted by violent programs. In fact, there was evidence to suggest that television violence after 9:00 p.m. had become even more violent than it had been a year earlier.

The Bird Committee Report on Television Violence

When the Standing Committee on Communications and Culture, chaired by Canadian federal MP Bud Bird, released its report, *Television Violence: Fraying Our Social Fabric* in June, 1993, it contained 27 recommendations. In addition to changes in the Criminal Code on slasher and snuff films it called upon the CRTC to supervise the development of a classification system for television programming, bearing in mind the possible integration with provincial film and video classification systems.[31] Building upon Beatty's 5-point strategy the Committee encouraged public discussion on all aspects of societal violence, more research, and more media literacy resources.

It recommended individual action through the availability of screening devices for both television sets and VCRs, and public information on complaints procedures through the Canadian Broadcast Standards Council. It urged the CRTC to exert pressure on broadcasters to demonstrate responsibility in purchasing and scheduling violent programming and to hold them "accountable" and subject to the Commission's sanctions with compliance to approved self-regulatory codes as a condition of license. Still, it favored "non-legislative" action.[32] Although it was stressed that the CRTC should "act" if industry self-regulation proved ineffective, no particular time frames were established. Just how the "threat of penalties" for industry breaches should be used in the event that self-regulation proved unsuccessful was unclear.

One year later the CRTC's credibility on the whole issue of violence was seriously undermined by its decision to exempt the Canadian subsidiary of the Japanese owned Sega Enterprises Ltd. from the licensing process entirely. Supported by the Canadian cable giant, Rogers Communications, it was excused on the basis that the normal regulatory process was "too complicated" for Sega Canada to qualify for a broadcaster's license.[33] Besides, the Commission explained, in this case it was giving the new technology a chance to develop.

The Bird Committee also called for cross-border discussions on television violence with American counterparts to promote collaborative and unified responses to the problem. Like the LaMarsh Commission, it pointed toward the need for federal government investment, through subsidies, in the production of Canadian television programs which would reflect the concerns about television violence and the objective of the Broadcasting Act to safeguard, enrich, and strengthen the cultural, political, social, and economic fabric of Canada.[34]

By 1996 all of these "potential" actions were beginning to disappear. One of example emerged when Pamela Wallin interviewed Robert Lantos, chief executive officer for Alliance Communications Corporation, for CBC Newsworld, on November 26th of that year, just prior to the Genie Awards Celebration in Toronto. Lantos spoke enthusiastically and confidently about Alliance's achievements, made possible through generous Telefilm grants, in carving out for Canadian film producers and distributers a "niche" in the global market by the use of "kinky" content as in the work of celebrated Canadian film producers, Atom Egoyan and David Cronenberg. In other words, relying on controversial industrial ingredients of sex and violence was becoming standard practice and supported by the taxpaying public as a matter of public policy.

Freedom with Responsibility: Can it Work?

On the broad subject of "freedom with responsibility," when she was interviewed for this work Trina McQueen commented on what she regarded as two significant developments since publication of the LaMarsh Report: the CRTC codes on sex-role stereotyping, and multicultural programming; both of which, in her view, had encouraged more responsible attitudes within the industry toward programming in general. According to her, Canadian television programming comes under regular review by the CRTC, which has always made some effort to hold broadcasters accountable on the issue of violence. She acknowledged, however, that while there had been a massive overhaul of the entire communications industry in Canada, that this had occurred for technological and economic rather than philosophical or ethical reasons. Apart from a few awards given out, said McQueen, there have been no specific financial incentives for better programming from the standpoint of higher social values. Furthermore, it has always been easier for Canadian broadcasters to import violent programming from the United States than to produce their own. Why have changes within the industry not been driven by ethical considerations? McQueen said:

> Television has managed to satisfy the great bulk of the public. There has not been a huge public outcry for something different...I don't think Canadian television is a big problem compared to that in other countries. American programs tend to be a problem. We need to address the excesses of networks like NBC, ABC and Fox Network. We have a mainstream public broadcasting system, and per capita, we spend more money than the British, although spending in general has been diminished somewhat by cutbacks.

> Environics Media Company have been surveying people on the subject of the public's trust of television right through the 1980s and indications are that it has grown steadily in the last 10 years. Television is far and away the most trusted media of communications for Canadians.[35]

It is impossible not to conclude, on the basis of this observation, along with the manner in which the CBSC was designed to accept feedback from the public, that the main reason the public seems so "satisfied" with the programming it gets is because the industry makes a point of keeping itself insulated from complaints. Also, the CRTC's refusal to respond to thousands of complaints about Howard Stern, despite the CBSC's inability to discipline its own members, demonstrates tacit collusion with industry. The possibility that the CRTC might really "step in" and discipline private broadcasters who violate their own conduct codes in the event that they demonstrate an inability to exercise self-regulation has evaporated—at least under the present leadership.

In her historical analysis of mass media in Canada, Mary Vipond has been critical of the CRTC for allowing controversies, generated by the subject of programming, to result in a concentrated preoccupation with the technological aspects of the communications industry. Where the issue of Canadian content is concerned, the emphasis has been on quantity rather than quality. Like David Ellis, she has pointed to the real constraint on freedom of expression in Canada as an economic one resulting from the growing concentration of ownership in media industries.

Generally, the *CRTC*'s cable policy has been faulted on two grounds. Firstly, for years the Commission allowed cable companies to expand in Canada on the basis of cost-free American programming, thereby fragmenting the market, hurting Canadian broadcasters and decreasing the total amount of Canadian programming on our screens. Its attempts to protect Canadian broadcasters were purely economic in nature; while fairly successful in protecting their revenues it did not address the overall threat to Canadian cultural content. Secondly, the *CRTC*'s assumption that cable is a "hybrid," half broadcaster and half utility, has been used to liberate these highly profitable companies from the most stringent regulations normally applied to both broadcasters and utilities.[36]

Vipond has commented on conclusions from the 1986 Caplan-Sauvageau Federal Task Force that more flexibility and effectiveness would result if the CRTC strictly enforced specific conditions designed for the particular circumstances of each licensee and left fewer matters to generalized regulations. Drawing upon the 1965 Fowler Committee Report on Broadcasting, she pointed out that the only thing that really matters in broadcasting is program content: all the rest is housekeeping.[37]

Classification of Films, Videos, and Television Programming

So far, LaMarsh Commission recommendations for a national classification system for electronic entertainment media, with research findings taken into account, continue to be ignored. Despite calls from the three international conferences on media violence held in Canada between 1992-3 for a national system, responsibility for any kind of classification of any product at all, remains at the provincial level. From time to time, over the past ten years, there have been attempts made by film and video distributors to initiate a national system. They have demonstrated a willingness to finance the process, independent of provincial governments, with whom they now share the expense of administration in Canada, and have argued that the development of a national classification system, administered solely at their own expense would be cheaper and much more efficient to operate.

This approach, according to the distributors, would eliminate the need for them to submit their films and videos to a number of different boards across the country.[38] At the present time broadcasters have their own inhouse codes which add to the lack of consistency in ways that classification criteria are applied once films originally classified by provincial boards for distribution in cinemas and video stores end up on movie network and pay-TV channels. On the whole, calls from both researchers on the subject of media violence and the public at large for changes in the mandate of classification boards and the criteria used, have generated no response at policy making levels either from provincial governments or private industry. Instead, the trend has been toward greater leniency in classification criteria. This has enabled distribution companies to reap the benefits from larger viewing audiences, with a stamp of approval from those mandated to act in the public interest.

Examples of public concern over these trends can be observed from Ontario legislative debates and news releases monitored in 1993. Considerable pressure was exerted on Marilyn Churley when she was Minister of Consumer and Corporate Affairs and responsible for administration of the Ontario Film Review Board (OFRB). Public pressure was also exerted on opposition critics Margaret Marland for the Progressive Conservatives and Diane Poole for the Liberals.[39] In the Ontario Legislative Assembly Marland summarized the major complaints she had received about the OFRB.

She made reference to the chairperson who held the public in contempt and attempted to withhold information on Board decisions which as a matter of policy were meant to be accessible to the public; irresponsible fast forwarding procedures for screening videos which made it impossible to adequately gauge content that might be in contravention of the Criminal Code; and indications that the Board was considering a motion that would lower its standards for the approval of adult sex videos. Said Marland:

> The OFRB says its first service is a direct service to the distributor, while its second service is an indirect service to the public—this is shown both in the internal memo and in the OFRB's response to a human rights complaint about slasher films—yet the public spends $750,000 each year for the board's operations…The board has approved for restricted viewing, and in some cases even younger audiences, AA-14 ratings for slasher films which glorify violence against women…and has not been exercising its authority under the Theatres Act to withhold its approval of films which contain graphic scenes of violence, torture, crime, cruelty, horror or human degradation.[40]

Marland concluded by calling for the resignation of the chair and a review of the OFRB's mandate and procedures. Although Dorothy Christian did resign as chair of the OFRB several months later, there is still no evidence of the review called for. In the end, Marland, Witmer and others who were so critical of the Board's mandate as members of the Progressive Conservative opposition at Queen's Park have abandoned the problem entirely since they formed the Government of Ontario following the election in 1995 and again in 1999.

The pro-industry approach taken by recent chairpersons of the OFRB and the credibility they have enjoyed in the courts was underscored in an Ontario Court of Appeal decision released in October, 1993.[41] The material in question contained scenes of simulated bestiality, sex as punishment, and scenes with dog collars and leashes on women forced to walk on their hands and knees.[42] It was reported that Robert Payne, who preceded Dorothy Christian as chair of the OFRB and served in that capacity when this particular case first came to trial, had testified that since 1990 the Board had allowed such material to be distributed because it was tolerated by the community at large.

Although the Crown had argued that the films in question were degrading and therefore created "a substantial risk of societal harm," the three judge panel determined that the Crown had failed to establish the element of risk which it said was essential to a criminal conviction and pointed to the role of the OFRB to determine such matters of public interest. Said the panel, "A provincial board, composed of a cross-section of citizens, does not consider films of this kind to be either degrading or dehumanizing, and trial judges must take this into account "regardless of how distasteful they personally may find the films."[43]

Bill Johnstone, a founding member of the Hamilton based organization, Canadians for Positive Community Standards (CPCS), argued that in this case, although the Court relied on the Board to gauge a reading of community standards, it had been misled. Said Johnstone, "We believe without doubt that the majority of the Canadian population would not tolerate this material. This myth of tolerance has developed because of the lack of knowledge of people who do not indulge in this kind of viewing."[44]

Johnstone's statement highlights the extent to which the OFRB and other agencies like it can and have been used as smokescreens, frequently established at taxpaying expense, for the purpose of legitimizing widespread distribution of harmful material under the guise of public tolerance. His point was amplified by Payne himself, who, after returning to his former job as a journalist for *The Toronto Sun*, criticized CRTC initiatives on the subject of violence on television, casting further doubt on his commitment to the public interest during his leadership of the OFRB. Referring to "zealots and crackpots" who tend to blame violent videos for violence in real life, Payne accused the CRTC of having "coerced broadcasters into a 'code of ethics' that serves up violence only to those who stay awake later than 9 p.m. and don't have cable."[45]

In addition to Johnstone and Ontario MP Margaret Marland, Valerie Smith, on behalf of the Coalition for the Safety of Our Daughters, also called upon Marion Boyd, Attorney General for Ontario prior to 1995, to investigate the possibility of appealing this particular Court of Appeal decision ruling.[46] She pointed out that the OFRB "routinely classifies extremely violent, sexually violent, and even pornographic movies for viewing by children," and added that because it was not operating in tune with social expectations, decisions and testimony from members should not be used as an accurate measure of community standards.

An example of how the OFRB is used by the industry to legitimize distribution of material to which the public at large objects, surfaced again with the Supreme Court of Canada's acquittal in 1995 of Randy Jorgensen, Canada's leading operator of the "Adults Only" chain of video stores. Jorgensen's company, which operates 39 video stores selling hardcore pornography in Ontario and 34 elsewhere in Canada was charged after police seized three videos that had been cleared by the OFRB. Although the Supreme Court acknowledged evidence of coercion and abuse toward women in the videos, it decided that the prosecutors had failed to prove the retailer knew the tapes included obscene material.

The court accepted Jorgensen's defense that he had not seen the tapes and had been relying on the classification board's approval. He was initially convicted in 1992 after undercover police bought several tapes from his Scarborough store one year earlier. When he later appealed that decision, the Ontario Court of

Appeal ruled that a film board's approval was not binding on a court and it subsequently upheld the conviction, which brought the case to the federal level. As a result of his acquittal by the Supreme Court of Canada, Jorgensen said he expected that doing business in the future would be "simpler."[47]

In the past, surveys were conducted within the province of Ontario to help determine what community standards are, but this is a practice that was discontinued when the Liberal Government assumed power in Ontario, in 1985. What these trends demonstrate is that the same province which initiated the LaMarsh Commission has, despite four subsequent changes in leadership, consistently ignored the LaMarsh recommendations on the mandate of the OFRB. On one point, however, concerning the LaMarsh Commission's recommendation that the OFRB's power to wield cuts to films be eliminated, Dorothy Christian refused to yield when she was still chairperson. She threatened to resign shortly after she was appointed in 1992 if this policy, recommended by the Ontario Law Reform Commission, as well, when it examined the mandate of the Board in 1992, was implemented. As she and others have observed, such a policy would have the effect of further enfeebling the ability of the Board to act in the public interest, essentially making it a publicly funded, legitimizing process on behalf of the industry, for the distribution of its products.

Nancy Toran-Harbin, a lawyer who served a two-year term on the OFRB, made the following observations in a personal interview in 1993:

> I first joined the Board hoping to act as a child advocate, thinking that as a parent, with a background in child development theory and law, I could make a contribution. But I feel that, for the most part, I wasted my time. However well meaning appointees are, I do not believe they can function effectively without some background and orientation in child cognitive development and research showing harmful effects. Furthermore, it is possible for members to become stagnant and desensitized and for that reason a rotating board would be a good idea. I also think the appeal procedure for a distributor who feels his product has been classified inappropriately needs to be reformed.

> At the present time, each film that comes before the board is reviewed by a panel of three members. However, if the distributor is not satisfied with the initial classification designation, the distributor can literally end up panel shopping until a panel is found that reflects the usual preference for the most lenient classification possible, maximizing the potential audience for it. In the process, the children of Ontario are not being well served.[48]

Toran-Harbin's experience provides a summary for the climate of discontent within the public at large that has surrounded the manner in which the ORFB has continued to function. It was reinforced by Eleanor Johnstone who resigned from the board in December, 1993, discouraged on the basis that those who pushed for tighter guidelines on sex and violence were being undermined.[49] Kelly Toughill, a journalist with the Queen's Park Press Bureau was similarly critical of Marilyn Churley in her capacity of Minister of Consumer and Commercial

Relations responsible for the operation of the Board during the Rae administration. Churley had acknowledged when first elected, that the link between pornography and violence against women was a "very important issue and a personal priority of hers, but none of her promises were kept."[50]

Toward the end of this period, however, Churley announced that Leslie Ann Adams, someone with extensive experience in journalism and television production and a background of work experience in health, environmental, and feminist organizations, had been appointed as chair of the Board. In response to her nomination, Adams said she was aware of the "tremendous power of film and video, the increasing concern within society about violence,"[51] and that it was "time to rate video games for sex and violence."[52]

This awareness was reflected somewhat in several subsequent board decisions which followed soon after Adam's appointment. The film *Hated* and the cartoon series *Little Red Riding Hood* are two examples of products that were refused approval and classification on the basis of excessive thematic material involving sex and violence.[53] In Saskatchewan a similar decision was made (although it was subsequently overturned when it was appealed by the distributor), to ban the film *Exit to Eden*, described as an erotic comedy involving scenes of sadomasochism.[54]

When the decision was first announced, concerning the latter, great emphasis was placed on how "out of step" the Saskatchewan Film and Video Classification Board (SFVCB) was with other provincial review boards. Even Saskatchewan Justice Minister Bob Mitchell said he found it 'odd' that his province "is the only jurisdiction in North America not to allow the film."[55] This observation by the Minister underscores two things. First, the continuing lack of awareness on the part of many politicians of widespread public concern about the proliferation of cultural commodities with themes of explicit sex and extreme violence. Second, the continuing reluctance of governments to take risks and act on that concern lest they be perceived as censors in the process.

By September, 1996, any optimism that Leslie Adams as the new chair of the OFRB would lead the review process in Ontario in a different direction was dashed. An article in that month's issue of *Toronto Life* dealt with the new trends in the city's burgeoning pornographic industry. Reporter Don Gillmor explained that the newest thing was CD-ROMs where interaction with women meant premature ejaculation was punishable by death. His research led him to the northern fringe of the city where two adult film distributors in a strip mall screened every video in their outlets as "de facto censors." They were screened with an eye toward the OFRB guidelines which list, among other taboos, scenes of incest, rape, coercion, degradation, humiliation, mutilation and the depiction of minors.

According to Gillmor, "There is room for interpretation on degradation and humiliation, but, for the most part, the board and distributors have reached an understanding on what will pass."[56] He pointed out that in the previous four years the Ontario pornography industry had grown into a business worth an estimated $50 million annually. In fact, critics have argued that one unfortunate side effect to the Butler decision handed down by the Supreme Court of Canada in 1992 was a new set of guidelines for obscenity that opened the door for an avalanche of graphic, hard-core material. In 1990, the OFRB screened 321 adult sex films. In 1996 it was estimated that they would screen 2,300.

It was further reported that the OFRB had, "refined its position," allowing consensual double penetrations and facial ejaculations, "two porn staples that other provinces already permitted" by 1995. The OFRB continues, to inoculate itself against the dull tedium of having to screen these videos by fast-forwarding segments, despite complaints made by Marland while she was opposition critic to Marlyn Churley as Minister responsible for the mandate of the OFRB during the Rae Administration. In other words, at the provincial level, lack of attention to the problem of media violence and appropriate classification criteria has gone from bad to worse.

When the Harris Government called an election in the spring of 1999, C-CAVE distributed a review of its record on violent entertainment products and crime prevention. On the latter, attention was focused on the Government's unrelenting emphasis on the need for boot camps; the need to sue parents, if necessary, to hold them accountable for the misdemeanors of their children; a tax subsidized legal challenge to the federal gun control legislation, despite evidence that it is supported by the majority of people in the province; and, in the fall of 1998, a decision to lower the age a youth can use a gun in the province of Ontario from 15 to 12 years of age.

In response to the highschool shootings in Littleton, Colorado and Taber, Alberta and a series of bomb threats throughout Ontario which followed in 1999,[57] it was announced that the board was considering the addition of an 18A category that would require adults to accompany teenagers between the ages of 14 and 18 interested in seeing a film deemed inappropriate for them. However, in a radio interview with CFPL News in London, Ontario on May 7, 1999, I questioned OFRB chairman Bob Warren's logic, first in concluding that they should be seen at all by those for whom they were deemed inappropriate; second, in assuming that teenagers are likely to submit to parental accompaniment in their movie going habits; and third, that managers of multiple theatre complexes such as Cineplex were likely to hire additional ushers to monitor compliance with this new classification. Existing criteria, for the most part, are already ignored in both theatres and video stores where those behind the counter are often seldom more than 18 years of age themselves.

My analysis of 281 films reviewed by the Board for the month of April, 1999, indicated that, despite increasing evidence of leniency in recent years, 159 were still classified as restricted; 139 of them with sexual themes.[58] In its report for 1997-8, Warren said that the main characteristics for the fiscal year were larger volumes of submitted product, especially of the adult sex genre. This was making classification decisions, he said, increasingly difficult as "film makers try to extend the boundaries of what is acceptable to the community." As a result, 1.8 percent had not been approved at all, a "slight" increase over the previous fiscal year.[59]

Generous Subsidies for Industry

As part of a blueprint for the television industry, a new multimillion dollar fund was approved by the CRTC during Spicer's tenure as chair, to create Canadian drama, children's programming, documentaries, variety shows, and music and dance programs.[60] It was reported that money for the fund would come from a levy that cable companies charged subscribers with the objective, according to Spicer, of reflecting Canadian values in a rapidly expanding television world. The fund was to be administered by an independent board of directors composed of industry representatives.[61] Repeated calls that the public, who would be paying for such a fund in the first place, should have input from educators and the community at large into decision making on the kind of programming that would be supported, were ignored. Canadians were still expected to adhere only to industry's interpretation of Canadian values.

By 1998, the fund was experiencing serious difficulties, despite an infusion of $50 million from the federal government. Various reasons were cited by the press. Canadian shows were being "frozen out of the line up for funds," most of them "grabbed" by a record number of Canadian producers of programs made in Canada largely for foreign markets: Telefilm and cable fund officials "hated" each other. This was perceived to be due, either to government officials "meddling" in the "creative" process or to Heritage Minister Sheila Copps *not* getting involved in how the funds should be dispersed; over reliance on government funds by broadcasters who tended to fuel over-production of programs; and large producers such as Alliance and Atlantis, publically traded companies who declared dividends and had their costs and profit margins covered through foreign deals, still getting public money.[62] Nowhere in this commentary was there any concern expressed regarding the *nature* of the content from the standpoint of violent themes, either for domestic or foreign markets.

The need for special criteria on how grants are awarded to film and television producers in a way that would reflect a concern for violence or other harmful elements in scripts, either by Telefilm, the Canadian Television Cable Production Fund (CTCPF) or provincial agencies such as the Ontario Film Development Corporation (OFDC) is increasingly urgent. There was criticism, for example, that public agencies helped to fund the film, *Paris France*, turned down by the Cannes Film Festival in 1993 because, according to the late Jay Scott, a film critic for *The Globe and Mail* at the time, "people were afraid of it." It was described as one of several *cult* films produced by Gerard Ciccoritti, director of CanCon vampire films:

> Written by three-day book-writin' local legend Tom Walmsley. The poster features Leslie Hope in leather drag, hauling Peter Outerbridge around by the neck. Real good choice of project to kick off a mainstream film career, eh? *Especially* in Canada. Ciccoritti just shrugs, and begs to disagree.[63]

While some have argued that *Paris France* is a serious, thought-provoking film that explores important social issues, the fact remains that indiscriminate promotion and funding of film and television production in Toronto, regardless of thematic material, has become part of an attempt to sustain Toronto as the third largest film center in North America, reputed in 1993 to be bringing in "$1.2 billion per year."[64] By 1996, this figure had grown to $2 billion nation-wide.[65] All of this underscores the extent to which the LaMarsh Commission observation that the film industry in Canada is badly uncoordinated remains a problem.

Responsibilities at the Municipal Level

So far, calls for greater responsibility and accountability on the part of government officials have been focused on either the federal or provincial levels. There are, however, things that can be done at the municipal level as well, if the political will exists. Given the extent to which major Canadian cities, particularly Toronto, have become key North American centers for television and film production, the need for better regulation of this process at the municipal level is more urgent than ever.

There is no doubt that economic considerations still tend to outweigh social costs in ways that were first pointed out by the LaMarsh Commission, but there is now greater potential for Canadians to address issues of content on a local basis. Canadian broadcasters, specialty channels, and cable carriers may still be in the habit of buying American programming, but in a growing number of cases these shows are actually produced in our own neighborhoods.

Although the Toronto Transit Commission adopted a policy some years ago to refuse a permit for a film crew with a script that it deemed too violent, on the basis that such a practice contravened the Commission's policy to make the transit system safer for women and children, there are no special criteria for how permits are given out by the city itself—nor has there ever been any inclination to develop any. Indeed, as demonstrated by the following news coverage, the opposite has occurred:

> "If it hadn't been for the efforts on behalf of the City of Toronto and Metro councils, we wouldn't have been here," said Kevin Gillis, executive producer of *Robocop, The Series.*
>
> Producers of the Toronto TV syndication considered U.S. cities but instead will spend $36.5 million here by next July.
>
> Toronto Councillor Anne Johnston, Metro's member of the Toronto film liaison group, is "thrilled" that her push last year to streamline the film location permit process is paying off.[66]

The intentions for this new *Robocop* series were described for Southam News as follows:

> Orion Pictures wants to widen the audience for the indestructible cyborg lawman who first crunched his way onto motion picture screens in the original *Robocop* back in 1987 and graduated to further cinematic mayhem three years later in *Robocop 2*. But with *RoboCop 3*, the producers are aiming to be—would you believe?—more family-oriented.

"The studio was adamant from very early on that we had to broaden the audience base for this picture," says director Fred Dekker.

"The original *RoboCop* and *RoboCop 2* were very hard, graphically violent films. However, the irony is that kids loved the character, but because of an R rating in most countries they couldn't go and see the pictures when they first came out." So a revised mandate faced Dekker in his capacity as director and co-screenwriter: he had to ensure that *RoboCop 3* would qualify for a PG-13 rating...previous films include *Night of the Creeps* and *Monster Squad*. Both these earlier items were affectionate celebrations of the B-movie horror and science fiction culture which so captivated him when he was growing up.[67]

Dekker explained that *Robocop 3* would be different—one that parents who are concerned about gratuitous violence "can bring their kids to and not feel bad afterwards." He said that, although there will still be plenty of "action," there will be more attention paid to "context" which, in his view, has been badly neglected in the past. Said Dekker:

> I think *RoboCop 2* was a science fiction movie because the villain was a big robot with a psycho-killer brain. This one I think of as a war movie, in the sense that instead of—say—occupied France, we have Detroit. Instead of Nazis, we have these mercenaries from the Corporate Rehabs, and instead of the French resistance we have the disenfranchised people of Detroit.[68]

Apart from the fact that these production trends do nothing to facilitate an opportunity for Canadians to tell their own stories through film and television programming, based on their own experiences, there are other ways in which this kind of community invasion by industrial interests is fragmenting neighborhood stability and cohesion. The residents of Toronto are expected to accommodate film crews and weather the usual inconveniences that come with production vans parked on residential streets blowing exhaust fumes throughout the neighborhoods, often with glaring artificial lighting and the noise of simulated gunshots heard well into the early hours of the morning, regardless of the content in the film or television script.

In addition, there is usually limited access to side streets and, in some cases, a person's own home and designated parking area. Other counterproductive, environmental problems include the material waste that results in garbage as elaborate set designs are used, blown up and later scrapped. At the same time, home owners themselves who offer up their houses as film locations in exchange for handsome profits regardless of thematic content, confident that any damage caused by cars blown up in their driveways or fake blood spattered on their walls will be repaired, are not blameless either.[69] On issues of violence, public education must be framed in ways that illuminate the serious social costs precipitated by these community disruptions on both an immediate, local basis when they are being produced as well as when they are reflected back into the home on the television screen.

Contrary to what the LaMarsh Commission recommended, from the standpoint of public money being used to support prosocial programming, we now actually have public money being diverted into the production of material that is known to be harmful to the community on a number of levels. This is occurring not only through tax subsidized production funds at both federal and provincial levels and by employees in the municipal public sector hired to process applications for permits and grants, but by elected officials who vigorously promote violence-filled productions like *Top Cops* and *Kung Fu: The Legend Continues*, in which fictional "bad guys" are being chased around Chinatown, Ontario Place, and Casa Loma in Toronto.[70]

When the contradictions in public policy were brought to the attention of both the City of Toronto Healthy City Task Force (HCTF) and the Safe City Committee (SCC) by C-CAVE in 1993, only the latter responded by initiating correspondence with the Toronto Transit Commission (TTC) and the Toronto Film Liaison Office (TFLO). In a letter on behalf of the TTC in October of 1993, A.F. Leach, former Chief General Manager, described the Commission's film policy as follows:

> There should be no adverse effect on the image of the TTC or public transit as a safe reliable form of transport by depicting scenes of violence or other unfavorable representation. If in the opinion of the TTC, such unfavorable portrayal is likely to occur, *script changes* will be required prior to filming, in an effort to resolve the matter. If there still exists a disagreement as to the script on the issue of unfavorable representation then the Commission shall be the final arbitrator.

In contrast, the letter received by the SCC from Commissioner Robert E. Millward on behalf of the City of Toronto Planning and Development Department one month later, on November 15, on the subject included the following explanation:

> David Plant of my Film Liaison Office has...informally discussed the topic with other film commissioners in Canada and the United States. It is generally agreed that federal and provincial bodies are responsible for reviewing and rating the suitability of programming for public distribution and that it would be inappropriate and impractical for any government body to set regulations that prejudged program content before such material was assembled into a finished form.

The puzzle, of course, is why it is appropriate for the TTC, like the New York Subway System, to have a policy on film production, but not Toronto and other major cities which host television and film production crews.[71] So far, the concept of "boycotts" is regarded by Toronto city officials as applicable only to private citizens, *not* municipal officials acting in the interest of private citizens. Prudent selectivity or approval of applications for production permits are not perceived, at this time, to be compatible with the concept of "self-regulation" as it might be encouraged for municipal authorities as well as industry in keeping with the spirit of the new code on violence developed by the CAB and the CRTC.

This kind of uncoordinated policy at municipal levels of government, with social costs receiving only marginal attention, underscores the extent to which much more vigilance is required at all three levels of government on the multifaceted ways in which our tax dollars are being spent to finance and reinforce harmful aspects of violence in popular culture.

News Media Concentration Accelerates

By 1996, more problems stemming from the growth of media concentration in Canada captured the public's attention. When Canadian media mogul, Conrad Black, expanded his empire by taking over Southam newspapers he radically altered the landscape of the entire Canadian print media. Not only does he now own all the newspapers in three Canadian provinces but he also owns 60 of the 105 daily newspapers throughout the country and 50 percent of English-language papers in circulation.[72] Compared to the United States, where eleven American corporations control 50 percent of American daily newspapers and the largest chain only has about 10 percent of circulation in the country, we have a much more serious problem in terms of diminishing diversity and what this means for democracy itself.

Canada is virtually alone in the industrialized world in having no legislation to prevent the concentration of newspaper ownership or cross-media concentration. Drafted by the powerful pro-industry lobby group, the Business Council on National Issues (BCNI), to regulate mergers and acquisitions and passed by the Mulroney Government, the Competition Act has a very narrow mandate and is skewed entirely in favor of big business. It can only be used to rule against a merger if the local commercial competitiveness of advertisers has been compromised.

Critics, Maude Barlow and James Winter, have pointed out that the Competition Bureau which administers the Act "refuses to examine whether editorial and news content diversity will be compromised, whether local news and the use of local reporters and columnists will be diminished, or even if a national chain will be able to control national advertising markets, thereby creating a monopoly and effectively diminishing competition at every level."[73] It goes without saying that whoever owns and controls the news media in society has tremendous power to hire and promote editors and journalists with views they deem to be "appropriate."

On the whole, it is apparent that changes within the communications industry since the LaMarsh Report was first published have been motivated primarily for economic reasons. Commitment to change as with recent initiatives on new codes of conduct, have been largely cosmetic. The onus of responsibility and accountability is still focused predominantly on the individual, either as consumer, parent or teacher. Government agencies have demonstrated little inclination to act in the public interest. Methods in which funding assistance is provided for television and film production go unchallenged. Provincial governments ignore the need for reform of classification systems. Municipal governments actively promote television and film production and continue to hand out permits indiscriminately. Meanwhile, concentration of media ownership and control of the cultural environment continues to grow, unimpeded by government regulation.

Notes

1. CRTC, 1991, 1992.
2. CRTC, 1991, 1992.
3. Beatty, 1993, Feb. 19, Ottawa: Communications Canada, p.1.
4. Department of Communications, 1993, April, p.2-3.
5. Department of Communications, 1993, p.3.
6. Comstock, 1991.
7. Walker, 1993, Oct. 8, *The Globe and Mail*, p. A16.
8. CBC Television, 1993c, Evening News with Stu Patterson.
9. Miller, Myers, Bruce, DallaCosta [MMBD], personal communication, December 13, 1993.
10. Despite several applications to the Ministry of Revenue in Ottawa for this charitable number and correspondence with various officials for a period of eleven years the federal government remains unconvinced that C-CAVE provides public education on the subject of media violence that is in the public interest. This situation provides an example of industry and government cooperation in hegemonically diffusing attempts on the part of concerned citizens to address the proliferation of harmful cultural commodities.
11. CRTC, 1993b, Oct. 28, Public Notice, 1993-149, Ottawa.
12. CRTC, 1993b.
13. CRTC, 1993b.
14. CRTC, 1993b.
15. CBSC, 1997, November 11; CBSC, 1998, March 25.
16. CBSC, 1994, Nov.1; Lacey, 1994a, Nov. 2, *The Globe and Mail*, p.C2.
17. CBSC, 1994.
18. Lacey, 1994b, Nov. 9, *The Globe and Mail*, p. C2.
19. CBC Newsworld, 1994, Nov.3.
20. CBC Television, 1994, Nov. 1.
21. FWTAO, 1994, Nov. 3, News Release.
22. Leland, 1993, Oct. 11, *Newsweek*, p. 50.
23. Leland, 1993, p.51.
24. "Beavis and Butt-head sparks," 1993, November 17, *The Toronto Sun*, p.S18.
25. Smith, 1993, Nov. 11, News Release, C.S.D.
26. Citytv, personal communication, January 21, 1994.
27. Citytv, personal communication, January 21, 1994.
28. Citytv, 1993b, In Your Face: Violence in Music, Director Moses Znaimer.
29. Citytv, 1993b.
30. Allemang, 1998, March 20, *The Globe and Mail*, p.C2.
31. Rec. No. 12, p.47.
32. Bird, 1993, p.44.
33. Magnish, 1994, Oct. 27, *The Toronto Sun*, p.11.
34. Bird, 1993, p.73.
35. Personal interview, May 21, 1993.
36. Vipond, 1989, p.175.
37. Vipond, 1989, p.181.
38. Canadian Motion Picture Distributors Association [CMPDA], 1992.
39. Ontario, 1993a, 1993b, 1993c, 1993d, 1993e, 1993f,1993g.
40. Ontario, 1993c, p.710.

41. *Ontario Gazette*, 1995.

42. Johnstone, 1993a, Fall, C-CAVE News, p.8.

43. Downey, 1993, Oct. 23, *The Globe and Mail*, p.A18.

44. Johnstone, 1993a, p.8.

45. 1993, Nov. 8, *The Toronto Sun*, p.28.

46. Ontario, 1993c; Smith, personal communication, October 25, 1993.

47. Van Rijn, 1995, Nov. 17, *The Toronto Star*, p.A3. When, on behalf of C-CAVE, I was interviewed about Jorgensen's acquittal on CBC Television, November 17, 1995, I said that unfortunately it sent a signal to all retail businesses that they need not always be considered responsible and accountable for the impact of their products on the public, particularly if they were not fully aware of what they were selling. Jorgensen was clearly being favoured over other retailers such as those in the chemical or pharmaceutical industries who are expected to test their products for toxicity before releasing them on the market in order to ensure the highest degree of public safety.

48. Personal communication, November 9, 1993. This and subsequent quotations from Nancy Toran-Harbin are derived from a personal interview for this study on November 9, 1993.

49. Toughill, 1994, Jan. 22, *The Toronto Star*, p.C4.

50. Toughill, 1994, p.C4.

51. Ontario Ministry of Consumer and Commercial Relations, 1994, July 7, News Release.

52. Rusk, 1994, Aug. 4, *The Globe and Mail*, p.C2.

53. Smith, personal communication, October 29, 1994.

54. "Saskatchewan bans," 1994, Oct. 12, *The Toronto Star*, p.D1.

55. "Saskatchewan bans," 1994, p.D1.

56. Gillmor, D. 1996, September, p.84, Fast Forward, Toronto Life.

57. Prete, 1999, May 11, *The Hamilton Spectator*, p.A4.

58. OFRB, 1999.

59. Warren, 1999, Sept. 30, Annual Report 1997-8, Ontario, p.2.

60. "TV Mega-fund," 1994, Feb. 11, *The Globe nd Mail*, p.D1.

61. "TV Mega-fund," 1994, p.D1.

62. Quill, 1998, April 26, *The Toronto Star*, p.F5.

63. Files, 1993, Oct. 28, *Eye Magazine*, p.25.

64. Chapman, 1993a, Nov. 26, *The Toronto Sun*, p.17.

65. Gray, 1996, July 13, *The Globe and Mail*, p.C1.

66. Chapman, 1993a, Nov. 26, *The Toronto Sun*, p.17.

67. Portman, 1993, Nov. 6, *The Kitchener Waterloo Record*, p.C6.

68. Portman, 1993, p.C6.

69. Kezwer, 1998, April 26, *The Toronto Star*, p.B1.

70. "Johnston gets," 1993, December, Teaside, Rosedale Town Crier, p.4.

71. Gerbner, 1994a&b.

72. Barlow and Winter, 1997.

73. 1997, p. 213.

Chapter 8

OUR CHANGING SOCIAL FABRIC

THROUGHOUT THE WORLD, cultural, social and economic transformation patterns, are now driven by communications technology. Institutional restructuring responses, occurring as a result, are dominated almost entirely by the dictates of the marketplace. For civil society itself, old infrastructures and regulatory procedures remain in place, or alternatively, are dismantled entirely. Meanwhile, as social disruption and fragmentation accelerates, so do the problems precipitated by the production and distribution of cultural commodities in which violence predominates. Consequently, the need for better collaboration between government, industry, social scientists, educators, parents and the health community on how these ominous trends should be addressed, is becoming increasingly urgent.

A Global Perspective
In 1968, following a United Nations Congress on the Prevention of Crime and the Treatment of Offenders, Peter Lyins examined ways in which different countries were responding to the issue of media violence. He reported that, out of 85 nations present, United States delegates found themselves pretty much alone on issues linking mass media and juvenile delinquency in two aspects.[1] First, they expressed lack of certainty on the effects of media violence and, second, they emphasized their aversion toward censorship and suppression of any kind of content. Concerns were expressed among delegates from developing countries over the importation of violent films, particularly those from Latin America, whose countries were recipients of United States aid and whose citizens consequently held the Americans in high regard.

In 1985, these concerns were amplified by Canadian writer William Stevenson. He described the kind of role modeling American popular culture was fostering in developing countries, on the basis of what was being perceived to be "typical" American behavior by impressionable young men fascinated with American habits and mores. He pointed out how pornographic films were teaching Latin Americans what they considered to be a northern way of life. With organized crime at the helm of film production and distribution, plenty of money, he explained, was being used to buy superior technology, stunning stars, brilliant effects, and expensive locations. The primary motive was money laundering through "fly-by-night" film production studios with films exported as part of a bargain package of cultural aid. Basically, said Stevenson, "the mob philosophy is being disseminated to encourage a macho approach to the proper order between the sexes involving domination and extreme violence."[2]

In 1995, for the first time since 1968, plans emerged for a one day workshop on the role of the media in crime prevention at the *9th United Nations Congress on Crime Prevention* held in Cairo, Egypt. Preparation by the Canadian delegation included a pre-congress consultation and information session in Ottawa. Evidence of success following the Congress was mixed. Mandla McHunu, director of the Socio-legal Studies Center at the University of Natal in South Africa spoke on the innovative Street Law Program developed by David McQuoid-Mason. George Gerbner, from the Annenberg School of Communication at the University of Pennsylvania, had been invited to participate but later expressed dissatisfaction with the outcome to the author.

Examination of the preliminary report, indicated that the agenda was, in the end, designed to serve, predominantly, industrial interests. Global Television news anchor Peter Kent, for example, was the moderator. There was, of course, a certain irony in Global Television's prominence at the Congress. At approximately the same time, at the annual Communications Conference at the University of Quebec in Montreal, Jacques Deguire of Laval University in Quebec was reporting on a study completed one year earlier which indicated that Global Television offered, by quite a large margin, the most violent programming of any broadcaster in Canada.

In recent years, concerns about the potentially adverse impact from the export of American popular culture commodities have been overrun by worldwide fascination with the American "dream factory." Its sophisticated technology has resulted in the emulation of American film, video and television producers on a global basis.[3] This trend, according to a 1991 UNESCO Report on the subject, is leading to increasing standardization and uniformity in productions with new forms of culture emerging out of interpretation of tradition and modernity. Some of the more ominous consequences of these developments have been described by George Gerbner:

> Concentration brings streamlining of production (denying entry to newcomers, reducing the number of buyers and thus competition for the products) and increasing the dramatic formulas suitable for aggressive international promotion. Program production is costly, risky, and hard-pressed by oligopolistic pricing practices. Most producers cannot break even on the license fees they receive for domestic airings. They are forced to go into syndication and foreign sales to make a profit. *They need a dramatic ingredient that requires no translation, "speaks action" in any language, and fits any culture. That ingredient is violence.*[4]

The nature of this concentration is generating unprecedented attitudes, values, and behavior patterns and is having an impact on cultural identities all over the world. Although the trans-nationalization of culture need not necessarily all be regarded as unhealthy, the fact remains that violence dominates United States exports. International data gathered by Gerbner and his associates in 1994 indicated that violence was the main theme in 40 percent of home-shown and 49 percent of exported programs.[5] What we now have on a global basis, as former U.S. army Lieutenant-Colonel David Grossman points out, is a breakdown in our violence immune system.[6] This is the inevitable result of steady heavy consumer habits of extreme violence in popular culture from an early age.

These production and distribution patterns point out the urgency for adoption, on a global basis, of policies that publicly supported, financial incentives for television and film production be confined to projects that do not involve excessive violence and other harmful messages. In addition, this same rationale should apply to production crews seeking permits from municipal authorities. Internationally approved criteria in this context would do much to create a "level playing field" for members of the industry now reluctant to cooperate in reducing their reliance on the cheap industrial ingredients of sex and violence because they do not wish to relinquish their competitive advantages.

For example, in the early 1990s it was pointed out by Thomas Radecki, child psychiatrist and founder of the U.S. based National Coalition on Television Violence (NCTV), that the cheaply produced, violence filled television series *Friday 13th* was actually filmed in Toronto. It was concerned Americans that eventually forced it off the air.[7] Such occurrences not only thwart the efforts of those attempting to act in the public interest in Canada, but in the United States as well, where most of these harmful products still originate. Instead, provision of tax credits and funding from industrial programs, such as the Canada Council, Telefilm Canada, and various regional film development agencies throughout Canada, for violence filled films is now standard practice. Some of these films, as Alison Vale pointed out in *The Globe and Mail* in 1999, have even become international award winners.[8]

Redefining Our Social Contract

Most people who live in pluralist societies, despite the fragmentation of postmodernizing change, are committed to democratic principles based on diversity and a broad spectrum of human rights. Although upheavals and transformation are underway, both within and among nations on a global basis, Canadians have been, and are likely to continue to be, bound together as individuals because of certain rules by which they have agreed to govern themselves. These fundamental principles continue to guide policy makers as well as the population at large, notwithstanding the fact that, as Chomsky and others have argued, democratic societies in which populations are not disciplined by force are subjected to more subtle forms of ideological control. In fact, there is an urgent need for these subtleties to be better understood and resisted.[9]

Because they have always been in the vanguard of moral and ethical leadership, at this critical juncture in our human history, more assertive leadership is required from social scientists, educators, and health professionals in the public debate over who should have the right to determine how our social and cultural environments are constructed in an information based economy. Grossman has commented on how civilized people, particularly young people, are currently socialized to become accustomed to killing others through role models provided by Hollywood:

> Manipulation of the minds of impressionable teenagers is a necessary evil that we accept only reluctantly and with reservations for combat soldiers but we need to face up to the consequences of it being indiscriminately applied to civilian teenagers.[10]

In his book *On Killing: The Psychological Cost of Learning to Kill in War and Society*, Grossman rejects the notion of violence in the media as either sublimation for innate aggressive tendencies or neutral entertainment. Drawing upon the theories of Freud, Pavlov and B.F. Skinner within the context of his own military experience and observations of how soldiers are trained, he calls it "classical conditioning, operant conditioning, and social learning."[11] In fact, it is argued by some behaviourists that, instead of catharsis, viewing tragedy, whether it is *King Lear* or brutal cinema, can reinforce feelings of victimization and helplessness. It discourages us from taking responsibility for our own happiness.[12]

In 1998, Canadian writer Gwynne Dyer commented on the ominous trends of these unrestrained practises in the promotion of popular culture to youth following the school massacre in Jonesboro, Arkansas involving accused killers 11 and 13 years of age. Noting that it was the fourth time in five months that American children had been accused of opening fire on their classmates with semi-automatic weapons, and that all the schools involved were not in big cities but in small southern towns, he pointed, not only to the obvious need for better gun control legislation, but to the diminishing reference in news coverage following these multiple shootings that young perpetrators tend to be influenced by films, television, or violent video games. Said Dyer, "Unless you pretend this is all such a mysterious phenomenon that nothing can be done about it, you have to take on some of the central shibboleths of American culture."[13]

Grossman has since analyzed this particular school shooting and noted the extraordinary degree of eye-hand coordination exhibited by the young perpetrators in handling the weapons used: a skill he attributes entirely to video game practice.[14] Frequently, it is a skill acquisition enthusiastically defended by industry apologists for violence in the content of these games.

The contradictions in our social contract within the Western World have already been well amplified by Canadian scholar, Elliot Leyton. Over two decades ago he pointed out that multiple murderers are not "insane" but very much products of their time.

> Rather than a randomly occurring freakish event, the act of the multiple murderer is dictated by specific stresses and alterations in the human community. Far from being deluded, he is essentially an embodiment of the central themes in his civilization, and his behavior is a reflection of that civilization's critical tensions. He is, as a result, a creature and a creation of his age.[15]

Leyton's analysis was underscored by American psychiatrist Brandon Centerwall in 1989, who concluded in his study that the mere introduction of television technology into Canadian and American societies has resulted in thousands of people being murdered.

The entire "developed" world was presented with an example of how these critical social tensions manifest themselves in the murder of a British toddler by two 11-year-old youths in Liverpool, England, in 1993. Although it is by no means the only example of murder or extreme violence and brutality committed by pre-adolescent children it is one that attracted worldwide attention.[16] In the court case that followed the English tragedy, Judge Michael Morland's reflections on why two boys would commit such a terrible crime resonated with similar speculations in related news coverage. He said, "It is not for me to pass judgment on their upbringing, but I suspect that exposure to violent video films may, in part, be an explanation."[17] The 2-year-old had evidently been doused in paint, battered to death and left on a railway line in a way that "bore a chilling resemblance to scenes from the video film, *Child's Play*,." *rented by one of the killer's fathers.*[18] It is frequently pointed out by researchers, community workers, and teachers that once these kinds of cultural commodities are in the home, children of all ages invariably end up with access to them.

The confusion and horror expressed by the public at large over this murder underscores the need for the information-cultural sector to become a priority field for attention from adult educators as communities on a global basis, committed to democratic principles, struggle to redefine basic freedoms and value systems as an integral part of our collective social fabric. In *The Toronto Star* these two 11-year-olds were described as "scapegoats for the sins of a society that itself is no longer able to judge what is 'right' and 'wrong' and which itself no longer understands the concept of logical consequences."[19]

Following this tragedy, over 25 leading psychologists in the United Kingdom were moved to reexamine their previous positions, and took a definitive stand on the issue of harmful effects from media violence. It helped to reinforce the position of the American Psychological Association (APA) on the issue, and once again, cried out for similar response from the Canadian Psychological Association (CPA) which remains conspicuous by its silence on this point. Although psychologist Leonard Eron from New York was invited to give a special lecture, open to the public, on the subject of media violence in February, 1996, by The Psychology Foundation of Canada (PFC), it was poorly attended and nothing in the form of positive initiatives followed.

In this context it would be useful to revive and reaffirm some of the findings and recommendations of the Ontario Psychological Association (OPA) in its brief to the LaMarsh Commission. Among these the OPA emphasized that regulation of the media industry may have to include regulation of individual contributors in the same manner as physicians, psychologists and others are now regulated in the service of public protection.

In the Canadian helping professions, there has always been a lack of consistency in policy positions on issues related to media violence. For example, at the Sunnybrook Health Science Center in Toronto a news conference was called in August, 1994, at which three top medical specialists sounded a public health alarm, urging the general public to treat the need for gun control as a major national health issue. According to Katherine Leonard, medical director of the teen clinic at the North York General Hospital, "Firearms are a leading cause of death among Canadian teenagers, and the majority of those deaths are suicides."[20]

This initiative on the part of medical professionals needs to be extended to integrate the issue of media violence. Although the Canadian Medical Association (CMA) and the Canadian Teacher's Association (CTA) made a modest start in 1994 when they joined grass roots community groups including Canadians Concerned About Violence In Entertainment (C-CAVE) in founding the Coalition for Responsible Television (CRTV) for the purpose of addressing the proliferation of violence in popular culture and its impact on violence in real life, neither the CMA, the CTA nor the CRTV have remained active on the issue.

The growing urgency for more definitive and well publicized health policies in Canada on the issue of media violence was demonstrated in coverage which followed a copycat crime committed by a 14-year-old boy in Saskatchewan, in 1995. Sandy Charles killed, skinned and cooked the flesh of his 7-year-old victim after being influenced, as his defending lawyer argued in the trial which followed a year later, by the movie "Warlock" which the youth had watched repeatedly prior to committing the crime.[21] In a feature story which followed in *The Toronto Star*, journalist Trish Crawford quoted a number of "experts." All of them focused on how: violence in the media is an issue only for the vulnerable few; for adolescents its mainly a social event; violence has always perturbed adults dating back to Bugs Bunny cartoons; its a chicken and egg, life versus art argument; blaming TV is too convenient; and poverty and neglect are more important factors in real life violence.

While no professional association can ever, nor should it ever, dictate the opinions of individual members, and irresponsible reporting will always, among other things, include self serving perspectives, in this and other similar cases, it would be much more difficult for helping professionals interviewed, to flaunt or ignore official position statements adopted by their own professional licensing bodies.[22] Gaps in consistency on public policy on media violence within the health community, preyed upon by profit-driven media interests determined to sustain collective denial on the urgency of the problem, help to reinforce public confusion. They also fragment and neutralize attempts in other sectors of society for the provision of public education, and retard the development of cohesive, cost-efficient, preventative, health care delivery.

Another example occurred at the Hospital For Sick Children in Toronto, in August, 1994. Despite the fact that staff psychiatrists and psychologists occasionally appear on panels confirming links between violence in the media and real life violence, it was reported on CBC's program, *Kids Culture*, that the Hospital had hosted a 30th birthday party for "G.I. Joe," a popular and controversial figure in a whole genre of violence-filled toys. A similar example of misplaced priorities in hospital administration policy was observed in Calgary, in 1994 when it was reported that the city's film commission was known to be "cooperative in the extreme in giving out permits. They'll shut down the city's intensive-care unit at 24 hours notice if you ask nicely enough."[23]

It is, of course, possible that film and television production in intensive care units of hospitals has nothing to do with themes of gratuitous violence, but the fact remains that its presence in these settings, to begin with, must inevitably be regarded as an intrusion into the operation of an institution whose priorities are health care delivery, not film and television production for entertainment purposes. Actual collaboration with industry to the detriment of the public interest within the health care delivery system has to be regarded as particularly counterproductive in the development of effective strategies for change.

Communications Management: A Global Challenge

Clearly, media violence is symptomatic of a larger phenomena of systemic violence within society at large, which has now manifested itself in every aspect of social, political, and cultural life. The extent and seriousness of these developments have been obscured and excused as necessary byproducts of democratic self-government opposed to censorship. Continuing opposition still clouds better clarity and understanding by the general public of how these critical developments have come about and how they should be meaningfully addressed. Economic interests have been allowed to override the public interest while politicians for the most part, have distanced themselves from involvement in the debate over policy on media violence, when it has come up at all. Meanwhile, evidence accumulates that systemic violence is being dramatically accelerated by the introduction of communications technology in an economy where popular cultural commodities are assuming ever greater importance.

No country is immune to the spiraling levels of violence that manifest themselves from concentration in global economic trends. Patterns of cultural and social transformation are inevitably influenced by factors such as poverty, overpopulation, and environmental degradation, which in themselves, are creating instability and predispositions to violence between and within weakening nation-states. However, an overlay of popular cultural commodities, marketed on a worldwide basis in which violence is *celebrated* and *glamorized*, inevitably exacerbates international tensions.

In addition, one must not overlook the historical connections between military policy and thematic content in cultural products. This is well outlined by Nancy Snow in her book *Propaganda Inc. Selling America's Culture to the World*. In it she traces the symbiotic relationship between Hollywood and the Pentagon based U.S. Information Agency which began during the Second World War for the purpose of winning popular support for U.S. entry into it.[24] In Canada, Joyce Nelson tells a similar story about the origins of the National Film Board (NFB) with the help of British documentary founder, John Grierson.[25]

Anti war movements have yet to seriously examine and address these links. In May, 1999, one had only to witness the hand-wringing and opposition to

NATO bombing in Kosovo in public forums, on Community Television, the Internet and CBC Radio. While critics vehemently opposed to NATO strategies made occasional reference to the hypocracy of President Bill Clinton pleading with American teenagers to use non violent conflict resolution strategies in the aftermath of the Littleton, Colorado, high school massacre while doing the opposite himself in Kosovo, the links stopped there. Observations of the growing popularity of Rambo designer sun glasses among Serb soldiers in Sarajevo, observed since the civil war in the former Yugoslavia erupted almost ten years ago, remains buried, for the most part, in the Spring, 1999, issue of *Adbusters*. In it, Bruce Grierson describes standard desensitization techniques for military training, compares them to popular culture consumption habits and matches them with rising evidence of violence on a global basis. The growing discordance between human society and the natural world, fueled by a morally vacuous global media industry and the subsequent need for models which offer new paradigms of social behavior is still poorly understood by the left.

Until public education is better channeled in this direction, serious world wide commitment from both government and industry to the development and implementation of codes on violence, classification criteria and blocking devices for all cultural commodities, whether these are television programming, films, computer games, or action-filled toys, is unlikely. For this to happen, social activism combined with research and media scholarship, must be accelerated and better supported within university communities themselves. This is, after all, where critical left wing protests and demands are usually based and nurtured.

Federal Regulatory Initiatives in Canada

There is now little doubt in anyone's mind that a "new" system for communications management for Canadians is more dependent than ever on what is happening on an international basis. Canadians are no longer the only ones being inundated with American cultural commodities. This is now happening on a global basis. But, having had more experience with the complications involved in trying to resist American cultural domination, Canada is in a position to make unique contributions to the development of a new international system. Unfortunately, no one acting on behalf of the public interest in Canada is rising to the challenge—with the possible exception of Heritage Minister Sheila Copps who, by introducing Bill C-55 into the House of Commons, made a valiant effort to protect the Canadian magazine industry from further American encroachment.[26]

While he was still chair of the CRTC, Keith Spicer's emphasis, internationally, on what he called "the Canadian example" was a step in the right direction. Unfortunately, little of any substance resulted from his commitment to the issue of media violence for a number of reasons. Despite his long-term goal of making violence on television as socially unacceptable as drinking and driving, pollution, and cigarette smoking, Spicer, himself, never enjoyed the full support of the entire Commission and his successor, Francoise Bertrand, has yet to demonstrate any real interest in the issue at all.

In fact, on the same day, May 17, 1999, that *The Globe and Mail* ran an article about how Canada has become a haven for criminals on the Internet, the CRTC released a decision, after ten months of hearings in 1998, not to regulate the Internet at all.[27] Bertrand said the Commission did not believe that regulation would serve the objectives of the Broadcasting Act, that the CRTC was "one of the first regulators in the world to clarify its position on the Internet" and that, where harmful content was concerned, tools such as Canadian laws of general application, industry self-regulation, content filtering software and increased media awareness, offered adequate protection.[28] In other words, the predominant emphasis would continue—in keeping with similar initiatives from federal and provincial governments—to be on sustaining a climate favorable to business and market incentives.

Spicer's approach in addressing the issue of media violence was, unfortunately, flawed from the beginning partly because he clung to the notion that violence on television is only a "children's issue." In the process, he ignored countless consultations and presentations from education and grassroots level organizations for whom the problem has always been much more complex. He always insisted that "censorship" was not the answer and he was "confident" that greater sensitivity from the industry would suffice. He spoke of striking "a reasonable balance between the right to freedom of expression and the right of children to a healthy childhood."[29]

The broader issue of cultural violence and, in particular, systemic violence that has become such a serious component to the problem as a whole, was ignored totally. The need for Canadians to recognize and reject corporate indignation and suppression of meanings as a ruse to protect profit-making potential, under the guise of protection for us all from censorship, was *never* a component in his rationale. Consequently, the LaMarsh Commission's hope that the CRTC would pick up where it left off has never happened—at least not yet.

Of course, as Spicer was fond of pointing out, a cooperative strategy involving all sectors of society in addressing critical cultural environmental problems is always preferable to a combative, legalistic approach. But it is unrealistic to expect to achieve this long-term goal by focusing solely on the protection of children, since children inevitably pattern themselves after adults and adolescents: many of whom are, themselves, already adversely affected by media violence. Also, in sticking to what he called a 'focused' agenda on gratuitous or glamorized violence and choosing not to 'diffuse efforts' by adding on 'sex, foul language, family values, specific feminist concerns or other distinct, more controversial issues,' Spicer trivialized existing codes of conduct for broadcasters. These codes already address all of the above and broadcasters are, at least in theory, expected to adhere to them.[30] Considerable public pressure has, in the past, contributed to existing codes on sex role stereotyping.

In a sense, Spicer was diminishing some aspects of broadcasting codes of conduct while trying to bump up the importance of others. A definition of media violence with emphasis on harmful effects for children alone, and an equally narrow definition of censorship—with no distinctions between individual freedom of expression and corporate freedom of enterprise—actually blocks progress for lasting change. Every sector of society is given a chance to shift the blame somewhere else. The cornerstone of a healthy democracy is that everyone learns to obey the rules collectively agreed upon and accepts responsibility for adherence to them. Anything less paves the way for anarchy.

Furthermore, on the whole subject of codes, despite claims made by the CRTC and Canadian industry spokesmen about the "stringency" of their own set on violence that went into effect in Canada, in January, 1994, the code designed and implemented by France was much better because it requires a ban on extreme violence up until 10:30 p.m. In Canada, the ban applies only until 9:00 p.m. when underage children are, in many instances, still watching television.[31]

Subsequent American Responses
Since Spicer's departure from the CRTC both American and Canadian broadcasters have stalled on development of the V-chip. In September, 1996, AGVOT reported at a meeting with C-CAVE that progress on classification criteria had been delayed due to "technical difficulties." According to spokesman, Peter O'Neill, "Americans are only interested in sexual content on television and Canadians are only interested in violent content."

Nevertheless, in December of that year the American television industry unveiled an age-based classification system with ratings in six categories. Said Jack Valenti, chair of the Motion Picture Association of America (MPAA), which had been asked to come up with the criteria, "Our goal was to create TV parental guidelines which would be simple to use, easy to understand and handy to find and we have accomplished it." The networks and distributors were generously allowed to rate their own shows, unlike the movie industry which is rated by an independent panel. Valenti said the association "hoped" that newspapers and TV Guides would print the definitions accompanying each category and themselves promised to print and distribute brochures to church groups, parents groups and local television stations.[32]

As American critics were quick to point out, this approach did not go far enough. It was vague, and furthermore, the fox was being allowed to guard the henhouse. Advocacy, public health, religious and education groups which include the Center for Media Education (CME), the National Parent Teacher Association (NPTA), the Children's Defense Fund (CDF), and the American Psychological Association (APA), said they intended to lobby for an approach in which letters such as V,S and L were used to denote levels of violence, sex and bad language.

George Gerbner dismissed it as a band-aid measure and called, instead, for an entirely different system: one that goes beyond a simple violence count to issues of fairness and equity. He took the opportunity to announce his plans to transform the Violence Index he developed 30 years ago into the Fairness Index which has since become a tool to assess how fairly people and action are represented on television. The important question to ask, he said, is "who is doing what to whom because violence is essentially a demonstration of power." It shows who can get away with what against whom as well as who the most likely winners, losers, perpetrators and victims are. Violent television content tends to create an unfair 'pecking order' with women, children, older people, and minorities at the bottom; a gross distortion, said Gerbner, of the true American picture.[33]

President Clinton advised critics to "try" the industry's age based ratings for 10 months before demanding changes and promised that top officials at the Federal Communications Commission (FCC) would be reviewing the ratings over a period of several weeks. If the industry failed to draft an "acceptable" plan within one year the FCC would, in keeping with the 1996 telecommunications law, set up an advisory panel to devise a rating system. The industry group made up of broadcast, cable-TV and Hollywood executives who devised the system, however, vowed to "fight any government-imposed system in court on First Amendment free speech grounds." In Canada, responding on behalf of AGVOT, whose deadline for a rating system was extended for a third time, until April, 1997, because for some mysterious reason the group found it necessary to conduct a public opinion poll, Trina McQueen said it would be impractical for Canada to adopt a classification system that was incompatible with the U.S. system.[34]

More recently, in the Spring of 1999, Valenti, and other Hollywood officials are, once again, embroiled in debates over media violence. These have reached a fevered pitch in Congress since the Littleton, Colorado, highschool shootings. Nevertheless, powerful Hollywood lobbyists have managed to dismantle one proposed legislative amendment after another as spokesmen such as Directors Guild of America President, James Shea, vow to resist Washington's "abusive" and accusatory statements. Said Shea, "One of the most important things the Guild can do is defend our members in the area of the First Amendment. We are going to put all of our resources on the line if directors are called upon by Congress or subpoenaed."[35]

Meanwhile, in Canada, on a more positive note, there is growing dissent within the film industry itself, particularly on the subject of cash rebates from the Ontario Government for U.S. violent, bloody, horror movies such as *Slice* about to be shot in Toronto. Talent agency president, Shari Caldwell, is objecting to this practice and refusing to submit her clients for roles in the production.[36] Three weeks earlier, on June 1, 1999, it was reported by Sid Adilman in *The Toronto Star* that, six prominent local casting directors had refused to work on a Telefilm funded teen slasher werewolf film because of the extra-ordinarily violent script.

Re-Inventing Federal Regulation

When he addressed the Canadian Association of Broadcasters (CAB) at their annual conference in Winnipeg, in 1994, Spicer congratulated the CBSC on their "courageous" step in ruling the children's program *Power Rangers* too violent for Canadian television and stressed the importance for all carriers to address the issue of *content* on the information highway, as well as *distribution*. He spoke of the challenges and uncertainty facing broadcasters as a result of technological convergence and market fragmentation occurring, but cautioned them to pay extraordinary attention to their audiences, an increasing number of whom are demanding less violence in programming. He recommended that "when in doubt" they should "go upscale" and offer viewers distinctively Canadian quality programs that would "stand out in the clutter of choices" from which viewers would soon be picking.

Once again he warned that if self-regulation was to be maintained as the preferred alternative to government intervention the public would expect to see results from relevant decisions. These, he said, must come not just from CBSC members, but from the pay and specialty services as well as the cable industry and eventual satellite operators, all of whom had promised anti-violence codes. So far any one of these challenges have yet to be taken seriously.[37]

Spicer's initiatives have dissipated into little more than public relations exercises in which the CRTC could be "seen" to be addressing the problem of media violence because institutionalized patterns of violence, ingrained within the economic activity of the communications industry itself, were ignored. He justified his course of action on the basis that Canadians wished to avoid ideological battles about "dancing on the head of a pin"[38] and instead were opting for broad consensus and cooperation. Certainly, there was no need to reinvent the wheel with another major inquiry such as the one conducted by the LaMarsh Commission. But now, in order to build on its work and what Spicer began, the CRTC must seriously examine the LaMarsh Commission's far reaching conclusions and recommendations. Also, at this juncture, public vigilance of *both* the CRTC and the industry is especially important, because we have the added component of having to unmask industry biased initiatives undertaken by the federal regulator in the past.

In this context, dissemination of disinformation, designed to trivialize the problem of harmful effects in the public mind, managed very well to keep pace with Spicer's initiatives on media violence. Misinformation promoting the message that "warning codes will solve most of viewers' problems with violent television," which the CRTC "fact" sheets themselves promulgated, quickly found their way into media literacy resource kits of one kind or another, designed for parents and teachers.[39] *Clipboard,* "A Media Education Newsletter from Canada" published twice a year in Toronto by the Canadian Association of Media Literacy Organizations (CAMLO) was one example. The Winter, 1993, issue was mailed to over 370 people in 38 countries with information contacts listed as: the CRTC, Public Affairs, Ottawa; C.M. Hincks Institute, Toronto; The Metropolitan Toronto School Board (MTSB); Action Group on Violence in Television (AGVOT), Ottawa; Alliance for Children and Television (ACT), Toronto; and the National Film Board of Canada, Ottawa. On the whole, it was fraught with contradictory information and industry congratulatory milestones of so called progress.

From an environmental perspective, Canadian ecofeminist, Joyce Nelson, has described a potentially effective strategy for the CRTC, if that is, we were to seriously address the role of the media in facilitating consumer-driven values now at odds with long-term human survival itself. On the subject of achieving "balance" in its rulings on programming, she has argued that, as environmental issues increasingly become "matters of public concern, CRTC rulings would logically suggest that virtually every product ad on mainstream radio and TV should be followed by a counter-ad pointing out the product's health and environmental dangers."[40] Now, the prevailing ideology within the mass media is that a message in support of the status quo is neutral, objective or "noncontroversial" while a message departing from the status quo position, or criticizing it, is typically considered to be biased or at the very least to "have a point of view."

This kind of reasoning has persisted within the Ministry of Revenue over the previous decade regarding C-CAVE's application for charitable status. There, the organization's concerns about the harmful effects of media violence are considered "biased" and "political." Detailed and repeated explanations that this position has been adopted for the provision of public education *because* the overwhelming weight of evidence points toward harmful effects have been ignored. Community education on social issues, in the view of the Ministry, is incompatible with controversy.

Concurrent Global Initiatives

In the early 1990s, New Zealand was the first country within the international community where the top-rated children's television show *Mighty Morphin Power Rangers* was removed entirely from the airwaves. This step on the part of the country's Broadcast Standards Authority was cited as an important precedent for removal of the show from Canadian airwaves as well.[41] In 1994, the Scandinavian Network TV-3 dropped the show from its broadcasts in Norway, Sweden and Denmark following the death of a 5-year-old girl after a game with three boys her age turned ugly, then later reinstated it on the basis of inconclusive links between the program and the tragedy itself.[42] However, Lasse Heimdal, Senior Consultant with the Norwegian YMCA, indicated later in a private conversation with the author that the program remained off the air in Norway. When it was ruled too violent for Canadian airwaves, the show was pulled off the air immediately, in its entirety, by the Youth Television Network (YTV), but Global Television continued to air it, after minor 'modifications' from American producers to meet Canadian standards, until the fall of 1995. At that time it was announced at CRTC hearings on media violence in Toronto that the show was being discontinued because of "high costs" involved in revising it to meet Canadian standards.

Despite Canadian officials occasionally priding themselves on the provision of international leadership in developing effective policy on media violence, there is additional evidence that Canada actually lags behind most industrial countries in addressing the issue. Unimpeded approval for distribution of films like Stone's, *Natural Born Killers*, although banned in other countries, is only one example. At municipal levels, film liaison offices continue to be indiscriminate in their accommodation of crews as Toronto grows into the third largest film and television production center in North America.[43] Frequently, generous funding is even provided from the public purse.

Meanwhile, in election campaigns, both political incumbents and new candidates who promise to address rising levels of crime in the city never make any reference to or even acknowledge their active promotion of it, when they pave the way for the production of violent films and videos which are known to exacerbate crime. These hypocrisies need to be exposed by members of a general public that are much more vigilant and media literate than is presently the case. Tendencies on the part of politicians to exploit the theme of "law and order" in their election campaigns simply reinforces what George Gerbner calls the escalating "mean world outlook" and crumbling of our social infrastructures.[44]

The Threat of Globalization

A legally informed and culturally fair global plan to protect cultural integrity in all countries is now also needed. This is necessary to offset trends in international trade agreements, such as the Multilateral Agreement on Investment (MAI), modeled after the precedent setting North American Free Trade Agreement (NAFTA) signed in 1993, which are paving the way for corporate rule. Provisions should include not only consideration of quotas but the need for every country to support its own creative media workers, protect jobs and independent media enterprises. Every country should be able to compete freely and fairly with the "cheap" American cultural products that now dominate the global market. The U.S., which now controls over 50 percent of the world's screens with mostly violent products while importing less than 2 percent, is preventing its own citizens from seeing the best that the rest of the world has to offer. Remarkably, objections from France, Canada and other countries to this state of affairs tend to be countered by American media conglomerates as unfair and biased.

Recent manifestations of this pro-corporate agenda, embodied in drafts such as the MAI are taking us in the opposite direction. Organizations and individuals in Canada and elsewhere have led a worldwide battle against this encroachment of corporate rule, but other, similar treaties, such as the looming Free Trade Area of the Americas (FTAA), continue to reincarnate. These trends are rapidly eroding the sovereignty of nations and their ability to act in their own public interest. The MAI, for example, would allow transnational corporations to virtually control health care, education, public utilities, provincial and municipal services as well as telecommunications and our cultural industries, with potential advantages over domestic interests.[45] The outright war on cultural rights, however, focuses on the fact that cultural sovereignty is rapidly becoming the new battle field for security and freedom in relation to the maintenance of national integrity.

The globalization of poverty and evidence that it is forcing growing numbers of children all over the world into the sex trade has prompted Canada, along with other countries to criminalize activities involving males who avail themselves of this form of child abuse. At local, community levels, however, evidence that better by-laws for restricting the sale, rental, and use of pornography as a preventative measure in addressing sex-related crime involving women and children continue to go unnoticed.[46] Meanwhile evidence accumulates that pornography is involved in most cases when women and children are victimized at home as well as abroad.[47]

In Canada, some progress has been made in Hamilton and Burlington, Ontario, with the implementation of municipal by-laws that would restrict the proliferation of adult video store outlets to selected centers. Licensees are now required to locate only within an industrial area, no closer than a radius of five hundred metres of a residential lot line and face stiffer penalties than they have in the past for rentals to underage children and adolescents. Drawing upon crime statistics gathered in the United States, the following observations have been made by a Hamilton based community group:

> Through new legislation and enforcement of existing laws, several cities and counties have been successful at lowering the rate of rapes and sexual crime. The Cincinnati area has closed adult sex businesses and has experienced a drop in sex assaults in the former areas of over 80%. Oklahoma county statistics show a drop of over 27% in rapes over a five year period, while the rest of the state experienced a rise of 19% over the same period. This was accomplished by the vigorous prosecution that resulted in the closing of over 150 sex oriented businesses in their county.[48]

So far, there has been little evidence of serious discussion for similar initiatives in other parts of the country.

Advertising and Reporting the Evidence

In print media, the predominant tendency is still toward vacillating coverage on issues involving media violence, in keeping with the time worn rule that controversy generates greater public interest. Over the past decade the scales have tipped back and forth in terms of acknowledged harmful effects. In 1990, solely on the basis of the economic trends involving the sale of cultural commodities, *Fortune Magazine* reported on the world's "insatiable appetite for Hollywood and rock and roll."[49] Japanese investment in American entertainment companies had led to expectations that popular cultural commodities, fuelled by new technologies would become the fastest growing global industry of the next decade. By 1994, articles in numerous popular magazines available on newsstands were featuring cover stories with discussion of social costs as well as economic trends.[50]

There have, at the same time, been countless examples of hegemonic diffusion of facts which might question established business practices involving cultural commodities. One involved reporting in *The Globe and Mail* soon after the CBSC ruled that *Mighty Morphin Power Rangers* was too violent for Canadian television. In the newspaper's criticism of the ruling it was pointed out that *Parenting* magazine came out in defense of the show, rating it as the sixth best one available on television for children. Furthermore, *Parenting* concluded that the *Power Rangers* offered "a rare mix of high tech and heart," that the violence in the program was "balletic" and that, essentially, they were like "little lambs frisking around on a meadow."[51] Public attention drawn to this observation, for Ken Stein, then president of the Canadian Cable Television

Association (CCTA), conveniently coincided with his statement in the same article that "cable operators are legally incapable and philosophically opposed to blocking out the show." Stein challenged the CRTC to change the rules, and implied that he expected to receive support from public opposition to "censorship."

In 1994, the toy company "Toys R Us" announced a voluntary corporate decision to stop buying and selling "extremely violent toys." By 1996, it was reported in *The Globe and Mail* that "Toys R Us" had decided to make fewer toys altogether and to become much more selective about movie-linked toys—not for any altruistic reasons involving corporate responsibility on the issue of violent themes—but because of what were described as "duds" from the previous summer which had been tied to Hollywood disappointments.[52]

One laudable exception to business as usual in this context has occurred in the Wal-Mart Store chain's approach to marketing popular music marked "edited," "clean," and "sanitized for your protection." Inevitably, this corporate policy has precipitated a barrage of criticism from members of the music industry who have vowed to fight for new "consumer protection legislation." Their interpretation of the latter would, in turn, prevent retailers themselves, from deciding what kind of merchandise they wished to carry.[53]

So far, some of the most successful and effective demonstrations of "consumer protection" have come from the Vancouver based magazine, *Adbusters*. On June 23, 1999, it was reported in *The Globe and Mail* that the magazine, which challenges consumer driven ethics, was recently named Canadian magazine of the year by the establishment based National Magazine Awards Committee.

Hegemony At Work

Until the Littleton, Colorado, and Taber, Alberta, shootings in April, 1999, made their impact, the news media themselves, had begun to lose interest in the issue of media violence. Occasional articles in which these observations were made filtered into my email box several months earlier. In this context, both *The Toronto Star* and *The Globe and Mail*, had begun to slide back into old habits of reporting, reminiscent of earlier decades. Gradually, credible authorities on the issue of harmful effects were no longer called. Only those who were prepared to excuse the media were consulted.

There was, however, a notable shift in these reporting patterns with the arrival in Canada, in 1998, of *The National Post*. This newspaper quickly picked up the lead on articles of community violence such as highschool shootings and made links to the consumption of popular culture. A newcomer owned by media mogul Conrad Black, *The National Post* relies less on advertising revenue from popular culture commodities than other Toronto daily newspapers and is, consequently, less vulnerable to the dictates of its clients.

The inevitability of bias where there is heavy reliance on such revenue from popular culture industries was explained by Jane Beddoes from the University of Saskatchewan at the height of criticism over the CBSC ruling on the *Power Rangers* in 1994.

The Globe cannot be expected to annoy its clients by representing the other case fairly, which is probably why it recognizes, in its three items on November 7, no opposition to violence on TV other than the fear that individual watchers might imitate particular violent acts. There is more at stake than this.[54]

At that time, these kind of observations were occasionally permitted in *The Globe and Mail*, but by 1999, C-CAVE had accumulated considerable evidence that editorial policy had shifted to one of censorship. Although letters to the editors of both *The Toronto Star* and *The Globe and Mail* refuting articles claiming no research evidence showing harmful effects have been sent in routinely, only one was published in *The Toronto Star* in August, 1998.

When *The Globe and Mail* published television critic, John Haslett Cuff's "memo" to Keith Spicer on January 22, 1996, telling him to "please stop" behaving in Washington like "a self-aggrandizing 'guardian' " by lobbying for cross border cooperation in development of the V-chip, it signaled a decisive change in future coverage. In fact, Haslett Cuff's call for someone to "put a muzzle" on Spicer, "give him the hook, the golden handshake or just kick him off the public stage before he can do any more damage" sent out a clear warning to Spicer's successor. Since then, when coverage has occurred at all in the newspaper, it has focused almost exclusively on *description* of the problem with any references to policy, apart from parental supervision and greater public "awareness," carefully evaded.

In fact, by the fall of 1996, examples of blatant disregard for public concern and emerging policy on restrictions of violence in popular culture surfaced in connection with coverage on high culture. Both *The Toronto Star* and *The Globe and Mail* carried extensive arts and entertainment section news coverage for celebrated Canadian film maker, Atom Egoyan's interpretation of the opera *Salome*, written by Oscar Wilde.[55] Full page advertisements, placed by the Canadian Opera Company included a prominent picture of a man's head on a platter with a knife beside it and began with the explanation that "WHEN ATOM EGOYAN YELLS "CUT!" AT THE OPERA, PEOPLE LOSE THEIR HEADS BUT AT LEAST THERE ARE NO CASTRATIONS."[56] It was explained that the ad was aimed at the first time opera goer with the promise that the controversial, shocking and provocative opera was being given "an even sharper edge." Copy focused on Egoyan's reputation for directing films "RIFE WITH VOYEURISM, FORBIDDEN DESIRES AND SEX," now transferred, for the first time, to the operatic stage.

Another retrograde step was taken in Canada, in the fall of 1996, as a result of the multimillion-dollar cost-cutting exercise in public broadcasting, when CBC President Perrin Beatty announced that advertising would, for the first time ever, appear along with prime time news on *The National*.[57] Commercials would begin to appear in shows that had until then been exempt. So far, children's programming is still exempted, but by even considering it Beatty demonstrated a radical policy departure from where he stood in the Mulroney administration as Minister of Communications when he was promoting his "5-point strategy" to protect children from harmful television.

An additional demonstration of a rapidly waning commitment to his own original strategy appeared on CBC television's *The National Magazine* in *How We Lost it at the Movies* on September 25, 1996. This soul-searching special on Canadian cultural identity, values, images, ideas and myths, hosted by Hana Gartner, concluded with commentary from Atom Egoyan and controversial Canadian film making giant, David Cronenberg, expressing indignation over collective "Canadian immaturity" that results in criticism of their celebrated images of voyeurism, violence and sexual eroticizing of children. On June 23, 1999, one of the sponsors for the CBC National News was the distributors for the controversial movie *Summer of Sam*. Scheduled to open in Toronto theatres on July 2, it is produced and directed by Spike Lee and is based on the exploits of a New York serial killer known from news coverage as the 'son of Sam'.

In the past, visual media producers have occasionally attempted to maneuver critics, such as members of C-CAVE, into promotion of material for public education purposes in which research findings on media violence are discussed as inconclusive, classification criteria and media literacy as the most important antidotes to the problem, television unfairly blamed and predominant emphasis on the responsibility of parents to address the problem. The Rogers Community Television production *Minding the Set: Stop the Silence on Violence* (1994), is one example and the YTV *Outreach Reel* (1993) was another. But there is an additional, more sinister trend in the issue of misinformation being circulated by the industry. Popular magazines, other than *Parenting* are, hegemonically, coopting the cautionary statements of critics and researchers to their own ends.

Consider the following slogans from eight glossy pages of advertising in *Entertainment Weekly* on September 17, 1993:

> Upon purchase of a **SEGA CD**[tm]**system** there may be a few questions you ask yourself about the future interdependency of man and machine, the emerging technological utopia, and our peculiar human desire for omnipotence. **But,** force yourself to get over any **philosophical crap** quickly, and just play **the coolest system ever made…**

> Is controlling the fate of actual persons **with a small black box** foreshadowing a future when we are merely pawns in some technical wizard's sick dream?

> **No, bonehead.** It's just some really bent fun, that's all.

> Could artificial sensory stimulation ever become so intense that it requires extreme new levels **of personal protection?**

> **Yeah…**to fend off everyone else who wants to play it.[58]

In spite of these forecasts for "an emerging technological utopia" and media reports on growing profits for the movie and television industry, some critics, among them Los Angeles film critic Michael Medved, see problems surfacing within the industry as a result of its own narcissistic excesses.[59] In his view, public disenchantment is directly related to declining programming quality and because of its persistent preference for the celebration of ugliness, Hollywood is committing cultural suicide.[60]

He made reference in the early 1990s to how box office figures are often inflated and how reports of "box office hits" have become a marketing strategy in themselves. He also pointed to evidence of diminishing enthusiasm among teenagers for "rock 'n' roll" while country music "with its earthy and unpretentious attempts to connect with the everyday concerns of Middle America" was growing in popularity.[61] Despite Medved's hopeful observations, however, accounts of "copycat" suicides among teenagers throughout North America which are linked to rock lyrics celebrating death continue to proliferate, and every year the messages become more vicious and anti-social.[62] One has only to consider the popularity of American shock rock band leader *Marilyn Manson* whose lyrics were implicated in the Littleton, Colorado, highschool shootings. Manson and his band members who style themselves after American serial killers and celebrate their lifestyles have an enormous following among young people throughout North America.[63]

Re-Inventing Classification

Medved believes that the mood of the American populace is beginning to revert back to the days that preceded the Hayes Code, originally designed to avoid perceived excesses in movie themes.

> The mid 1960s saw major changes taking place in the entertainment industry, as well as the entire makeup of American culture. The role of the church was dwindling as an influence in Hollywood, and, as this vacuum widened, the opportunity for self-regulation without the constraints of the Protestant, Baptist, and Catholic film offices looked appealing to the studios.[64]

By the end of the 1960s the Hayes Code was replaced by a more lenient, industry run, ten-point movie code that, at the time, came under considerable criticism for its vague definition of maturity and emphasis on parental responsibility for restricting what children watch. Nevertheless, it was adopted and has remained the standard for film classification in the United States ever since.

On the whole, apart from warning labels for violence and parental advisories, there has never been any indication of serious discussion either in Canada or the United States among those who control and administer existing review boards to redress the prevailing classification systems for film, video, television, or computer games on the basis of a broad and growing range of health concerns. Classification criteria being developed to accompany new "V-chip" technology, either for television or in the form of "net nannies" for the Internet has always been focused on giving parents 'choice' rather than acknowledgment of harm.

Despite heightened public awareness at the time on the subject of media violence, a report on film classification in Canada released in 1994 by the federally appointed Council on the Status of Women, before it was disbanded, was devoid of any recommendations for classification criteria that would take into account research findings as well as community standards. On the whole it reflected an appalling degree of ignorance in view of the debate on standards going on within the country. While the Report provided a review of differences and similarities between the various provincial systems across Canada, it was, nevertheless, essentially a re-invention of old documentation on the subject. Public education was still perceived to include only information about classification itself, and no mention was made about the need for it to be related to research findings.

For most films, the movie theatre anywhere in the world today is only a short stepping-stone to the television screen in the home, either through networks, cable systems, satellite transmission or videotape cassettes. Age restrictions are seldom strictly enforced, particularly where paid entry into one, as in the case of North American Cineplex theatres, facilitates the opportunity to walk in and out of several others. Hollywood producer Oliver Stone's controversial film *Natural Born Killers*, about how the media turn serial killers into celebrities has been cited in a number of copycat murders around the world, and is currently the subject of a lawsuit for damages in the U.S. Although it was banned in Ireland and widely objected to throughout Canada, it was, nevertheless, approved for distribution by all provincial review boards within the country. In fact, there was no evidence of controversial discussion over the matter of approval for the film anywhere in Canada, such as the kind that took place within the British Board of Film Classification (BBFC).[65] The LaMarsh Commission recommendation that a panel of "expert consultants" be set up at the Ontario Institute for Studies in Education at the University of Toronto to devise a suitable classification system for television programs for the guidance of parents, teachers, and members of the general public has yet to be seriously considered by anyone.

The traditional role for review boards would be more acceptable to the general public *if* research findings were taken into account and, for example, a model like the one developed by the American based International Coalition Against Violent Entertainment (I-CAVE) for rating films, videos, programs, computer games, and toys was adopted.[66] Designed under the leadership of child psychiatrist, Thomas Radecki in Urbana, Illinois, this model would require the addition of several new categories, among them one labeled "unfit." To say it is unlikely that the industry would ever agree to such a profit-impeding, but nevertheless practical and honest approach, to the process for the purpose of protecting children, would be an understatement. Although information on this more research-based model for classification criteria has been provided by C-CAVE to the Ontario Film Review Board (OFRB) and to the Ontario Law Reform Commission (OLRC) in its 1992 review of the OFRB's mandate it has yet to be reflected in proposed classification criteria anywhere in Canada.

Stretching the Boundaries of Parental Responsibility

Both Mary Winn and Miriam Miedzian noted that throughout the 1980s American reformers had shifted from trying to improve television programming to parent education and the introduction of courses on media literacy into schools. These same trends have been evident in Canada as well. The LaMarsh Commission stressed that a predominant emphasis on parental responsibility and accountability is both absurd and unfair. Even when there is a full-time parent in the home, this is an inexcusable imposition. Television programs that encourage violence are permitted under the guise of freedom of expression or economic necessity, and then parents are told that it is their responsibility to restrict the negative influence and to undo the damage. An additional problem lies with the message about societal values that children derive from such an approach.

Media researcher and educator, Sandra Campbell of Viva Associates in Toronto has said that in her work with children who confide their fears and nightmares from watching violence and horror shows on television, often for the first time, she is asked, "If this is so scary and bad for me, how come I'm allowed to watch it?"[67] To children it soon becomes obvious that the people who control the media are more interested in profit than in their welfare. Instead of being restricted from harming children, these people are very handsomely rewarded. They become rich, powerful, and respected, and are beyond the control of parents, teachers and political leaders who can only issue warnings.

The rationale that unabated violence on the screen is the sole responsibility of parents to monitor, block out or interpret for their children is, to put it mildly, convoluted. Few would disagree that parents in their homes have an obligation to influence their children's viewing habits. Certainly they must learn to rely less on television, videos, or computer games as electronic babysitters and be more assertive in *what* their children are allowed to rent from video stores, but their responsibility does not end there. As child expert Benjamin Spock has pointed out, pediatrics is politics not only for doctors but for parents as well.[68] All responsible adults must better acquaint themselves with existing and well publicized research on the subject of media violence and what can be done in the home to mitigate harmful effects.

However, they must also be vigilant about misleading information and object to its production and distribution in the first place. The innumerable media literary resource kits that have been developed within the industry since the CRTC announced approval of the CAB code on violence have much of value to contribute in assisting parents but some of them are also misleading and counterproductive because the emphasis is concentrated solely on individual responsibility. This line of reasoning greatly exaggerates what parents and teachers are able to accomplish without the help of government and industry. It amounts to manipulation of parental perceptions while industry is let off the hook and allowed to appear as a benevolent contributor to parental responsibility. In this way the industry works at cross purposes with adult educators attempting to respond to the need for better public awareness among the adult population, in general, on how the media operate.

Until parents themselves develop better critical *thinking* skills about how the mass media work, calls for media literacy among children will be of marginal value. This point has been stressed frequently by educators both nationally and internationally.[69] In England the Professional Association of Teachers (PAT), following a survey of teachers' perceptions of the effects on children of the new entertainment technologies, concluded that "the overwhelming responsibility for improving things lies with the adult community."[70] As the LaMarsh Commission observed, parents are under enormous constraints in attempting to control their children's media diets and cannot be expected to assume the burden without the help of industry and government.

An additional dimension to the problem has arisen from the fact that, since the LaMarsh Report, many young parents have had their addictive dependence on television and other electronic media carefully cultivated. This has obscured their perceptions of harmful effects on the basis that they too grew up on animated cartoons such as the *Road Runner* and *Bugs Bunny*. An added dimension to the problem is that adults who have developed a dependence on violent entertainment in their youth themselves are often those most vehemently opposed to its restriction or any evidence of its harmful effects. This trend, alone, underscores the urgent need for the media industries, like the food and drug industries among others, to demonstrate that their products are *not* toxic and harmful to the general public *before* they are put on the market.

Moreover, it is a well known fact that, at best, parental monitoring and interpretation of television program viewing only works in conventional home settings when two parents are prepared and in a position to allot considerable amounts of their time to screening television guides, purchasing and applying blocking devices, and carefully perusing various kinds of promotional material for toys, computer games, and related cultural commodities such as T-shirts and lunch boxes. Even in these ideal situations it must be acknowledged that much of the advertising for these products, to begin with, is aimed predominantly at their children.

Unfortunately children most at risk because of steady heavy viewing diets of television and related forms of amusement tend to come from single parent homes in which there is little supervision or diversionary activity, and communities in which high levels of violence already exist. Furthermore, although many extremely violent films may appear on television with advisory warnings, they can still be recorded on video or rented and viewed at any time of the day or night within the home by older siblings with less inclination to prevent younger children from watching than their parents might exhibit.

In addition, as pointed out by Winn in 1977, and observed again in the PAT survey in 1994, there is evidence to suggest that when parents or other adults watch extremely violent movies or television programs with children who have not yet developed adequate cognitive and emotional skills to process the relevant messages, the joint activity can, in itself, be harmful and counterproductive. The very nature of harmful entertainment becomes "normalized" in ways that contribute to a collective form of cultural desensitization. It can happen in the home as readily as in the classroom, where media literacy courses are taught with predominant emphasis on technique rather than content. In this context, nothing is as effective as abstinence or simply turning the television set or computer off, yet this is seldom a parental strategy discussed in the media literacy kits developed by members of the industry or media literacy educators in collaboration with them.

Even when parents do resort to the strategy of turning a television set off entirely, it still does nothing to protect their children in other people's homes, the values-free classroom where violent media messages are being decoded and deconstructed under the guise of appropriate media literacy instruction, or the lack of safety in the community at large that is fostered and reinforced by the cultural pollutant of media violence or harmful addiction to the technology itself as in the case of the Internet.[71] The message from industry that research findings are inconclusive and that the most effective approach is for parents to sit down and watch *any kind* of programming with their children also creates the danger of parents being lulled into a false sense of security about the gravity of the problem. An additional harmful effect presents itself in feelings of parental helplessness, apathy, and alienation.

In fact, there is growing evidence of mistrust and lack of confidence in the industry on the part of parents. In a Gallup poll conducted by The Family Channel, in 1994, on America's television viewing habits, it was found that an overwhelming majority of the American public were aware that television programming contributes to violence, sexual activity, and profanity, but doubted that promises from broadcasters to use disclaimers notifying viewers about questionable content was doing much to improve the situation. Impressions that depiction of harmful materials was increasing in television programming were corroborated by actual measurements of amounts of violence on several programming outlets. In a survey dating back to 1991, Gallop found that more American adults than ever were restricting their children's viewing habits due to offensive content. Two unrelated studies, also reported on, from the Center for Media and Public Affairs (CMPA) and the Harry Frank Guggenheim Foundation found that violent acts on television increased significantly between 1992 and 1994.

An examination of how parents can address the problem of media violence necessitates reflection on the fact that many people within the industry are also parents. The inconsistent application of codes of conduct in day to day business practices with what conventional wisdom says should be taught to children in private life is nothing new. However, if serious attempts to improve the cultural environment are to be made, these inconsistencies have to be addressed. Consider the following examples of contradictory parental behavior and how they cloud the issue of "parental responsibility." In July, 1993, when he was interviewed on the subject of the company's distribution of the interactive video-game *Night Trap* on CBC Midday, Jeff McCarthy, vice-president of Sega, argued that Sega was demonstrating good corporate citizenship by adding a warning label that the game was not appropriate for children under the age of 12 years. When he was asked by host, Laurie Brown, if he allowed his own young sons to play the game he said, "Yes, but they never lose." Losing this game means that the heads of scantily clad female coeds are ripped off instead of the head of the serial killer. Surely this is neither mature parenting nor responsible corporate citizenship.

The second example involves renowned actress Meryl Streep's foray into the production of the "action" movie *The River Wild*, with a plot that revolves around a marriage gone dead and a family stalked by sinister robbers while on a river-rafting vacation. Although this movie is by no means the most violence-filled production involving a leading Hollywood actor or actress to be released on the market it was reported that, Streep wielded the cars in this unaccustomed action role with a "flair" that rivaled Schwarzenegger.[72] As an actress, as well as a mother of four children, we can only speculate on how she addresses the problem of media violence in her own home in relation to her career choices, but, because she is a talented and world renowned adult, what about her larger responsibility as a role model for children? When interviewed, Streep said she was "too old to have to explain" her actions in order to be properly "understood" and that for her the work of acting "is having an unshakable conviction like children in the grandeur of their pretend games."[73] Why should Streep's behavior either as an actress or a parent be excused while vigilance and application is being demanded of other parents?

The tragic consequences of this kind of illogical compartmentalization of "responsibility" as a defensible safeguard for individual rights and freedoms, without accountability being considered, was illuminated, in 1994, in a four part series on rock star Michael Jackson's obsession with "little boy friends."[74] Parents as well as employees of the rock star appeared to have been seduced into either overlooking, ignoring, or excusing his sexual abuse of children because the truth was too inconvenient, unpleasant, or threatening. Society has an obligation to assist parents in socializing and caring for their children. As Gerbner and others frequently point out, parents and their immediate communities are no longer the principle story tellers for the young. It is the mass media. Consequently, to focus primarily on the responsibility of parents in the home to monitor and interpret their children's viewing diets merely underscores the extent to which denial continues to cloud collective consciousness on matters of public policy related to media violence.

Notes

1. Lyins, 1968, p.168, in O.N. Larsen, ed.

2. Stevenson, personal communication, May 4, 1995, *Influence*, 1985.

3. The 1991 UNESCO report, *New Communications Technology Research Trends* stated that: "The American production format is tending to become the norm all over the world." Jouet & Coudray, 1991, p.35.

4. 1994a, p.393.

5. Gerbner, Morgan & Signorielli, 1994a, p.393.

6. Grierson, 1999.

7. NCTV News, November 1989-January 1990; Radecki, 1992.

8. Vale, 1999, may 17, *The Globe and Mail*, p.D1.

9. Achbar & Wintonick, 1994. Producers, Necessary Illusions, Montreal.

10. Dyer, 1994, Nov. 19, *The Toronto Star*, p.B8.

11. Grossman, 1995, p.324.

12. Doidge, 1999, May 5, *The National Post*, p.B5.

13. 1998, March, *The Toronto Star*, p. A15.

14. Grierson, 1999.

15. Leyton, 1968, p.269.

16. "Boys, 6, suspected," 1994, Oct. 18, *The Toronto Star*, p.A21; Bunyan, 1993, Nov. 26, *The Globe nd Mail*, p.A14; "France seeks," 1993, Dec. 2, *The Globe and Mail*, p.A10, "Boy killed," 1996, June 9, *The Torono Star*, p.A3.

17. "Case brings," 1993, Nov. 26, *The Globe and Mail*, p.A14.

18. "Case brings," 1993, p.A14.

19. Rosenkrantz, 1993, Nov. 29, *The Toronto Star*, p.A23.

20. Bragg, 1994, Aug. 25, *The Toronto Star*, p.A1.

21. Roberts, 1996, June 20, *The Globe and Mail*, p.A8.

22. Crawford, T. 1996, June 23, *The Toronto Star*, p.A1.

23. "Why Vancouver," 1994, Sept. 28, *The Globe and Mail*, p.A13.

24. Snow, 1998.

25. Nelson, 1988.

26. Scoffield, 1999, April 27, *The Globe and Mail*, p.A1.

27. Ross, 1999, May 17, *The Globe and Mail*, p.A3.

28. CRTC, 1999.

29. CRTC, 1994, p.2.

30. CRTC, 1994, p.2.

31. CRTC, 1993a, 1993b; Dyson, 1994a.

32. "New TV ratings," 1996, December 21, *The Globe and Mail*, p.C4. TV-G for suitable for all ages; TV-PG for parental guidance suggested; TV-14 for parents of children under 14 strongly cautioned; TV-M for mature audiences only and two categories applying to children's shows: TV-Y for all children and TV-Y7 for kids seven and older. This was an effort, said Jack Valenti, president of the Motion Picture Association of America (MPAA) and head of the industry group that developed the television ratings, grounded in honourable purpose.

33. Gerbner, G., 1996, December, 19. News Release, CEM, Philadelphia.

34. "U.S. TV ratings," 1996, December 19, *Bloomberg Business News*, Washington, D.C., p.1; Atherton, T. 1996, December 18, *The Globe and Mail*, p.E5.

35. Madigan, 1999, June 21, *Variety*.

36. Adilman, 1999b, June 22, *The Toronto Star*, p.E6.

37. R. Cohen, J. DeNew, R. Dyson, P. O'Neill, personal communications, November 15, 1994.

38. CBC Radio, 1994, Jan. 18, Morningside with Peter Gzowski; National Council of Churches, 1994; Rogers Community Television, 1994a, Jan. 8, Violence on Television, Host: John Tory.

39. *Clipboard*, Winter, 1993, A Media Educaton Newsletter Fom Canada, Toronto.

40. Nelson, 1989, p.134.

41. "Spotlight: Power," 1994, Aug. 28, *The Toronto Star*, p.B2; Walsh, 1994, Nov. 21, *Time*, p.78.

42. "Boy, 6, suspected," 1994, Oct. 18, *The Toronto Star*, p.A6.

43. Chapman, 1993, nov. 27, *The Toronto Sun*, p.3.

44. National Council of Churches, 1994, personal communication, July 14, 1995.

45. OECD, 1997; Graham & Speller, 1997.

46. Speirs, 1994b, Nov. 17, *The Toronto Star*, p. A1.

47. Johnstone, 1993b.

48. Johnstone, 1993b, p. 1.

49. Huey, 1990, Dec. 31, *Fortune*, p.50.

50. Examples include the following: *Time*, May 7, 1990 (Corliss); *Newsweek*, April 1, 1991 (Plagens, Miller, Foote, & Goffe); *Peace*, May-June, 1992 (Dyson); *Maclean's*, December 7, 1992 (Jenish); *New Yorker*, May 17, 1993 (Auletta); *Maclean's*, July 19, 1993 (Brady); *Mother Jones*, July-August, 1993 (Cannon); *Time*, August 2, 1993 (Hull); *Time*, September 27, 1993 (Elmer-Dewitt); *Newsweek*, October 11, 1993 (Leland); *Time*, November 1, 1993 (Hornblower); *Wired*, May 1994 (Wolf); *Maclean's*, August 19, 1994 (Kaihla); and *Maclean's*, October 24, 1994 (Bergman).

51. Lacey, 1994b, Nov. 9, *The Globe and Mail*, p.C2.

52. Pereira, 1996, Feb. 2, *The Globe and Mail*, p.B6.

53. Strauss, Neil. 1996, November 12, pp.1-4. Institute for Global Communications, email: labornews@igc.org

54. Beddoes, 1994, Nov. 16, *The Globe and Mail*, p.A22.

55. Gerstel, J., 1996, Sept. 22, *The Toronto Star*, p.C1; Everett-Green, R. Sept. 21, 1996, *The Globe and Mail*, p.C1.

56. Advertisement "HEY! THIS ISN'T" 1996, Sept. 13, *The Toronto Star*, p.C13.

57. Winsor, H. and C. Harris, 1996, Sept. 19, *The Globe and Mail*, p.A1.

58. *Entertainment Weekly*, 1993, p.45-52.

59. "U.S. movie industry," 1993, Jan. 5, *The Toronto Star*, p.C5.

60. Medved, 1992, p.5.

61. Medved, 1992, p.7.

62. CFRB Radio, 1994; Berardini, personal communication, November 24, 1994.

63. CFRB Radio, 1994; Berardini, personal communication, November 24, 1994, C-CAVE News Release, 1997.

64. Baehr & Grimes, 1990, p.34.

65. "Britain allows," 1994, Oct. 20, *The Globe and Mail*, p.C2; Greig, 1994, Oct. 20, *The Sunday Times*, p.2-8; Lees, 1994, Oct. 23, *The Sunday Times*, p.5; "Stone film," 1994, Oct. 28, *The Globe and Mail*, p.D6.

66. C-CAVE, 1993, Fall News.

67. C.M. Hincks Institute, 1993; IPCA, 1993; Roger's Community Television, 1993, interview with Sandra Campbell.

68. Levine, 1994, Sept. 10, *The Toronto Star*, p.D1.

69. MacDougall, 1993; Millar, 1994, Oct. 19, *The Toronto Star*, p.A11.

70. PAT, 1994, p.22.

71. When more than 13,000 psychologists met in Toronto in August, 1996 for the 104th annual convention of the American Psychological Association one of the issues discussed was the emerging evidence of addiction to the Internet among adolescents (Hall, 1996). Aug. 10, *The Toronto Star*, p.A2.

72. Hipschman, 1994, Sept. 30, *The Toronto Star*, p.C1.

73. Hipschman, 1994, p.C1.

74. Andersen, 1994, Nov. 13, 14, 15, 16, *The Toronto Star*, Parts One-Four, p.C1;C5;D1;C1.

Chapter 9

NEW INSIGHTS

THE OBVIOUS QUESTION IS why, with so many warnings for several decades now about where communications technology without responsible regulation is leading us, has there been so little progress on the problem of violent content? The fact that self-serving responses from industry have consistently clouded consensus on the research demonstrating harmful effects is one reason. But many men and women, health professionals, educators and otherwise, in a number of countries, have agreed upon excesses involving media violence causing social harm and have tried to do something about it.

Nevertheless, confusion over what constitutes harm and how it should be addressed is still predominant. What these trends do, is illuminate the need to reexamine our civil liberties, redefine what we mean by censorship, accelerate the Cultural Environmental Movement (CEM) and implement the kind of proposals which would take us in a new direction advocated by the CEM and other similar organizations.

What Have We Learned?

In her book, *Boys Will Be Boys: Breaking the Links Between Masculinity and Violence,* published in 1992, Miriam Miedzian considered the pattern of dedication and commitment to change exhibited by a number of groups acting in the public interest in the United States over a period of 20 years. These groups included Action for Children's Television (ACT), the National Coalition on Television Violence (NCTV), the American Medical Association (AMA), the National Parent-Teacher Association (NPTA) and the National Council of the Churches of Christ (NCCC), all of whom have declared themselves over the years as being opposed to censorship. This, in her view, was the key reason for their lack of progress. Despite their activism, these groups have not, adequately clarified what they mean by the word censorship or stressed the point that they are *for* responsible regulation. They have used too strict an interpretation of the First Amendment. As a result, tireless efforts to influence the Federal Communications Commission (FCC) to use its rule-making and licensing power to decrease television violence has had little effect.

In Canada, patterns of protest and subsequent diffusion of them by vested interests have been similar. When the LaMarsh Commission conducted its hearings in 1977, it was reported that over 8,000 people attended. More than 800 participants made either oral or written presentations or both. Over half of these came from community groups and individuals not affiliated with specific institutions in education, research, religious organizations, industry or government. Although since then, there has been some ongoing public activity in attempts to address the problem of media violence in Canada, for the most part, the momentum of public concern built up by the LaMarsh inquiry has not been sustained. This has occurred largely for two reasons. First, the work of the Commission was immediately discredited by the news media, and second, the initial leadership of the LaMarsh Center established at York University in Toronto ignored the central purpose for which it was intended and developed its own agenda for research on the subject of violence.

Canadians Concerned About Violence In Entertainment (C-CAVE) itself was formed in 1983, five years after the Commission's Report was released, largely as an outgrowth of encouragement and support from its American counterpart, NCTV, founded by Illinois based, child psychiatrist, Thomas Radecki. The organization has always been linked with other Canadian organizations attempting to improve the quality of popular culture and reduce levels of violence in society, particularly for women and children. It has never, however, enjoyed the same kind of support and generous funding as other organizations, such as the Alliance for Children and Television (ACT) and the Association for Media Literacy (AML), focused exclusively on alternative television programming for children or values-free analysis of the media.[1] As a result, its mandate to provide public education on what the research shows on media violence, based on overwhelming evidence pointing toward harmful effects, and solutions that include strategies to address systemic violence as well as alternative programming and individual responsibility, has been marginalized.

In 1990, when the issue of media violence began, once again, to receive attention on a widespread basis in Canada, dozens of additional community-based groups sprung up, and while they lasted helped to amplify calls for change that went beyond the parent, the teacher, and alternative programming. Unfortunately, there has not been much lasting impact. Similarly, although the number of individual researchers and journalists with an appreciation of how mass media work in contemporary society has grown, this has been offset by increasing evidence of desensitization, particularly among young journalists, such as those reviewing video games. For many this entertainment has been normalized through diets of media, heavily laced with "action" from a very early age, and is having an impact on their social orientation, in spite of the fact that, as a generation, they are better educated and much less inclined to accept conventional notions of "censorship" than their predecessors were two decades ago. Also, although more women are now employed within the media industries and have brought new feminist perspectives to issues, framing them in different ways, some, like their young male counterparts, argue in defense of violent content.

In 1998, in the *New York Times*, American journalist Lawrie Mifflin discussed evidence of unprecedented levels of excesses in television programming while public outcry appeared to be diminishing.[2] At the same time, similar observations were made in Canada's national newspaper, *The Globe and Mail* by journalist Sandra Martin. She wrote of trends in popular culture involving unprecedented excesses in the use of sexual themes. Nevertheless, analysis in both cases was still carefully framed to conclude with emphasis on "opposition to censorship."[3] This pattern tends to repeat itself over and over again in ways that seem designed more to placate editors than because they offer sound conclusions to the overall analysis. As long as this unvaried approach is adhered to, eloquent hand-wringing, whether it is practiced by mainstream journalists or community activists will only continue to serve the hegemonic purposes of dominant interests.

In the United States, the Littleton, Colorado, massacre, reminiscent of the Montreal Polytechnical Institute shootings in Canada, in 1989, helped to galvanize all sectors of American society into responses to the mushrooming problems of violence in society. While American print coverage focused on the re-introduction of gun control legislation, another round of Senate hearings on media violence, passage of a juvenile justice bill designed to prevent and punish youth crime at the state and federal levels, voluntary removal of violent video games by arcade owners, and negligence lawsuits, in Canada, it was predominantly on successful 'containment' of subsequent eruptions of school violence by police and school officials.[4] While in Manitoba a $100,000 awareness campaign was launched to "help" the industry based Entertainment Software Rating Board, formed in 1994, keep violent and sexually explicit video games out of the hands of children, in Ontario, with an election underway, Minister of Consumer and Commercial Relations for the Harris Government, David Tsubouchi, concluded that the subject was a non issue.[5]

In Canada, evidence of Federal Government interest in issues involving media violence is, now, virtually non-existent. The Canadian Radio-television and Telecommunications Commission (CRTC), in its report on the Internet, concluded that there were already adequate Criminal Code provisions and self-regulation to handle on-line crimes such as the production of hate literature and child pornography. Besides, said Ms. Bertrand, Chair of the federal regulator, regulation would "cripple" Canada's vibrant, competitive and productive Internet industries.[6] In Ottawa, federal officials reached a "compromise" with Americans over the issue of Canadian advertising allowances in their split-run magazines with Heritage Minister, Sheila Copps, promising tax breaks for everyone regardless of content.[7] The Toronto Police morality squad declined an opportunity to lay obscenity charges against the sexually violent book *American Psycho*, in this case citing the Butler decision as their *reason* while the entire matter was ignored by the media despite a news release from C-CAVE.[8]

Meanwhile, media scholars, community activists and concerned journalists with a more critical perspective continue to exchange views and calls for decisive action to stem the flow of profit driven cultural commodities with lifestyles and conflict resolution strategies which are plunging us into world wide chaos, whether it is in Kosovo, Colorado, or Taber, Alberta. Clearly the Internet is offering new channels for quick and widespread information exchange that is unfiltered by the agendas of dominant corporate interests and this unprecedented window of opportunity must be utilized and extended as effectively and quickly as possible.

Responsible Re-Regulation

Promises of industry self-regulation, alone, without government intervention have never worked well. In the United States, in October, 1990, the 20,000 members of ACT had convinced Congress to pass the Children's Television Act. The law, which came into effect a year later, stipulated that broadcasters had to serve the educational and informational needs of children or face the risk of losing their broadcast licenses. However in December, 1992, *Maclean's* reported that by August of that year, a review by consumer groups of 58 stations revealed that no broadcasters had produced new programming to comply with the law. "Instead, they had simply re-labeled existing programs, in many cases cartoons, as educational."[9]

In 1996, in the middle of the presidential campaign, a similar pledge was extracted by Clinton from the American broadcasters to commit to a minimum of three hours of "quality" children's programming each week, but again, with no clear assurance that progress on implementation of this new policy would be closely monitored. In June, 1999, based on findings released by The Annenberg Public Policy Center of the University of Pennsylvania, which has tracked the quality of children's television programming on U.S. TV networks since 1996, it was found that one in five television shows aimed at young people has little or no educational value at all.[10] Minor signs of improvement were, however, noted. In 1998, 26 percent of the shows were deemed to be of low quality compared with 36 percent in 1997.

These same patterns of extremely marginal change for the better have been evident in Canada as well. Objections to the violence in the television program for children, *Teenage Mutant Ninja Turtles*, were diffused by replacing it with the *Mighty Morphin Power Rangers*, which is similar in content. For Global Television, accommodating the CBSC ruling on the program being too violent for Canadian television meant minor modifications to, basically, the same thematic material with even the title itself retained, until some months later it was discontinued entirely, ostensibly due to costs involved in making the modifications. Until stringent guidelines and enforcement are provided by government acting in the public interest this kind of insignificant modification in programming content will continue to flourish.

Community Dialogue with Industry: How Meaningful Is It?

In the 1970s a major setback experienced by community activists on the subject of media violence, both Canadian and American, resulted from the wave of deregulation that characterized the "Reagan years." Deregulation of children's television programming led to a scenario where many half-hour programs became 30 minute commercials, filled with violence, most of them infiltrating Canadian airwaves. In the process, some of the avenues for dialogue that were established in that decade in Hollywood were dismantled simply because they were no longer required. Campaigns to reduce sex and violence, though highly publicized, enjoyed only brief success because the trend toward deregulation was accompanied by the justification that the public interest would be better served if marketplace forces were allowed to operate freely. By the late 1980s, as Kathryn Montgomery has explained, "skillfully fashioned industry strategies had transformed advocacy groups from a disruptive force into what network executives referred to as a 'feedback system'."[11]

In Canada, C-CAVE first established communication with the CAB in the early 1980s and provided input for the new code of violence which was approved by the CRTC in 1994. In the end, however, the code fell short of expectations by a considerable margin. At that time, through their societal issues chairman, Peter O'Neill, the industry based association sought assistance in "coordinating a list of concerns" and those of other groups with whom C-CAVE worked. These were then discussed in a closed circuit TV dialogue among broadcasters in 1994, with a videotaped copy of the conference later given to the author. Essentially the dialogue involved an exchange of recycled information among industry spokesmen on various initiatives being undertaken to address the issue of media violence in response to pressure from community organizations.

In compiling the list of 'suggestions and concerns'—among them the reminder of findings demonstrating that adults as well as children are affected by violence—Joan DeNew, founder of C-CAVE, informed O'Neill that several activists had flatly refused to "dialogue" with the CAB at all because they considered it a waste of time. In terms of serious policy implementations for self-regulation through widespread adherence to its conduct code approved in 1994, nothing has yet occurred to change their minds. Although C-CAVE sustained a series of meetings with industry spokesmen until Peter O'Neill was downsized as a result of an industry merger in 1997, which were attended by representatives from other community based organizations as well, in the end, nothing was accomplished. O'Neill's identified replacement, CTV Vice President, Bev Oda, has not demonstrated any interest at all in sustaining this dialogue. An invitation to Ms. Oda to participate in a panel coordinated by the author for the 1998 Canadian Communications Conference at the University of Ottawa on 'Regulation of the Media for the Good of the Public' was accepted but subsequent follow-up phone calls were ignored.

These experiences resonate with Montgomery's warning that even when members of the industry are willing to "dialogue" with advocacy groups, as part of their continuing strategy for deflecting pressure, without effective political leverage, these groups are unlikely to have their demands and concerns taken seriously.[12] Along with many others, she has stressed that the economic marketplace is not synonymous with a marketplace of ideas and that present trends are paving the way for the marginalization of more and more groups of citizens. The challenge now, in all countries, particularly as film, television and video production converges and locations for this economic activity mushroom around the world, is to reinvent and extend these channels for communication and to avoid previous pitfalls. This needs to happen between all sectors of society, including industry, with firmly established links and networks between community activists on a local, national and international basis under the auspices of international umbrella organizations such as those first initiated by the International Coalition Against Violent Entertainment (I-CAVE) and currently being build upon within the Cultural Environment Movement (CEM).

In Canada, such an opportunity was nominally provided by Bill Graham, chairman of the House of Commons Standing Committee on Foreign Affairs and International Trade. In the early months of 1999, he conducted a series of cross-country consultations on international trade priorities and concerns in preparation for major World Trade Organization (WTO) ministerial conferences planned for later in the year, but there is no evidence that Graham, himself, understands the impact of globalization on cultural issues. At an International Forum on *The Challenges of Globalization* held at Bishop's University in Lennoxville, Quebec, in conjunction with the Congress for the Social Sciences and Humanities in June, 1999, when he spoke at a luncheon, he was flippant and dismissive of any links between harmful cultural products and more liberalized trading patterns, despite receipt of numerous submissions on the subject from the author in the past, which included the aforementioned consultations.

In the Report itself, entitled *Canada and the Future of the World Trade Organization*, the only reference made to C-CAVE at all in the chapter on cultural issues, is within the context of an old issue concerning control of content, such as violence portrayed in audiovisual media, manifesting itself in a new way because of technological change. Said the authors, "It has a trade dimension because of the ease with which digital signals can cross borders."[13] This was hardly a new, ground breaking observation on the problem. What is now urgently needed is some representation on the cultural industries Sectoral Advisory Group on International Trade (SAGIT), lauded in the Report as a key component in preparations for the future from the non-profit sector of the cultural community, so that appropriate regulations for the protection of cultural sovereignty *and* the cultural environment can be introduced into trade talks on a global basis.

From the standpoint of public education, broad, transparent public consultations are needed in order for the crucial choices and decisions that are now facing all countries and international bodies engaged in increasingly complex, multilateral and regional trade liberalization processes to be better understood. But they are essential to serious collaboration between representatives in all sectors of society committed to meeting the challenges of the new information age and the impact of violent content upon it.

Minor steps taken so far for North American co-operation on strategies such as blocking devices for parents must be reinforced. Despite widespread concerns that the telecommunications bill approved by the U.S. Congress in 1996 paves the way for media conglomerates to seize greater control of the emerging information superhighway and sets a precedent for similar bills in other jurisdictions, the bill endorses emerging V-chip technology. This is an important gain if only because it is an acknowledgment from industry that media violence is, indeed, harmful. It signals a slight departure from previous assertions that research findings are inconclusive or that the problem is a moral issue only and should be dealt with entirely by parents. In other words, however minuscule, it is an indication of some movement toward consensus from government and industry as well as parents and educators that we, in fact, have a serious and growing health and social problem.

Unfortunately, the section within this U.S. telecommunications bill, which would have made it a crime for people to knowingly send "indecent" material to minors over the Internet through the Communications Decency Act (CDA), was struck down almost immediately.[14] However, when the successful court challenge was reported on in the September, 1996, issue of *Internet World,* there was also reference to ways in which the problem, once acknowledged only in the home and school was growing within the work place as well, as Internet "addiction" siphoned time and energy away from job related activity. This was a clear indication that the problem is growing and not about to go away on its own.

When the U.S. Supreme Court ruled the CDA unconstitutional in 1997, Congress responded in 1998 by passed the Child Online Protection Act, which would criminalize the posting of any material deemed "harmful to minors" on a commercial Internet website. Critics of the Act continue to claim its effect on speech would not be much different from that of the CDA, an assertion the lower courts have basically agreed with, and the new legislation is now pending a hearing in the Third Circuit Court of Appeals.[15]

Bills have also been introduced requiring any library or school receiving federal funds to install filtering software on any computer terminal accessible to the general public. Again, in 1998, a federal district court ruled that a library in Virginia had violated the guarantee of free speech when it decided to install the Internet filter X-Stop on all of its computer terminals and called for such devices only on computers designated for use by children. In spite of this fierce opposition, American legislators continue to cast about for solutions in the post-Littleton mood and are, so far, undeterred by arguments that the only answer to bad speech is more speech.[16]

Advertiser Boycotts
While speech alone is not and cannot be the whole answer, the potential for useful information exchange on issues of mutual concern on an international basis is growing. In 1994, exchanges between the Norwegian YMCA and Canadian community organizations on CAB codes of conduct helped to inform the campaign

launched in Canada, in October, 1996, urging advertisers to boycott two new violent series in the TV season that fall. Letters were mailed to seventy of Canada's largest advertisers, in which the Coalition for Responsible Television (CRTV) urged companies to boycott the ultra violent series "Poltergeist: The Legacy," purchased by CTV, and "Millennium," purchased by Global TV.

The CRTV pointed out that working with the CRTC and broadcasters had not proven to be even remotely productive and that a new direction was needed. Simultaneously, the public was urged to "point the finger of blame for harmful programming at the corporations who underwrite violent shows with their advertising dollars" and to demand greater responsibility and accountability from them for what goes on the air. "Without advertising," said co-president, Jacques Brodeur, "programming cannot exist." One year later "Poltergeist" was taken off the air due to "poor ratings," according to CAB spokesman, Peter O'Neill, and "Millennium" was moved from a 9 o'clock to a 10 o'clock time slot. In May, 1997, a CRTV news bulletin announced the results of its campaign encouraging the boycott. Out of 25 sponsors of the television program, *Millennium*, 13 agreed to pull their ads.[17] Meanwhile, in the business section of *The Globe and Mail* it was reported that Peter Swain, President of Media Buying Services Ltd. in Toronto, had issued the following warning:

> Advertisers are becoming more sensitive to the negative implications of being associated with violent programming...in most corporate board rooms, it's not worth the price of admission to be seen as exploiting violence. It's too dangerous...It doesn't take much to create a bandwagon effect and go after an advertiser.[18]

Similar attempts on the part of C-CAVE, working in cooperation with both the CRTV and the CEM, to remove the Howard Stern show from the air on Q107-FM in Toronto and CHOM-FM in Montreal by encouraging advertiser boycotts, have also been somewhat successful. The Stern Show was taken off the air in Montreal, prevented from proliferating throughout the country, canceled for late night television in Toronto by CHUM Ltd., and although he remains on the air in Toronto, an extra producer has been hired to screen out what the CBSC deems to be unacceptable on the basis of Canadian codes of conduct.

In this case, partial success was due to some assistance and cooperation from competing radio station owners as well. Ironically, the success from these advertiser boycotts has come under criticism within the Cultural Environment Movement itself. At the second International Convention, held at Ohio University in March, 1999, these Canadian initiatives were criticized by American media scholars concerned that industry sources of funding for research projects might be threatened by advertiser boycotts.

Re-examining Our Civil Liberties

As early as 1969, in the United States Lange and his colleagues made the point that the policies of the First Amendment can no longer be secured simply by keeping the government out. They also argued that analysis is not values-free in research any more than reporting is in journalism. This is an observation that is repeated more and more often in recent literature on a whole host of social and environmental issues. Warnings are also being made that freedom of expression is paradoxically, in grave danger, *because* there is a lack of serious response to the problem of media violence. One of these surfaced in Comstock's 1991 analysis of research on knowledge, beliefs and perceptions resulting from greater exposure to violent media. He and his colleagues concluded that it is associated with an ideology favorable to the use of force and indifference to civil liberties.

Many scholars have argued that traditional media give us our perceptions of the world around us and have challenged the enduring myth that media provide "a free marketplace" in which everyone's ideas and opinions can be aired. In democracies, developed on the basis of classic liberalism, the media are expected to take an active role in the process of governance through criticism and vigilant observance. These functions have traditionally been encouraged by giving the press and other media of expression the same freedom of speech that we enjoy as individuals. Yet, today more than ever there is evidence that this is no longer tenable as more and more ownership of the media is concentrated into fewer and fewer hands. Certainly there are some mitigating influences from alternative and independent media, made possible by the wider availability of new communications technology, but for the most part, the mainstream media are controlled by dominant corporate interests unresponsive to social concerns.

The prevailing mood of the general populace tends to be one of confusion and resignation on the basis of beliefs that effective regulation is not possible either because of the nature of new technology or because of the potential threat of "censorship." Others, including Canadian financial journalist, Linda McQuaig, argue that new communications technology, such as the Internet, offer greater potential than ever before for regulation in the interest of people rather than corporations and financial institutions.[19] Simplistic definitions merely add to the problem of public confusion and mitigate progress toward effective, long-term solutions that address issues of content as well as issues of ownership, copyright and privacy.

In fact, there is increasing evidence that censorship works best when it is least recognized. The cornerstone of a successful democracy is that its members learn to obey the rules that they collectively give themselves. Also, they must learn to *recognize* the rules that they have collectively given themselves and distinguish them from rules that are being imposed upon them by dominant corporate interests under the guise of collective freedom and choice for everyone. One of the most important jobs facing adult educators today in the provision of public education is facilitating a better understanding of this crucial distinction. The main emphasis must include challenging the notion that corporations or enterprises are "persons" and therefore entitled to liberties guaranteed to persons. Anatol Rapoport, founder of a four-year peace and conflict studies program at the University of Toronto, and author of *The Origins of Violence* has spelled out some of the fundamental differences involved. There are stringent laws against killing persons.

Corporations are routinely killed by other corporations (as in "hostile take-overs"), and there are no legal defenses against such "murders." Corporations can change heads. They do not have a natural life span. Unlike persons corporations don't have children, at any rate, are not responsible for lives of entities that might be regarded as their children. Therefore arguments invoking "freedom of expression," which must be taken seriously when applied to human individuals, should have no force with regard to corporations.[20]

Legal scholar, Stephen Sedley, has argued that there is little to be learned about either the philosophy or the policy of civil liberties from the general run of mass media and that there is a danger in letting political commentators and leading writers dictate or even shape our views on the subject. Most of the principles now accepted and supported by the media were, in fact, fought for and won by predecessors with a much broader concept of freedom of speech. Press freedom, for example, is seldom echoed by much press stridency in defense of the freedom of others to voice their views in a similar manner. Every day, newspaper editors decide which news items will be included and which ones will be rejected. Are they not practicing a form of censorship? Basic civil liberties have always had to be fought for in society on a more popular, widespread basis.

In his analysis of the political economy of the mass media, Noam Chomsky does not blame the press for limited discourse in Western society and explains that it has happened in every society since biblical times. Anyone who refuses to be subordinated to power will be marginalized and, while there are huge differences between the mechanisms and severity of social control in different societies, what is striking, he explained to *Peace Magazine* editor Metta Spencer in an interview, in 1995, in Toronto, is that the results are much the same in both free and totalitarian societies.

Certainly *principle* in defining civil liberties is fundamental, but it is not a unitary body of timeless criteria. It is a complex and shifting concept. The way in which anti-racism has become a principle because consensus has made it one is an example. Slavery is no longer perceived as a "right," as it still was by white European males who drafted the First Amendment in the United States. The genesis, consensus, and rationale of principles and rights are a complicated web of divergent ideas and movements over a period of decades that change as time passes. We have experienced modifications in our collective perceptions involving rights and freedoms in relation to cigarette smoking. There are countless examples of how language, defined as "sexist" is being tolerated less than it once was.

At the same time, ecotheologians such as Thomas Berry in the U.S. are calling into question the concept of democracy, itself, and recommending that it be replaced with the concept of "biocracy." In such a framework our entire legal system, which now fosters a sense of human beings having rights on a level that ignores the rights of other species in the natural world and the rights of future generations of humans, would need to be reexamined. According to Berry, "all our professions and institutions must be judged primarily by the extent to which they foster a mutually enhancing human-earth relationship."[21]

As a society, we have become more critical of what we perceive to be infringements on our basic freedoms and less cognizant of our duties, responsibilities, and obligations as citizens. In 1993, on behalf of the Government of Ontario, police superintendent Kenneth Turriff reported on his review of public perceptions of duties, responsibilities and obligations for Canadian citizenship. He argued that democracy, as we now know it, was in danger because of both the growing public demand for more privileges from "the system" and the Government's attempt to satisfy these demands.

From his computer search, Turriff discovered that the majority of treatises on freedom that included reference to either duties, responsibilities, or obligations, were written in the 1940s and that these gradually faded in number as the search moved into the area of publications of the 1970s, 1980s and 1990s. He also noted that "following the proclamation of the Charter of Rights and Freedoms in 1982, the primary focus of the literature pertaining to citizenship is on rights and freedoms." What Turriff's observations underscore is an increasingly simplified perception of what it means to live in a democratic society.

The diminishing appreciation for the cost of freedom, its importance in our lives and the ease with which it may be lost, needs to be reversed. More vigilant protection of our basic civil liberties becomes especially urgent upon close examination of the current information-based economy, not only because of the extra-ordinarily powerful influence the new communications technologies exert, but because of the growing complexity which surrounds their converging erosion of our democratic way of life. More questions need to be asked as to whether or not it is possible to pursue democracy and social justice at all when corporations are allowed to control so much wealth and power.

Following initiatives for a "Democracy Teach-In" at University campuses throughout the United States in October, 1996, Vigdor Schreibman reported on the CEM listserv that the breakdown of American democracy was visible everywhere. At the same time, he said, it was being pervasively denied because of its complexity and because of the "calamitous implications for the American myth."[22] In a survey done one month earlier it was discovered that very few faculty members appeared to be willing to speak out either in public or on their own campuses. This, in turn, was leading to a lack of student interest and activities in anything other than sports. The ideals of young Americans didn't even seem to include democratic politics anymore. Instead, they were adopting the attitude that there is no rational purpose for them to participate in a rigged and lopsided political system. Said Schreibman, "The bottom line is clear: when the next American generation becomes this nation's leaders, in the absence of fundamental reform, there will remain not even the ancient dream of democracy."

In this context the legal challenge launched against the Canadian Government by British Columbia lawyer, Connie Fogal, and the Defense of Canadian Liberty Committee in April, 1998, over negotiations of the Multilateral Agreement on Investment (MAI) then at the Paris based OECD, and now back at the WTO, offers an important opportunity for clarification of civil liberties, rights, and protection. In this case both the content of the Agreement and the process engaged in by the Canadian Government are being challenged. It is being argued that the MAI is a mechanism and structure that restricts—possibly even eliminates—the capacity of the Government to make and continue domestic law in the interest of citizens and the public good; that it paves the way for the spending of public monies without parliamentary approval; and that it is a vehicle which would eliminate adherence to the Constitutional framework and imperatives of Canada. Essentially, it would give:

> [S]overeign rights, without responsibilities, to international corporations and financial institutions, and it impedes, if not eradicates, mechanisms to maintain control over local, provincial property and civil rights, and renders impotent our judiciary with respect to these matters...It will have the effect of granting corporations, non-natural persons as well as the minority of natural persons, rights over Canadians, their governments, and their courts, when those same corporations may be foreign owned and controlled by foreign "parent" affiliates.[23]

The kind of concerns, which the MAI has sparked globally, are precipitating a re-examination of democratic principles which may ultimately help to save them.

Progress Toward Harm Based Definitions

Many Americans have pointed out, that in helping to frame the First Amendment, Thomas Jefferson emphasized that their legal system must be responsive to changing historical conditions.[24] In 1986, in his book, *Amusing Ourselves to Death*, Neil Postman called for a ban on political commercials along with cigarette and liquor commercials. For those objecting on the basis that such a ban would violate the First Amendment he suggested a compromise not unlike the one proposed by Joyce Nelson for the CRTC two years later: "Require all political commercials to be preceded by a short statement to the effect that common sense has determined that watching political commercials is hazardous to the intellectual health of the community."[25] Throughout the world the rights of tobacco companies to advertise their products under the guise of freedom of expression are being challenged and these trends need to be broadened to encompass other toxic cultural messages as well.

In Canada, despite progress on harm based legislation for the protection of women and children, the debate over freedom of expression surrounding issues of pornography and the harmful impact of advertising on children is far from over. Although the courts are beginning to acknowledge that collective freedom from fear and abuse must take precedence over someone's right to amuse himself in any way he chooses, or sell anything for profit, regardless of the consequences, as ruled in the Butler and Irwin Toy cases, there is still very little evidence of real change in business and social practices. In 1999, the Butler decision was actually used as an excuse by the Toronto Police Force to ignore distribution and sales of the ultra violent novel *American Psycho*.

In her analysis of the debate over censorship as it applies to pornography, American legal scholar, Catherine Mackinnon, has discussed "the sexual politics of the First Amendment." She argues that, "Written by white men who owned slaves and regarded women as chattels it was drafted to guarantee *their* freedom to keep something they felt at risk of losing."[26] In actual fact it is harm-based rather than content-based and society at large is still fraught with disagreement as to whether women are or should be subordinated to men, especially in a sexual context. "The struggle against pornography," says Mackinnon, "is an abolitionist struggle to establish that just as buying and selling human beings never was anyone's property right, buying and selling women and children is no one's civil liberty."[27] Mackinnon has led the debate within the legal community, joining the themes of harm and equality in an effort to remove female pornography from the realm of First Amendment protection. Her assessment of the ongoing struggle against pornography, within the context of entrenched perceptions of civil liberties skewed in favor of dominant male interests, applies equally to the ongoing struggle against violence in the media. Just as pornography eroticizes hierarchy, media violence glamorizes it. In both cases the central dynamic is inequality on the basis of dominant-submissive relations.

In fact, the problem is reaching unprecedented proportions. When she testified on behalf of the Mahaffy and French families during their application hearing to have a section of the Criminal Code that allows the public access to evidence altered, Mackinnon said the tapes of the sexual assaults and murders of their daughters were no different from the ones on video store shelves only in this case we all knew how they had been made. As with other forms of pornography where bondage is often used to heighten the male's aggression and sexual arousal, it is extremely damaging to society.[28] There is no difference if the victimization involves real people as opposed to staged performers.

Despite warnings over the past decade from researchers such as Miedzian, O'Connor, Dyer and Grossman on how civilian youth is socialized to be warlike and violent, the profit-driven appeal of violence as an industrial ingredient on a global basis continues to serve a patriarchal, male-dominated model for social and political organization. As many scholars including Berry have observed, the term "patriarchy" is now useful "to designate the deepest and most destructive level of determination in the Western perception of reality and value."[29] Subsequent criticism of these manifestations are now widely identified with the rising consciousness of women which, in turn, has given rise to popular post-secondary studies in "ecofeminism." Scilla Elworthy, founder of the Oxford Research Group in England, offers an insightful analysis of these connections in her book, published in 1996, about women entitled *Power & Sex*.

Freedom of Expression Not Corporate Freedom of Enterprise

The premise that better distinctions have to be made between individual freedom of expression and corporate freedom of enterprise is rapidly becoming a cruel understatement. Confusion between the two which allows for the blatant exploitation of children's value-systems, as in the case of "O.J. Halloween" costume items marketed for children in the fall of 1994 during the height of publicity surrounding the trial of O.J. Simpson in the State of California, along with distortions of civil liberties in mockeries made of fair-trial rights, as occurred in the Bernardo, Homolka and Simpson trials, must be better addressed by adult educators.[30]

There are other dimensions to media excesses which must also be addressed. It was not only the legal principle involving the "presumption of innocence" which was eroded by media opportunism when American Olympian athlete, Tonya Harding, was charged as an accomplice in the attack on rival skater Nancy Kerrigan as they both competed for prominence in the 1994 Winter Games. In that case, systemic violence which has infused professional sports was also a factor as it was when Canadian competitive athlete Ben Johnson was charged in 1988 with the illegal use of steroids. The pressure to win, fueled by the glamour of media attention, exacerbates and promotes these kind of deviancies.[31]

A more recent example emerged with the accidental death of World Wrestling Federation (WWF) performer, Owen Hart of Calgary, Alberta, in May, 1999, when a cable wire snapped while he was being lowered into the ring for a match in Kansas City, Missouri. It drew attention to the extra ordinary lengths to which Federation promoters will go in order to create a spectacle and draw audiences—all under the guise of 'spectator sport'.[32]

These examples illustrate how the ethical underpinnings to some of our basic institutions are in need of critical reexamination if we are serious about reclaiming our democratic freedoms in the current cultural environment. At the very least, it must be acknowledged, that while our news gathering media preoccupy themselves with sensationalism and trivial details, we are being unfairly distracted from more urgent matters such as the growing threats to our long term survival as a species from other forms of environmental degradation. But until we address the issue of cultural degradation it is unlikely that we will make much progress in other areas. Furthermore, as American Technical Consultant Jeff Robbins argued at the *New World Order Conference* in Toronto, in June, 1999:

> Television, arguably the hands-down most successful and powerful panderer to the principle of least effort ever invented, is also the number one engine driving consumption around the globe...advancing technology is rendering people and human social structures increasingly addicted to consumption. It is this exponentially mounting dependency that will render futile any and all proposals for a sustainable future unless recognized and dealt with very soon.[33]

As Berry has pointed out, the creation of a new cultural coding in an ecological context is the current challenge in our collective human experience.

Full Cost Accounting

LaMarsh Commissioner Lucien Beaulieu's assertion that the onus of proof of harmful effects from media violence should rest within the industry rather than with the public at large, is becoming increasingly urgent. Fortunately, in society as a whole, evidence that human health and well-being is linked to the health of the natural environment is growing. Advocates in all sectors are now calling for primary prevention research and policies which respond to "zero discharge" of all persistent toxic products. These include the principle of reverse onus, or proof required that a substance is not toxic before it's release into the marketplace. Since 1977, this is what Beaulieu has advocated for media violence as well.

It would be useful for the media industries to examine and adopt a model for "responsible care" such as that developed by the Canadian chemical industries who have at least begun to acknowledge their role and responsibility in the provision of public safety, zero emissions, risk perception, research, and development of alternatives to extremely toxic products. They have also established verification protocols to assess levels of compliance in a way that far outstrips anything even considered thus far by the media industries.

Media industries have no more right to unfettered cultural pollution of the airwaves than the chemical industries have to the degradation of water, air and soil. Pharmaceutical or food industries, among others, are held liable and accountable if they produce and distribute products that are inadequately tested to determine risk factors. The same should hold true in the media industries. Greater expectations of the media industries from the general public for protection from their own toxic productions would, in themselves, do much to facilitate better public awareness on the extent to which our basic civil liberties are unacceptably skewed in favor of dominant corporate interests.

The Cultural Revolution

In 1991, recognizing the need for new responses to issues involving media violence, Gerbner first held discussions in Washington, D.C., for the purpose of launching the Cultural Environmental Movement (CEM). The founding Board of Directors assembled a group of advisors and consultants from a variety of professional, media-orientated, health-related, women's minority, environmental, labor, religious, academic, and other citizens groups. A series of policy meetings resulted in an approved prospectus, a survey, an outreach program and a general direction for the CEM. Initial start-up grants and a contract for cultural indicators research with the Center for Substance Abuse Prevention, processed through the University of Pennsylvania, made it possible for office space to be obtained at the University's Annenberg School for Communication. Funds for that particular research project were instrumental in supporting the outreach activities of the CEM. By 1994, these involved intensive networking on the Internet both for direct inquiries through the office e-mail address and for interactive communication and dissemination of information through a large international list of contacts.

The aim is to address the problems of an increasingly centralized, globalized and mass-marketed media environment, and to move toward a more democratic cultural policy. In the CEM's prospectus it is stated that:

> The majority of viewers who watch more than three hours a day have little choice of thematic context or cast of character types. There is no historical precedent, constitutional provision or legislative blueprint to confront the challenge of a coherent new cultural environment into which children are born, in which most people live and learn, and which is drifting out of democratic reach.[34]

Gerbner continues to explain that the present situation, where media are tailored to fit the marketing strategies and priorities of dominant corporate interests, did not emerge spontaneously. It has developed despite significant public opposition over the years. The CEM is concerned, he says, with distortions in the democratic process where taxation occurs without representation and where payment is divorced from choice. Taxation without representation triggered the first American revolution and the same process on a larger, global scale and with a deeper human impact is needed once again.[35]

To bring about change, concerned citizens are urged to mobilize as effectively as commercials mobilize us all to act as consumers: to build a new coalition of international media councils, teachers, students and parents, human-rights groups, minority groups and religious organizations, environmental and legal associations, consumer groups, creative voices in the media, arts and sciences and others committed to broadening the freedom and diversity of the media mainstream. Resisting censorship, both public and private, includes exposing the media's use of the American Constitution's First Amendment and similar legislation in other countries as a shield for power and privilege, and extending rights and facilities to interests other than the most powerful, profitable and popular. Media literacy, awareness, critical viewing and reading are essential educational objectives at every level and should include both adults and children.

Gerbner made many of these points when he spoke at the first of the three international conferences initiated by the CRTC in Montreal, in November, 1992; at a public lecture sponsored by C-CAVE and Science for Peace at the University of Toronto in July, 1995; and again in Toronto at an international conference on television violence held at the Ryerson Polytechnical Institute in May, 1998. The role of government, he argues, is to better facilitate this process of public awareness by providing appropriate regulation on the basis of new trends in technology invention and use. Total reliance on free market forces has not and cannot work.

The national consultation on youth and violence convened by American Attorney General Janet Reno, Department of Education Secretary Richard W. Riley and Department of Health and Human Services Secretary Donna Shalala in Washington, D.C. in July, 1993, was an important initiative. According to Gerbner, it was the first high-level, government-sponsored group of health, youth and education professionals, writers, and independent producers to consider media policy. Said Gerbner:

> The group concluded: "The issue of media violence is really just the first phase of a major cultural debate about life in the 21st Century. What kind of people do we want our children to become? What kind of culture will best give them the environment they will need to grow up healthy and whole?" The group recommended that citizens "take lessons from the environmental movement to form a 'cultural environmental' movement."[36]

Following through with his own initiative for such a movement, a test mailing of 1,500 was conducted, in November, 1993, and, as of August 15, 1994, 2,765 names were in the database. Representatives of 88 different organizations from various states and countries notified CEM in writing of their interest in affiliation. These ranged from small local groups to large national and international associations.

Canadian organizations included the Alliance for Children and Television (ACT) in Toronto—a national, nonprofit organization dedicated to enhancing the television experience of Canadian children; the Association for Media Literacy (AML), Weston, Ontario—the first comprehensive organization for media literacy teachers in Canada; C-CAVE, described as the major Canadian critical media advocacy group dedicated to increasing public awareness about the effects of entertainment violence on society; the Center for Literacy, Montreal—a resource and teacher-training center; Jesuit Communication Project, Toronto—established to promote and develop media education in schools across Canada; The Media Foundation, Vancouver, publishers of *AdBusters, The Journal of the Mental Environment*; MediaWatch CANADA—a national, volunteer, feminist organization that works to eliminate sexism in the media; and The United Church of Canada, Division of Communication, Toronto—the integrated communications arm of Canada's largest Protestant denomination.

Strategic planning for a period of over three years involved activities related to organizational development and the provision of information. In Canada, regional meetings held at the University of Toronto in July, 1995, and February, 1996, helped to stimulate local activity and preparation for a national "Founding" Convention held in March, 1996, at Webster University in St. Louis, Missouri. The purpose of the Convention was to assemble, for the first time, interested individuals and representatives of affiliated organizations from the U.S. and abroad. The program included internationally prominent keynote speakers; working sessions to develop areas, targets and priorities for joint action; and the formation of a Steering Committee with representatives of affiliated groups.

Three documents, which express CEM's basic policies and programs, were approved at the Convention: the "People's Communication Charter," which spells out international standards for cultural policy making; the "Viewers' Declaration of Independence" which sets out the urgent reasons for the coalition; and the Agenda for Action which makes strategic recommendations.[37] The Second International Convention was held at Ohio University, in Athens, in 1999, and a third is planned for Quebec City, 2002.

Canadian Support

The challenges for Canadians posed by Gerbner and his colleagues are many. Collaborative projects on cultural indicators research within Canadian universities, such as those in American universities, would be useful in a way that was envisaged when the LaMarsh Center for Study on Conflict and Violence was first set up at York University. Coalition-building among community, medical, church and education-based groups begun under the auspices of the CRTV needs to be accelerated. As an affiliated association, C-CAVE was the Canadian co-sponsor of the first CEM Convention, participated in the second one and continues to collaborate on various projects with the CEM Board of Directors.

For more than a decade C-CAVE has been active in forging links with other organizations such as the AML, ACT, NFB, IPCA, United Church of Canada, MediaWatch, Canadian Association for the Study of Adult Education (CASAE) and the Canadian Communications Association (CCA), among others. These have been reinforced by participation in regular board meetings and participation in CEM Conventions. The Founding Convention in St. Louis was preceded by the first International Summit on Broadcast Standards with Keith Spicer, former chair of the CRTC, and Ron Cohen, chair of the CBSC among those who attended and spoke. Another Summit should now be coordinated for the purposes of evaluating progress made in various countries, first, in developing standards, and second, in adhering to them.

One recommendation that grew out of a workshop at a C-CAVE sponsored conference on media violence, in 1994, on newsletters was that a Canadian contribution be developed for inclusion in the *Cultural Environment Monitor* now being published on a periodic basis by the CEM directorate, based in Philadelphia at Temple University.

Another example of outreach and networking activities, in keeping with CEM objectives was a national "Safety Net" conference on crime prevention, public safety and justice reform coordinated by CAVEAT, in Hamilton, in September, 1994. Over 100 invited participants from across the country included members of the media, lawyers, elected politicians at all three levels of government, law enforcement officers, civil servants, educators, and representatives from other grass roots level organizations.

The executive summary began with a statement from CAVEAT urging the Federal Minister of Justice to "support the enactment of legislation prohibiting the manufacturing, production, distribution and possession of materials including all serial killer cards, serial killer board games, pornographic materials and other like materials." It was recommended that the exemption for child pornography in Section 163, Subsection of the Criminal Code involving "artistic merit," be deleted on the basis that consideration of harmful effects must take precedence over artistic significance. Restriction of violent and sexually explicit material in newscasts, broadcasting and advertising to appropriate adult viewing hours of 10 p.m. to 6 a.m. was also recommended.

In fact, three out of seven preliminary recommendations adopted by the conference addressed the issue of media violence: a rare example of a summit or conference focusing on crime prevention that included substantive policy recommendations involving the issue of media violence. The attention of elected and appointed officials focusing on issues involving crime and prevention, whether it is re-examination of the Young Offenders Act, incarceration of perpetrators, or their rehabilitation, at federal, provincial and municipal levels should now be directed to these recommendations. So far, any attempts to do so have proven to be futile.

An advisory panel for parents, teachers and journalists established at the Ontario Institute for Studies in Education (OISEUT) based at the University of Toronto, as first recommended by the LaMarsh Commission, is long overdue. Objectives within the Transformative Learning Center at the Institute need to be broadened to include such an initiative. The Center emphasizes the need for development of effective counterbalances to present economic globalization tendencies as nation states become less and less capable of regulating the new forms of economic activity.

Budd Hall, chairman of the Department of Adult Education at the Institute has stressed the important potential that exists for international non-government organization (NGOs), each responsible for its own administration and funding, and accountable to its own members, not to any government, in the facilitation of positive social and cultural transformation. One of the perceived strengths of NGOs is their capacity to respond to rapidly changing global contexts and issues because, unlike governments, they are relatively unencumbered by bureaucratic structures.[38] The potential for this kind of collective activity was demonstrated by the opposition marshaled on a global basis to the MAI. Nevertheless, as stressed by Connie Fogal and others at the *New World Order Conference* at Ryerson Polytechnical University in June, 1999, activity through NGOs must not *replace* political involvement through dialogue with elected representatives. With all its flaws, the democratic political process requires that those who campaign for the support of constituents are, in the final analysis, at least accountable for their actions in ways that non-elected officials, however well meaning they may be, are not.

The Information Super Highway: Who Will Define Content?
One of the most critical as well as urgent reasons for the acceleration of the Cultural Environmental Movement springs from growing commercial struggles for control of the new converging technologies. Various aspects of this looming economic phenomena were evident at a conference on "Powering Up North America" held in Toronto, in February, 1994, cosponsored by the Information Technology Association of Canada (ITAC) and the Canadian Advanced Technology Association (CATA). Heavy promotion of the event included a 12-page advertising supplement in Canada's national newspaper, *The Globe and Mail*. Jon Gerrard, Secretary of State, at the time, focused on the commitment of the Federal Government in "Building the Canadian Information Highway."

Immense media attention was generated by his announcement that a chair and members of an advisory council on information and communications infrastructure would be appointed. The battle between telephone and cable companies over control of the new information highways connecting homes and businesses quickly became a war of corporate behemoths with the impact on ordinary citizens largely overlooked. As a result, a Coalition for Public Information (CPI), initiated by the Ontario Library Association (OLA), sprung up to protect the public interest.[39]

The paradox in the commercial rush for control over cyberspace is that all the free speech rights intended for individuals and communities are becoming the exclusive property of business. Jeffrey Chester, executive director of the Center for Media Education, a Washington, D.C., based advocacy group fighting for open electronic media, is among opponents calling on governments to set aside channels for local, civic, and national communications and individual access.[40]

In 1995 the Canadian Government asked the CRTC to hold public hearings on the subject of the information highway. It was anticipated that issues for examination would include content and the use and sharing of facilities. Regional consultations were held throughout the country in October of that year, specifically, on the issue of violence in television programming. The purpose, according to Spicer, was to invite further public input "before taking the issue any further." A key problem identified by him was foreign signals distributed by the cable industry who were not governed by the CAB code on violence.

There was one possible solution, he said, to leveling the playing field for Canadian broadcasters and for ensuring that Canadian TV violence standards applied equally to all signals watched by Canadian viewers.

> This approach would require distribution undertakings to curtail or encode any program which has been found to violate an approved code on violence. This would apply to cable companies...as well as to other distribution undertakings such as direct-to-home (DTH) satellite services or multi-point distribution systems. One means of implementing this approach would be to amend the Cable Television Regulations, which currently prohibit any undertaking from altering any programs they distribute. It may also require modifications to industry codes to ensure that all licensees are bound by any prohibition against a specific program.[41]

Public discussion on these possibilities initiated by Spicer must be revived. Similarly, the concerns expressed by the Information Highway Advisory Council, representing thiry business, education, and cultural leaders, about the growing volume of violent, racist, sexist, and abusive traffic on the Internet must be addressed.[42]

On the whole, one of the most alarming manifestations in the rush for inclusion on the Information Super Highway can be observed as the nation's teachers, school board trustees, politicians, and parents eagerly embrace the concept of Internet education with few qualms about the consequences. In the process, they are opening up their classrooms and homes to an avalanche of electronic advertisements as students arriving at the new Electronic Library are immediately entreated to "meet their new classmates."

In 1995, *The Toronto Star* reporter Naomi Klein encountered some of them at one advertisement site described as, "the Trix rabbit, the Honey Nut Cheerio bee, the Lucky Charms leprechaun, and Count Chocula."[43] She reported on other educational sites as well, with advertising links to Honda, Sunny Delight orange drink, and Disneyland Hotel along with computer game and software manufacturers. Klein posed the question of whether or not educators could block out commercials while still accessing valuable learning experiences through the Internet, such as museums, libraries and link-ups with other schools. "If we can screen out sex and violence with programs like Net Nanny," Said Klein, "surely somebody could develop technology to block ads."

Trends Within the Canadian Broadcasting Corporation

The changing economic climate, within the communications industry at large, has precipitated challenges for public broadcasters and these of course include the CBC. From the standpoint of violent content, although as a public broadcaster it is exempt from many regulations now governing private broadcasters, despite statements of principle to the contrary, the CBC has occasionally aired programming that is just as objectionable as that seen on private stations. An example emerged on November 28, 1994, in Toronto, when action shots from the *Mighty Morphin Power Rangers* appeared, before the watershed hour of 9:00 p.m. established by the CRTC for private broadcasters, on the CBC in a commercial for CD-ROMs, which promised more exciting and entertaining adventures. Similarly, at the height of the public debate over the CBSC ruling about the program being too violent for Canadian television, the author was contacted by a CBC affiliate in Red Deer, Alberta, and invited to discuss the local public broadcaster's decision to air the *Power Rangers* program simply because it was exempt from CAB criteria that governs private broadcasters.

In March, 1995, the CBC launched a highly criticized bid to make broadcasting history in Canada by carrying live coverage of the Bernardo trial.[44] C-CAVE was one of several organizations opposing the network's plans and one month later CAVEAT called upon Prime Minister Jean Chrétien to investigate whether or not the CBC was acting within its mandate on behalf of the people of Canada. Legal counsel was retained to determine if the actions of the CBC were in contravention of broadcasting regulations.

Two months later, John Haslett Cuff, television critic for *The Globe and Mail*, accused the CBC of betraying its mandate by "choosing [at taxpayers expense] to divert increasingly scarce programming dollars to ersatz Canadian productions with most of the equity and profits from sales outside Canada."[45] This was the easily predictable outcome of a decision on the part of the public broadcaster to open up a Los Angeles office to foster co-productions.

Another departure from its mandate occurred with the announcement from president Perrin Beatty, in the fall of 1996, that in order to make up a budget shortfall of nearly $200 million, more commercials would be introduced into areas where they had not existed previously.[46] While the promise of more Canadian content always has wide popular appeal politically, in actual fact what followed within a week of this particular announcement was prime time public affairs programs on both CBC National TV and CBC Newsworld focusing attention on some extra-ordinarily violent examples of Canadian content, namely the productions and work of Atom Egoyan and David Cronenberg. What is obviously needed is adherence from *both* public and private broadcasters to a more broadly applied code on violence such as the one already adopted by the CAB in order to enhance the potential for the production and distribution of less violent *Canadian* content, both domestically and internationally.

As Marc Raboy, director of the Communications Policy Research Laboratory at the University of Montreal has pointed out, public broadcasting remains a key institution for democratization in the context of globalization. Broadcasting was conceived for commercial purposes, but *public* broadcasting was introduced for purposes of cultural development and diversity. In the April, 1998, special issue on the Cultural Environment Movement of the *Gazette: The International Journal for Communications Studies*, Raboy said, "As media politics go global, public broadcasting must be rethought and new structures and mechanisms put in place at the global level."[47] One of the most important contributions made by public broadcasting is that it helps to raise the standard for the entire market, acting as a catalyst and serving as an example to all broadcasting services. According to John Allemang, television reporter for *The Globe and Mail*, this is precisely what is beginning to happen as U.S. networks begin to look to the CBC, in spite of it's flaws, as a model for their own 21st-century strategies.[48]

Public Funds for Canadian Content
In a report based on discussions and debates at eight public forums that took place across the country in 1994, Friends of Canadian Broadcasting (FCB) offered several key recommendations. These addressed both the increasingly beleaguered CBC and the need for support for Canadian programming. FCB recommended reduced CBC reliance on advertising revenues and creation of a $400-million Canadian content fund to be supported by existing and emerging players in the industry, including cable monopolies.[49] In the fall of 1996 Heritage Minister Sheila Copps unveiled a new television-production fund involving $200 million a year. It was to incorporate $100 million from a combination of the existing cable television production fund and the television-production budget of Telefilm Canada.[50] The additional money injected into the fund corresponded approximately to the money the government was then receiving through the CRTC for various broadcasting fees. The emphasis of support, however, was not for inhouse CBC producers but for independent production houses, and in particular, young producers.

These funding approaches were accompanied by shifts in policy decisions within Telefilm Canada, itself, with less money expected in investments for TV series and specials, and greater expectations for Canadian exporters of programming to pay their own way in international film and TV markets.[51] Previous criticisms aimed at Telefilm for fostering cultural imperialism in attempts, through centralization of funding support for productions based in large centers such as Toronto and Montreal, were ignored.[52] This practice, perceived by observers to be making "about six producers extremely rich at taxpayers expense" with the rest of the country, particularly western Canada, ignored, was being reinforced instead of reversed.

In 1994, FCB spokesman Ian Morrison called for the cable industry's
voluntary programming fund which was then increased from $50-million to
$60-million a year and being allocated by the cable companies, to be redirected
for public purposes.[53] He countered criticism from the Canadian Cable
Television Association (CCTA) over fears of a consumer revolt if the
recommendation for a two dollar increase in cable fees by industry to make this
possible was implemented by pointing out that Canadians, "didn't object when
cable bills went up to give [Rogers Communications' executives] Phil Lind and
Ted Rogers million dollar bonuses, so why should they complain about a teeny
weeny increase to give Canada a bonus?"[54]

In April, 1998 public indignation over CRTC performance resulted in
appointment by Minister of Heritage Sheila Copps, of a special parliamentary
committee chaired by Sarmite Bulte, Toronto MP for Parkdale-High Park. The
Committee was expected to investigate how appointments are made to the
CRTC on the basis of concerns that almost all of these originate from private
industry and involve individuals who are least likely to make decisions that favour
the public interest, particularly on issues involving rising telephone and cable
rates. So far, there is no evidence that this committee has accomplished anything
that has translated into meaningful change in the make-up of the Commission.
Nevertheless, this initiative is one that must be supported and strengthened
before any significant shift in decision making on the part of the Commission can
be anticipated.

Many of the same recommendations made by FCB in 1994 surfaced in the
Juneau Committee Report released on January, 1996. Appointed by Prime Minister
Jean Chrétien several months earlier, it was expected to review the mandates of the
CBC, the NFB and Telefilm Canada. On the whole, although an important
initiative for change, the Juneau Report proposed little that was particularly far
reaching. Although it recommended a reduced emphasis on sports for example,
already extensively offered on private television, it still said that the CBC should
stay in hockey, the Olympics, major Canadian events like the Grey Cup, and the
Briar Curling Championship. Like the CBC itself, the Juneau Committee was
accused of trying to be all things to all people and in the process missed the
opportunity to revitalize and streamline Canadian public television. There was no
specific reference in the Report to the issue of violence. Telefilm was urged to
become "less industrial and more culturally focused" by actively encouraging and
nurturing small and medium sized companies in all regions of the country. Said the
Committee, "We believe that Telefilm has a responsibility to manage its resources
with an eye to maintaining what might be called an ecology of creativity."[55]
Precisely what kind of creativity they had in mind was not specified.

In October, 1998, the CRTC announced hearings in Ottawa for a "major
re-examination of policies governing Canadian television," described as the most
sweeping since "the mid-1980s."[56] Although I was among those invited to appear
before the Commission, and gave examples of objectionable Canadian content,
paid for from the public purse, one year later there is still no evidence of a Report

from these hearings. Instead, it was reported in 1999 that not only Telefilm but the Canada Council and various regional film-development agencies have been generously providing tax dollars to a number of sex and violence filled Canadian productions, among them some of the following:

David Cronenberg's Cannes-prize-winning *Crash* (fetishized car wrecks); Lynne Stopkewich's *Kissed* (necrophilia); John Greyson's *Lilies* (plenty of unabashed gay sex); Bruce Sweeney's *Dirty* (drugs, explicit oral sex, sado-masochism); and Atom Egoyan's triple-header, the Oscar nominated *The Sweet Hereafter* (incest), *Exotica* (teen strippers) and *Family Viewing* (voyeurism and masturbation); Cynthia Roberts' *Bubbles Galore* (pornography star Nina Hartley turning porn producer); and *Bride of Chucky*, the $25-million comedy-horror sequel to *Child's Play I and II*, *(supported by the Ontario Film Development Corporation).*

Arguing in *defense* of these trends, Alison Vale pointed out in *The Globe and Mail* that Canadian film would "be no where without sex and violence" supported by tax dollars. Certainly, the prevailing attitude on the part of both government and industry still tends toward the notion that if the content is "Canadian" it is above reproach regardless of its nature.

The growing revolt against such funding practices within the industry itself, must, however, be supported and encouraged. The six Toronto based casting directors reportedly shaken by highschool murders in Colorado and Alberta who in June, 1999, refused to work on the teen slasher-werewolf movie, *Ginger Snaps*, planned for filming in the city in September of that year, must be nurtured for their courage as rare trend setters. In addition, Telefilm Canada officials such as Bill House who defended the government agency's investment in the script, saturated with themes of sex and violence, by saying, "We think this one will be very commercially oriented and that's partly what we're all about," must be exposed and challenged.[57] Clearly, Telefilm Canada's criteria for funding the country's film industry must be revised.

Notes

1. Haslett Cuff, 1998, May 2, *The Globe and Mail*, p.C6.

2. 1998, April 6.

3. 1998, May 4, p.D1.

4. Chan, 1999; Mitchell, 1999; Obmascik, 1999.

5. Howell, 1999; Kuxhaus, 1999; C-CAVE, 1999.

6. Tuck, 1999, May 18, *The Globe and Mail*, p.A1.

7. Scoffield, 1999, May 2, *The National Post*, p.A3.

8. C-CAVE, May 26, 1999.

9. Jenish, 1992, Dec. 7, *Maclean's Magazine*, p.44.

10. Children's TV…,1999, June 29, *The Globe and Mail*, p.C2.

11. Montgomery, 1989, p.216.

12. Montgomery, 1989, p.222.

13. Canada, June, 1999.

14. U.S. bill rips, 1996, Feb. 2, *The Globe and Mail*, p.A11.
15. Brown, 1999.
16. Brown, 1999.
17. Canadian Teachers Federation/CRTV, 1996.
18. "TV violence ," 1997.
19. McQuaig, L. 1998. *The Cult of Impotence*, Toronto, London, NY: Viking.
20. Personal communication, December 7, 1995.
21. Berry, 1988, p.212.
22. Schreibman, V.1996. Oct. 21, personal communicaton.
23. Fogal, C., 1998, April 26, cfogal@netcom.ca; dweston@island.net
24. Miedzian, 1991; Postman, 1986; Schiller, 1989; Toffler, 1980.
25. Postman, 1985, p.159.
26. Mackinnon, 1987, p.206.
27. Mackinnon, 1987, p.213.
28. Rankin, 1996, p.A8.
29. Berry, 1988, p.141.
30. "Sister-in-law," 1994, Oct. 18, *The Toronto Star*, p.A20.
31. Rasminsky, 1994, Feb. 10, *The Globe and Mail*, p.A25.
32. Mitchell, 1999, May 25, *The Globe and Mail*, p.A1.
33. Robbins, 1999, june 5.
34. Gerbner, 1994, p.1.
35. Gerbner, 1991a, 1991c, 1993, 1994a, 1994b; National Council of Churches, 1994.
36. 1993, p.2.
37. CEM, 1996.
38. Boulding, E., 1988; Boulding, K.E., 1985, Hall, 1993.
39. Jeffrey, 1994, March 3-9, *Now Magazine*, p.18.
40. Zerbisias, 1994, Jan. 29, *The Toronto Star*, p.B1.
41. CRTC, 1995.
42. Klein, 1996, Oct. 14, *The Torono Star*, p.A13.
43. "Information highway", 1995, April 22, *The Ottawa Citizen*, p.E2.
44. Jenish, 1995, March 14, *Maclean's Magazine*, p.35.
45. Haslett Cuff, 1995, May 15, *The Globe and Mail*, p.C1.
46. Winsor, H., 1996, Spt. 7, *The Globe and Mail*, p.A1.
47. Raboy, 1998, p.168.
48. Allemang, 1999, July 6, *The Globe and Mail*, p.C1.
49. Zerbisias, 1994, Jan. 29, *The Toronto Star*, p.B1.
50. Winsor, H., 1996, p.A8.
51. Adilman, S., 1996, Sept. 18, *The Toronto Star*, p.B2.
52. Lee, 1995, Sept. 9, *The Globe and Mail*, p.D2.
53. Winsor, 1994a, Nov. 1, p.A8; 1994b, Nov. 30, *The Globe and Mail*, p. 13.
54. Zerbisias, 1996, Feb. 1, *The Toronto Star*, p.B7.
55. Canada, 1996, p.253.
56. Fraser, 1998c, April 29, *The Globe and Mail*, p.A6.
57. Adilman, 1999a&b, June 1&22, *The Toronto Star*, p.A1&E6.

Chapter 10

EDUCATION FOR SOCIAL CHANGE

GLOBAL EDUCATION FOR social change and a sustainable future, requires reexamination of our approach to values education in schools. Alvin Toffler first pointed out, in 1970, that as a reaction against clerical education, educators have relied on teaching the facts and letting the student make up his or her own mind:

> Cultural relativism and an appearance of scientific neutrality displaced the insistence on traditional values. Education clung to the rhetoric of character formation, but educators fled from the very idea of value inculcation, deluding themselves into believing that they were not in the values business at all.[1]

Media literacy instruction in Canada has tended to reflect these delusions of neutrality. The challenge now is to develop a rationally moderate position on what is right and what is wrong for students, now born into a media saturated society, regardless of political, religious or nonreligious persuasion, ethnic background, or economic status, with an aim to seek out a middle road between totalitarianism and a moral vacuum.

Relegation of the concepts of truth, goodness and evil to the status of subjective relativity has not worked.[2] At this critical juncture in our human history, appropriate education requires a deep understanding of how and why our world is changing and of how people and cultures around the world are responding to these changes. While the process of inquiry into what divides cultures, classes and nations ought to be tolerant and empathetic it cannot, as Paul Kennedy has argued, be values-free.

> In the end, it is not enough merely to understand what we are doing to our planet, as if we were observing the changes through a giant telescope on Mars. Because we are all members of a world citizenry, we also need to equip ourselves with a system of ethics, a sense of fairness, *and* a sense of proportion as we consider the various ways in which, collectively or individually, we can better prepare for the twenty-first century.[3]

Today more than ever, commercialized mass media and popular culture are competing with classroom educators attempting to facilitate deeper understanding of global trends. However, neutrality on matters such as media violence merely paves the way for marginalization of the formal education system to serve economic interests. In the U.S., evidence that over "135,000 children take guns to school each day," resulting in tragic consequences, has accelerated calls for decisive action on gun control, but these must be matched with similar attention to the exacerbating influences of media violence.[4] Politicians, law enforcement officers and, in particular, classroom teachers, who are confronted with the magnitude of the problem on a day to day basis must all be held accountable and not be permitted to shift the blame onto each other.[5]

At a conference held in Toronto on safe schools in 1994, Durham Police Services Board member Sara Macdonald said, "We need to go back to teaching values—letting young people know what is right from what is wrong."[6] According to Robert Heath, Superintendent of the Scarborough Board of Education in Metropolitan Toronto, the main reason for the explosion of youth violence and discontent across North American in the 1990s is because both adults and the mass media have failed to offer children positive role models.[7]

Although progress in addressing youth violence is being made according to Stuart Auty, a former school vice-principal and the executive director of the Canadian Safe Schools Association (CSSA), denial is still a problem.

> There was a time when school principals worried about what people would think if a police cruiser parked outside a school; now the police are actively encouraged to come in and establish links with students and teachers before something goes wrong.[8]

Clearly, closer cooperation between public institutions, whether they involve law enforcement or the education of youth, is necessary. Instead, new federal gun control legislation passed in Canada, in 1995, similar to what already exists in a number of other countries around the world, is now facing a legal challenge from the provinces of Alberta, Saskatchewan, Manitoba, Ontario, and the Yukon.[9] It was announced days after a coroner's jury in Vernon, B.C., following the murder and suicide of ten people, made a number of recommendations to improve police procedures and firearms registration. Nor has this legal challenge been withdrawn on the basis of subsequent reports of tragedies involving children killing other children with guns due to easy availability such as the one in Taber, Alberta, in 1999.

Within the school system itself there has been some evidence that the Scarborough Board's much criticized policy of zero tolerance for violence has been working. By the fall of 1996, violence and weapons-related incidents were down by 60 per cent. Adoption of the policy has meant automatic expulsion of students possessing firearms or using weapons for the purposes of intimidation or assault. Other schools have reported similar evidence of success since police have been invited into the schools with students, and parents have also become actively involved in confronting the issue of violence.[10] These policies now have to be broadened to address glorification of violence in popular culture and normalization of it among youth *before* it precipitates these violent behavior tendencies.

Many have argued that new approaches to doing business in an information-based economy are rapidly emerging but that regulatory frameworks are still predicated on old models of governing.[11] The same can be said about old models of education and, in particular, values-based education, whether it is being considered within the formal classroom setting or within the context of popular education through the mass media. Traditional approaches to education are being coopted in an economy where aggressive marketing of popular cultural commodities includes marketing of lifestyle itself. Communications technologies are converging and precipitating unprecedented changes along with critical environmental and social costs that threaten human survival.

It seems patently obvious that a new paradigm for social, political and "ethical" or "spiritual" organization is required for long term human sustainability. Consequently, the old arguments that, like the poor, violence and crime have always been with us and that plurality inevitably necessitates the accommodation of diverse opinions, need reevaluation. Human arrogance has led, not only to our current civilizational crisis from an environmental point of view, but to widespread confusion of "rights" over "privileges" and this development is urgently in need of analysis and clarification.

Conclusion and Recommendations

Professionals in a variety of disciplines along with media scholars now view the matter of media violence as a critical mental health and societal problem. A number of studies, both before and since the LaMarsh Commission released its Report in 1977, have addressed and helped to clarify some of the reasons involved in a world where social and cultural organization is increasingly dominated by communications technology. In Canada, the LaMarsh Report provided a springboard for the development of policy on communications technology that can continue to help us prepare ourselves for the 21st century. Although some of its recommendations have been implemented and some need to be updated, most have been ignored entirely and remain both relevant and urgent.

The challenges posed by these circumstances for adult educators, in particular, are obvious. Everyone today is confronted by the urgency for decision-making procedures that take into account the larger life cycle and mutually enhancing human-earth relationships. Consequently, it is necessary for educators involved at all levels of human development to address the problems of degradation within the cultural environment as an integral component related to other, equally critical areas of the environment requiring attention. There is no doubt that defining "appropriate" patterns of behavior for cultural and social transformation poses difficulties but they cannot be side stepped.

Thomas Berry has reviewed the traditional roles of postsecondary institutions of learning, their historical shortcomings, and called for greater emphasis on the development of "new stories" at this critical juncture in our human history. A new mode of cultural patterning is needed, he says, with emphasis on "the college years," because students at elementary and high school levels are not yet capable of the required capacity for reflexive reasoning.[12] Essential in this process is a serious understanding of Western cultural traditions, given the extent to which the entire world of life, thought and values has been influenced by them. The tragedy, says Berry, is that "the dark, destructive aspect of Western patriarchal civilization has become virulent" at the same time that the influence of the West has become so pervasive throughout the human community and when "its technological capacity for plundering the earth has become so overwhelming that all the basic systems of the planet are being closed down."[13]

On cultural issues, a number of specific challenges and opportunities exist in all sectors of society. Many of them overlap and require cooperation and commitment on joint projects involving government, industry, NGOs, educators, researchers, health professionals, parents, and members of an informed public. Initiatives such as "Days of Action for the Cultural Environment," parents' marches, teach-ins on college campuses, and meetings in town halls would help to raise the profile and urgency of these multi-faceted issues on long term sustainability.

Applied Research and Development
The joint initiative on the part of the CRTC and the CAB to develop a code on Violence was an important step in the right direction but the public must learn to demand that they *themselves* take it seriously. For this purpose it is critical that the research community, itself, participates in monitoring implementation of the code and that it become a focus and inspiration for other segments of the popular cultural industries as well as the private broadcasters. It will be necessary to harness the appropriate research techniques and skills at the postsecondary level either through the existing LaMarsh Center on Violence and Conflict Resolution at York University or through the establishment of another university based center such as the Ontario Institute for Studies in Education at the University of Toronto, where the appointment of an advisory council for parents, teachers and members of the media was first recommended by the LaMarsh Commission. Judy LaMarsh's first choice for a center on studies in media violence was the Ryerson Polytechnical University which now has access to impressive technology for communications and journalism-based degree programs through the Rogers Communications Center, but the primary focus of its studies remains in the area of skills acquisition and application rather than critical theory development and instruction.

In 1994, it was reported in the *New York Times* that the monitoring of violence in TV programs and video games may "prove a boon to social scientists who have been most critical of these industries' efforts at self policing."[14] Clearly the potential for greater cooperation between industry and the research community in addressing the problem of media violence exists. Important models for this purpose have already been developed by George Gerbner and by the NCTV in Champaign, Illinois. In order for this kind of relationship to be fruitful, however, sufficient autonomy must be guaranteed for the research community, to ensure that the focus of inquiry does not become bogged down in endless analysis with subsequent evasion of serious policy recommendations that might jeopardize industry based funding sources.

Regardless of where and how media violence monitoring processes are established in various countries including Canada, these should be done in cooperation with those already in existence in order that duplication and unnecessary additional costs be avoided. The Cultural Indicators Model developed by Gerbner, and more recently expanded into the "Fairness" Indicators Model, was used, for example, by Paquette and Deguise at Laval University in Quebec in a study completed in January, 1994, entitled *Index Violence on Canadian Television.*[15]

The provision of vigilance on whether or not government incentives for industry self-regulation are taken seriously cannot be left entirely up to underfunded and over-extended grass roots level community groups. When former CRTC chairman Keith Spicer encouraged coalition-building between such groups in 1994, and appealed for assistance in monitoring implementation of the CAB Code on Violence, it was stressed that such activity could not be effectively undertaken by anyone without a budget, appropriate administrative staff and research personnel.

What is also urgently needed is a Second International Broadcast Standards Summit of CEM affiliates and supporting organizations, media executives, and representatives of producers and creative workers in participating countries, to develop a mechanism for regular consultation and broad adherence to a set of mutually agreed upon media policy standards for international trade. The first Summit, held in March, 1996, in St. Louis, Missouri, in conjunction with the CEM Founding Convention, included participation from CRTC and CBSC officials in Canada and their counterparts from France, Germany, England, Croatia and Hungary. The dialogue which began at this time needs to be sustained, enlarged upon and funded with appropriate representation from all sectors of society, not just industry and government officials.

As Spicer emphasized at the meeting in Canada, in January, 1994, unless grass-roots level activism on media violence and television program monitoring along with coalition building is sustained, the likelihood of coordinated efforts on the part of government, industry and the community at large being sustained, would begin to fade. Although the establishment of the Media Awareness Network through the National Film Board (NFB) office in Ottawa, with funding from the Ministry of Justice was an important initiative, it will always have certain limitations. It does not and cannot provide the kind of critical, pedagogical perspective that an academic institution can, through research which includes participatory, action-oriented methodology. The NFB's principle mandate is to make films, not to provide public education on media violence. Despite the Board's laudable record on the provision of public education on how the media work through many of its productions and video anthologies, it does occasionally become embroiled in public controversy where conflict of interest is inevitable.

In all countries, the challenge is to build on public education and community awareness that community organizations have already initiated. An essential component in the provision of public education and greater public awareness involves discussion of research findings through mainstream media itself. In this context, education should be provided within schools of journalism on the value of prevention, the impact of desensitization and other causal factors. Also, more research is needed on how cooperative working relationships between all sectors of society in addressing the problem of violence in the media can best be developed. This is necessary at both national and international levels.

In other words, research is required on new patterns evolving from the trans-nationalization of culture on a global basis as popular culture assumes greater importance in the global economy. Within this context, Gerbner's research findings, replicated year after year, indicating that most people do *not* prefer violent television programs when they have a choice need to be better amplified. Cross-national comparative studies documenting trends in global homogenization versus diversification need to be done in addition to exploration of mechanisms used by democratic societies to support independent voices through journalism and the production of cultural commodities.

A Global Marketing Awareness Task Force to expose the "dumping" of cultural products worldwide that drive out home-produced and quality materials should be set up in all countries, including Canada, in cooperation with the CEM Board of Directors. This initiative should include regular global monitoring of media ownership, employment and content, and release of annual reports on the health and diversity of the cultural mainstream. These reports should include assessments of, and guidelines for, diverse and equitable media ownership and employment practices with fair and realistic gender, racial, ethnic, aging, disability and mental illness portrayal. On health-related issues, presentations in both advertisements and regular content should be monitored for the depiction of addictive substances without harmful consequences, promotion of prescription drugs to the public, the aggressive marketing of pharmaceutical products as "miracle drugs" and other inducements for "pill popping" that, together, make for a drug culture. Similarly, fast and reckless driving, both as a dramatic and as a sales feature; violence with incidious patterns of victimization and without realistic consequences or suggestions for alternative approaches to conflict resolution; and, impossible standards of beauty, especially for high fashion, diet programs, cosmetics, cosmetic surgeries, and other products that imply human defects, particularly in women, should be exposed and criticized.

All of these potential initiatives were incorporated into the CEM Agenda for Action and approved at the Founding Convention in 1996 by over 150 independent organizations and supporters from 64 counties around the world on the basis of recommendations from 15 different working groups.

Better Contributions from Non-Governmental Organizations

More evidence of position statements on the harmful effects of media violence from professional health associations and organizations, as well as parent-teacher associations, in all countries, would do much to enhance and reinforce what has already begun in this context in the United States. To observe the difference in commitment in this regard, between Canada and the U.S., one has only to check out the web sites for both the American Medical Association (AMA) and its Canadian counterpart.[16] The Founding of the Coalition For Responsible Television in Hull by C-CAVE, and other groups, in 1994, was a beginning. It included the following organizations: Canadian Teachers' Federation, Girl Guides of Canada (Ontario Council), London Family Court Clinic Inc., Canadian Medical Association, Canadian Association of Principals, Canadian Conference of Catholic Bishops, Toronto Board of Education, several Ontario Women Teacher's Associations and C-CAVE. One year later the coalition's membership list included over 54 organizations, 25 individual members, nine endorsing members and three donors. Since then, further progress has been arrested, unfortunately, due to lack of funds. The Coalition might be encouraged, for example, as a vehicle for enlarging its membership *and* fundraising, to explore the feasibility of a Charter of Rights challenge to the give-away of public airways for private profit.

Attention given to the issue of media violence and its harmful effects by the Canadian Pediatric Association, Canadian Physicians for the Prevention of Nuclear War (renamed Physicians for Global Survival [Canada]), Federation of Women Teachers Associations of Ontario and each international counterpart needs to be extended and better supported.[17] Also, the far sighted recommendations made to the LaMarsh Commission by the Ontario Psychological Association in 1977, have, so far, been ignored. Its observation that licensing boards for journalists and other key members of media industries should be considered on par with law societies who govern entry into the practice of law and colleges for physicians, surgeons, nurses and teachers who set and maintain adherence for standards practiced by those professions should be re-considered.[18]

Resource material on the current nature of the mass media should be developed for parents and others involved in child rearing activities, with attention paid to the ways in which advertising is profoundly changing our civic culture into a passive consumer-driven democracy. Such material should be made broadly available through doctor's offices, child care centers, hospital waiting rooms and newly created resource centers focusing on the contemporary nature of the mass media. Steps should also be taken to ensure the accuracy of information on the environmental impact of various cultural commodities. Misinformation circulated under the guise of media literacy for public relations purposes designed to rationalize the existing media system should be challenged and exposed.

As a component of public education and action, boycotts of retail outlets selling harmful cultural commodities should be encouraged. Conversely, retail outlets adhering to industry codes of conduct should be supported. Collaboration on such action should be explored with media workers' unions to develop labor participation in the Cultural Environment Movement. At the same time, public support for diversity in representation should be created and additional policies that result in loss of jobs in the cultural industries avoided. Complaints about sponsorship of violent content should be directed to advertisers as well as companies and governments whose products or services are being promoted. Experience has shown that purchasers of advertising are extremely sensitive to consumer concerns. Frequently the parties on whose behalf the advertisements are purchased are not even aware of precisely which television programs or violent video games their advertising dollars are supporting, especially when large blocks of advertising spots are purchased through advertising agencies or media buying services.

Governance for Public Education and Protection

Appointment of additional commissions to study the issue of media violence for harmful effects—at least in Canada—should be avoided. Instead, there is a much more urgent need for assessment of relationships between federal regulators such as the FCC in the U.S. and the CRTC in Canada, the industries they regulate and how their performances interface with the public interest.[19] Recommendations from previous inquiries should be reviewed and fused for effective policy development. In Canada, apart from the LaMarsh Report, these include the Federal Report from the Standing Committee on Communications and Culture, *Television Violence: Fraying Our Social Fabric*, in 1993, and another study completed in the same year by the Royal Commission on Violence Toward Women, *Changing the Landscape: Ending Violence and Achieving Equality*.[20] What is also needed, is an assessment of various measures taken in different countries to address media violence in order to ensure that success stories in one jurisdiction help to reinforce and accelerate similar measures in others. In addition, cooperative development of standards for practices related to the media by all levels of government should be undertaken at once—both nationally and internationally. As the Report published by the Canadian Government in 1993 on *Television Violence: Fraying Our Social Fabric* pointed out, the need is for the predominant focus, at this juncture in the debate, to move to policy and implementation of regulations.

Central to any serious initiatives on the part of either educators, health professionals, politicians or the community at large, is the critical need for attitudinal changes toward the high levels of tolerance of violence in the community whether these involve the natural environment or fellow human beings. In 1993, the Royal Commission on Violence Against Women, as a part of their national action plan, urged that a policy of "zero tolerance" toward violence be adopted by all levels of government and every organization within society. So far, it has only captured the imagination of a few school board officials. It stressed the need for both systemic and individual responsibility in attempts to address the issue of violence against women. In order for the principle to be adopted more generally, forums should be held on a widespread basis with community leaders and media professionals committed to the creation of alternatives to the cult of violence and brutality that cultivates meanness, glorifies domination, deforms masculinity, and sexuality and polarizes society.

Violence prevention policies already being introduced into schools must be publically supported and appropriately funded. These include procedures for reporting weapons-related incidents to police and assurance that when students are suspended or expelled, the relevant information is included in their official school records so that these measures do not result in students with problems being shunted from one board to another. Also, that remedial programs for those expelled be provided and that the impact of media violence be appropriately acknowledged and addressed.[21]

In schools, media literacy programs should incorporate the aim to prevent violence and should be undertaken at the provincial or state rather than individual board level to ensure some degree of consistency and consensus on what is being taught. Public education initiatives for the reduction of media violence, both within and beyond the school, should include explanations of the human, social, and economic costs and be appropriately funded. At both secondary and post-secondary levels of formal education, courses should be designed that teach students how media-driven consumer lifestyles have a harmful effect on the natural as well as cultural environment. Media literacy in this context should include advertisement-free as well as war-toy free zones in schools. On the whole, use of school time and space for commercial messages should be vigorously opposed in all media forms including the Internet. Also, a regular review of research findings on media violence should be integrated into policy and program planning at all levels of government and public service organizations dealing with the education and welfare of children.

The need for more "ombudsmen" or public "watchdogs" to offset corporate encroachment into civil society is becoming increasingly critical. In Canada, as in other countries, federal mandates for special auditor-generals to keep watch on government as well as industry "stewardship" of the environment should be created and extended to address cultural degradation as well.[22] Gratuitous violence in the new communications based global economy should be considered every bit as critical and urgent as global warming and saving old growth forests. In an era of growing deficits and shrinking budgets, social costs should be born by sectors of the communications industry that help to foster and reinforce them. New definitions of economic growth are being demanded by environmental groups on a whole host of pressing issues polluting our human habitat. It is no less critical for inclusion of the same kind of accounting on matters of cultural importance. Such auditor-generals could, in turn, do a great deal to help redefine the meaning of productivity in society in its broadest sense. The value or harm involved in productivity should be taken into account to reflect calculations of either damages or improvements to health and social improvement or decline.

Obviously this would require inter-ministerial as well as intergovernmental attention and cooperation. This needs to happen on both a national and global level. In this context, the CEM Agenda for Action developed at the Founding Convention in 1996, should be widely circulated. A formal complaint procedure to investigate and publicize violations of the People's Communication Charter should be instituted immediately along with a People's Media Inquiry.[23] The latter might be administered in collaboration with local and regional CEM affiliated and supporting organizations, with open hearings held each year followed by publication of a report. The existing CEM listserv and website, with interlocking Internet addresses, already provide avenues for such initiatives on a global basis.

These infrastructures for monitoring complaints on an international basis would need to interface with institutions controlling financial and trade patterns such as the World Trade Organization. Current discussions for a new financial architecture at globalization forums such as the one held at Bishop's University in Lennoxville, Quebec, in June 1999, still tend to focus exclusively on things such as reform of the World Bank and the International Monetary Fund. Economists searching for new ways for us to govern ourselves, socially, politically and financially must incorporate the concept of full cost accounting which includes stewardship of civil society. Growing concerns on a global basis for cultural protection in response to encroachment from huge U.S. media conglomerates has prompted Canadian Heritage Minister Sheila Copps to initiate discussion on strategies for protection of cultural diversity with other countries, but there is still no evidence that the underpinning pull toward the use of more and more harmful content in joint ventures between foreign and domestic production companies is being seriously addressed or even acknowledged.[24] In Canada, the prevailing wisdom still is that if its Canadian content it is above reproach.

One initiative for the provision of public education on media issues on a global basis that could be undertaken in collaboration with present CEM leadership is the development of a center to serve as an information service, clearinghouse, speakers bureau, and newsletter editorial office to coordinate action on national and international levels. A calendar of events could be published, to link independent producers committed to CEM objectives and like minded editors of independent publications, to local communities with notification of teach-ins, town meetings, open hearings, policy briefings, and activities of national CEM affiliates.

In Canada, as well as other countries where they do not yet exist, resource centers for parents, educators, students, the media and members of the general public could operate in conjunction with an advisory council. Such a center could include the identification and cataloguing of resources on research findings and media literacy already developed by TVOntario, NFB, AML, MediaWatch, IPCA and C-CAVE among others. The Center should have a permanent, full-time staff and a 1-800 telephone number for easy accessibility across the country and be designed to operate in co-operation with similar initiatives from the CEM and supporting international affiliates. At the very least, the cost for the 1-800 number should be absorbed by one of the major telephone companies as a demonstration of good corporate citizenship on the issue of media violence.

Standards should be developed and incorporated to protect the environment, both cultural and natural, in treaties and international trade agreements. Within this context, limits should be established on whom we give permits to for film and television production in our cities and communities, particularly with respect to publically owned property. A code of ethics should be drafted to which all liaison offices operating on a global basis are expected to adhere. It should be compatible with the People's Communication Charter and the Viewer's Declaration of Independence approved at the International Founding Convention for the Cultural Environment Movement in 1996.[25] Negative-option marketing should be prohibited in all countries. Telephone and cable companies should not be allowed to "impose" any kind of services, whether these are unwanted channels and video games, violent and otherwise, or 1-800 numbers for pornographic services at higher cost onto their unwitting customers.

International TV violence standards should be adopted to apply equally to all signals watched by viewers, both domestic and foreign, and legislation developed in each jurisdiction to ensure their adherence. Before distribution, any program which has been found to violate an approved code on violence in any given country could then be curtailed or encoded. This should apply to cable companies as well as to other distribution undertakings such as direct-to-home (DTH) satellite services or multi-point distribution systems. Existing regulations for this purpose should be amended where necessary.

Legislation developed in the province of Quebec banning advertising directed to children thirteen years and under should be adopted by other provinces in Canada and considered in other jurisdictions as well. Any attempts to introduce advertising into children's programming by public broadcasters, such as the CBC, should be strongly protested along with media literacy kits that endorse the value of advertising as an important source of revenue for children's programming. One example of the latter is a resource kit called "Prime Time Parent" put out by Alliance for Children and Television with the support of Health Canada.[26] Media education for everyone of all ages ought to focus on the extent to which television programs exist in the first place—because people want to sell you things. Although television is a source of news and cheap entertainment, it isn't free. We pay for it, mostly in time, but also in psychological clarity and independence from enslavement by the consumer driven economy television is designed to sustain.

Blocking devices should be mandatory on all television sets sold anywhere. The confusion and stalling over classification systems used to rank levels of violence, sex and foul language in programs, either due to border complications or technical difficulties should be quickly resolved. In Canada, these excuses arose among industry officials at the same time that expectations began to grow on the part of the public as to just what could conceivably be blocked out, apart from violence, such as entire categories of shows or advertisements.[27] Rather than using these expectations as an excuse for further delays, the industry should, instead, recognize the extent to which dissatisfaction with the present state of TV programming and distribution is growing and act accordingly.

Industry Initiatives and Accountability

In Canada, better adherence to policies developed for industry self regulation to eliminate gratuitous violence in programming, to reduce sensationalism in reporting it, and to support its prevention generally, should also be accompanied by the development of alternative family news programming aired in prime time, both on radio and television. Promotion of anti-violence initiatives such as the creation of public service announcements by industry through co-operation with public service organizations and the scientific community should also be encouraged. In addition, a 1-900 telephone number should be provided for easy public access in filing complaints about existing programming. A small surcharge could be applied to prevent abuse of the service and to finance it. This could become a component in the present complaint process on television violence, established through the CBSC, making usage much easier for members of the general public. Adherence to self-regulatory codes on violence within the media industries should be a condition for license renewals along with required demonstration of initiatives to develop or purchase programming alternatives to those involving high levels of violence.

Classification Boards and Criteria

The mandates of film and video classification boards need to be expanded to include other cultural commodities such as video games, CD-ROMs and computer software. Films submitted for entry into both domestic and International Film Festivals should be subject to the same review procedures as all other films, videos and computer software prior to distribution. Similarly, additional award categories should be established which take into account levels of either prosocial or compassionate thematic material. The mandates of film and video review boards should be expanded to provide accurate information on the cultural environmental impact of various commodities to consumers. Such information should also reflect the integrated policies, priorities and objectives of other ministries such as health, welfare, social services and education.

Input from health and social science researchers that takes into account existing knowledge on emotional and cognitive responses for people of all ages is needed in the development of both government and industry regulated film and video classification systems. Criteria reflecting research findings and child development theory would assist board members in making informed decisions and prevent them from relying solely on some vague notion of community standards of morality. These boards should, in turn, include members appointed on a rotating basis to avoid desensitization from review of the material and to ensure the broadest possible reflection of community standards.

Periodic public surveys should be conducted to help determine existing community standards in order to avoid total reliance on politically appointed boards, too often far more sympathetic to the objectives of distributors than the public interest. This would also help to avoid scenarios where, in court cases, judges rely primarily on "expert opinion" from board members. Now, these opinions are arrived at entirely on the basis of individual preferences with no input at all from either the research community or the public at large. In addition, measures should be taken to ensure that decisions disliked by industry officials are not easily overturned as is now the case with provincially operated review boards in Canada.

Review boards should retain the right to return to the distributor any commodities that cannot be accommodated by classification criteria, particularly those containing extra-ordinarily brutal and violent content. Fast-forwarding in the screening process of films and videos for objectionable material or language should not be permitted. This approach, as it has been used in Canada, despite objections from the general public, makes it impossible to adequately monitor language and images.

In-flight screening of movies for airlines to ensure their suitability for child viewing should be enforced. Similarly, periodic checks should be conducted in movie theatres for enforcement of the "spirit of classification" in which attempts are made to screen out productions deemed inappropriate for children and requiring adult accompaniment. These should be insisted upon by parents, teachers, health professionals, airline officials and movie theatre operators. Amendments to the Criminal Code are needed to stem the proliferation of extremely harmful forms of violent entertainment such as snuff and slasher films and serial killer trading cards. Appropriate changes for compatibility should, in turn, be made to Customs Tariffs. In addition, existing exemptions for artistic merit should be removed.

Regulation of Production, Distribution and Retailing

Discretion should be used in the provision of violent media entertainment in correctional institutions where inmates serve time, especially when crimes of violence have been committed. Appropriate regulation should also be developed to require all video stores and retail outlets to demonstrate community responsibility and service by providing sections which include educational resource videos that would help to familiarize parents and other consumers with what the research shows on harmful effects. This is just one of many ways in which better provision of public education could be coordinated without necessarily adding to the already overburdened budgets of existing health and welfare agencies. At the same time, video distributors and retailers would have an opportunity, at the very least, to "be seen" doing something to address the problem.

As the mandates of broadcast standards councils are expanded beyond network television to include other aspects of industry such as cable and specialty channels they should, in turn, interface with inter-ministerial and intergovernmental councils to facilitate the development of integrated policies and priorities with existing film, video and other, similar, review boards. These measures should also coincide with better defined incentives for producers of prosocial cultural commodities. Governments at all levels should agree to eliminate existing incentives for the production and distribution of socially harmful cultural commodities within the economy and adopt better ways to quantify their effects on the community. In Canada, this was first recommended by the LaMarsh Commission over 20 years ago. Public expenditures that subsidize and encourage culturally harmful activities such as funding for gratuitously violent films and television programs through Telefilm, the Cable Television Production Fund or regional development corporations should be discontinued.

All member states of the United Nations should introduce clear, accessible legal provisions within a treaty to limit pornography according to an equality, harms-based approach where the exploitation of women and children in pornography and the subsequent violation of their rights is taken into account. The growing global child sex slave trade partly due to the globalization of poverty is making this increasingly urgent. Initiatives from Canada and other countries to prosecute citizens for sex crimes committed against children abroad should be supported and accelerated.[28] All universities and other educational or public institutions should adopt policies governing use of the Internet that includes blocking pornography from computer bulletin boards.

In this context there is a critical need for more women to be involved in decision-making roles concerning cultural matters given their historical aversion to violence and the predominance of their participation in various peace initiatives around the world. As pointed out to the CRTC at the regional public consultation in Toronto, in October 1995, by Janis Alton, United Nations representative for the *Canadian Voice of Women for Peace and Social Justice*, U.N. studies for 1992 demonstrated that a critical mass of women in any decision-making body must exceed 35 percent before the priorities of women begin to surface in matters of public policy.

Summary

Effective action on pornography and media violence will only be possible if the required political will exists to implement recommendations emanating from countless studies already done over the years in various countries around the world. In Canada these both predate and follow the LaMarsh Commission Report released in 1977. One major weakness in most of these inquiries is the lack of adequate follow-up to implementation of recommendations. This, of course, is particularly difficult because of the extent to which the mainstream media usually work to discredit them. In Canada, the LaMarsh Commission's mandate was under attack from the very beginning and its Report further discredited by the initial direction taken within the LaMarsh Center at York University itself.

Now, however, as we face the new millennium, discussion within the research community, the public domain, and the communications industry is beginning to change. With each new outburst of violence, either in a school or the community at large, concern and acknowledgment of the problems posed by media grow. To a much larger extent, the debate now revolves around what needs to be done and by whom rather than whether action is warranted at all. The challenge is to avoid having the blame shifted back and forth with the predominant focus on what parents and teachers can do. Everyone has a part to play including those within the media industries themselves.

Although national regulation of what is permitted may be even more difficult now than it would have been several decades ago, there are other compensations. The proliferation of technology has resulted in the potential for greater access to information and education on the subject for more people on an international basis. Journalists, researchers, producers and editors now have greater range for the expression of opinion and selection of issues for examination on public affairs programs and themes in fictional programming, despite prevailing trends toward mergers and conglomeratization. Community television options present themselves as avenues for adult educators to participate in public education through the use of sophisticated new technology. Similarly, the Internet offers enormous potential for organization, cooperation and collaboration on an international basis. Alternative options in media diets need to be supported and reinforced. Many members of the media are better educated on communications research in general than used to be the case.

The fundamental challenge is first, for educators, health professionals and policy makers, committed to the public interest, to regain control of the debate on the whole spectrum of what makes up the mass media today. Second, it is for those acting in the public interest to demand more control over how it is being developed and distributed. The point of the debate and program for change is to move the locus of the existing political and economic control of information from private, corporate decision-making to public participation and accountability. Keeping the emerging electronic frontier free of legal shackles in the midst of rapid convergence of information and pressure for its commercialization is not an option. If we are to have a sustainable future we need some rules on the highway.

On the whole, the public must accelerate demands that the news media provide clear ideas for rational alternatives to the critical damage that media violence inflicts on the cultural environment. Lester Brown of the Worldwatch Institute, a close observer of trends and progress on a host of issues relating to human sustainability, has reminded us of the need to step up the pace of change. We do not, he argues, have time for the traditional approach to education which involves training new generations of teachers to train new generations of students because we don't have generations to work with, we only have years left.[29] The communications industry is the only instrument that has the capacity to educate on the scale needed and in the time available. Not only does media violence pose serious problems which need to be addressed within the context of degradation to the cultural environment but the problem is compounded in another way. Aside from distorting value systems that are incompatible with long term human survival, seduction into the production, distribution and consumption of media violence, particularly as entertainment, also diverts critically needed human, financial and technological resources from other urgent environmental issues. For educators and policy makers intent on facilitating greater public awareness and action on any number of pressing global issues, working with and within the mass media becomes essential.

Notes

1. Toffler, 1970, p.417.
2. Bloom, 1987; D'Souza, 1991; Gow, 1985; Kilpatrick, 1993.
3. 1993, p.341.
4. Millar, 1994, Oct. 19, *The Torono Star*, p.A11.
5. Mackie, 1994, Nov. 25, *The Globe and Mail*, p.A11; Millar, 1994.
6. Millar, 1994, p.A11.
7. Lewington, 1994, Oct. 22, *The Globe and Mail*, p.A11.
8. Galt, 1996, Feb. 22, *The Globe and Mail*, p.A1.
9. Sheppard, R., 1996, Oct. 8, *The Globe and Mail*, p.A19.
10. Small, P., 1996, Oct. 7, *The Toronto Star*, p.A1.
11. Crook, Pakulski, & Waters, 1992; Ellis, 1992.
12. Berry, 1988, p.99.
13. Berry, 1988, p.103.
14. Kolbert, 1994, May 9, *New York Times*, p.D7.
15. Ségun, 1994, June 4, *The Globe and Mail*, p.A1,6.
16. http://www.ama-assn.org/ad-com/releases/1996, http://www.cma.ca
17. CPS News Bulletin, Feb., 1990, Ouellet, January, 1990, Hammell and Santa Barbara, November 19, 1991; FWTAO, December-January, 1991; August-September, 1992; October-November, 1992.
18. Ontario, 1977, p.26.
19. Fraser, 1998a, April 29, *The Globe and Mail*, p.A6.
20. Marshall & Barrett, 1990.
21. Lewington, 1994, Galt, 1996.
22. Speirs, 1994b, Nov. 17, The Toronto Star, p.A1,36.
23. People's Communications Charter, CEM Monitor, 1996.
24. Crane, 1999, June 17, *The Toronto Star*, p.B2.
25. CEM Monitor, 1996.
26. Lacey, L., 1995, Aug. 24, *The Globe and Mail*, p.C1.
27. Saunders, D., 1996, Oct. 11, *The Globe and Mail*, p. C1.
28. "Kids at risk", 1996, Oct. 7, *The Toronto Star*, p.A14.
29. Brown, Durning, Flaven, Herse, Jacobson, Postel, Penner, Pollcek, Shea, & Starke, 1989.

BIBLIOGRAPHY

AS A GENERAL RULE, THE REFERENCES for this book follow the format of splitting citations into Notes and Bibliography. In the case of books and periodicals, the Notes generally contain the last name of the author, the date of publication, and particularly in cases where direct quotations are used, the page numbers as well. The full citation is included in most notes where press and other media sources are used. In other words, not all references in the Notes contain information such as the author's first name, the title of the book or article, and the publisher or periodical, which are listed in the Bibliography. Where there is more than one publication by the same author in the same year, these publications are identified by letters after the date, in alphabetical order. Many notes contain additional information or quotations that would have interrupted the flow but that may be of use to interested readers. This Bibliography is by no means a complete list of the works I drew upon in research for this project. A more extensive one appears on the Black Rose Books Internet website (http://www.web.net/blackrosebooks/mind), along with: A Review of the Literature; information on Canadians Concerned About Violence in Entertainment (C-CAVE); and two documents approved at the founding Convention of the Cultural Environment Movement (CEM), the People's Communication Charter, and a Viewer's Declaration of Independence.

Achbar, M., & Wintonick, P. (Producers). (1994). *Manufacturing Consent: Noam Chomsky and the Media* [Video recording]. Montreal: Necessary Illusions.

Angus, I., & Jhally, S. (Eds.). (1989). *Cultural politics in contemporary America*. NY: Routledge.

APA Commission on Violence and Youth. (1993). *Violence and youth: Psychology's response (Vol. 1, Summary)*. Washington, DC: Author.

Attorney General's Commission on Pornography. (1986). *Final Report of the Attorney's General's Commission on Pornography*. Washington, DC: U.S. Government Printing Office.

Baehr, T., & Grimes, T.W. (1990). *The Christian family guide to movies and video (Vol. 2)*. Brentwood, TN: Wolgemuth & Hyatt.

Bandura, A. (1973). *On aggression: A social learning analysis.* Englewood Cliffs, NJ: Prentice-Hall Inc.

Bandura, A., Ross, D., & Ross, S. (1961). Transmission of aggression through imitation of aggressive models. *Journal of Abnormal and Social Psychology, 63*(3), 575-582.

Bandura, A., Ross, D., & Ross, S. (1963). Imitation of film-mediated aggressive models. *Journal of Abnormal and Social Psychology, 66* (1), 3-11.

Barlow, M. and J. Winter. (1997). *The Big Black Book.* Toronto: Stoddart.

Barritt, L.S., Beekman, T., Bleeker, H., & Mulderiz, K. (1983). *A handbook for phenomenological research in education.* Ann Arbor, MI: The University of Michigan Press.

Barron, J. (1992, November 12, 13). Towards ethical questioning of audio-visual violence. Paper presented at the *International Symposium on television, film and violence: Constitutional theory and the direction of research.* Quebec Institute of Research and Culture, Montreal: CRTC and Ministry of Communications.

Beck, C. (1990). *Better schools: A values perspective.* NY: Falmer Press.

Berkoff, F. (1993, October). My battle with bulimia. *Modern woman,* 12-13.

Berry, T. (1988). *The dream of the earth.* CA: Sierra Club Books.

Bird, B. for Standing Committee on Communications and Culture. (1993, June). *Television violence: Fraying our social fabric.* Ottawa, ON: Ministry of Supply and Services.

Bloom, A. (1987). *The closing of the American mind.* Toronto: Simon & Shuster.

Bogart, L. (1980). After the Surgeon General's report: Another look backward. In S. Withey, & R. Abeles (Eds.), *Television and social behavior: Beyond violence and children* (p. 103-134). Hillsdale, NJ: Lawrence Erlbaum.

Bogdan, D. (1992a). *Re-educating the imagination: Toward a poetics, politics, and pedagogy of literary engagement.* Portsmouth, NH: Boynton-Cook-Heinemann.

Bogdan, D. (1992b, Fall). Reading as seduction: The censorship problem, and the educational value of literature. *The Association of Departments of English, Bulletin of the Modern Language of America (102),* p. 11-16.

Boulding, E. (1988). *Building a global civic culture: Education for an interdependent world.* NY: Teachers College Press, Columbia University.

Boulding, K.E. (1985). *Human betterment.* CA: Sage.

Brown, L.R., Durning, A., Flaven, C., Herse, L., Jacobson, J., Postel, S. Penner, M. Pollcek Shea, C., & Starke, L. (1989). *State of the world 1989: A Worldwatch Institute report on progress toward a sustainable society.* NY: Norton.

Brown, J. (1999, May 30). *Forum Connection* @civilrightsforum.org.

Canada. (1999, June). *Canada And The Future OF The World Trade Organization.* Ottawa, ON: Standing Committee on Foreign Affairs and International Trade.

Canadian Broadcast Standards Council. Decision 97/98-0001+ and Decision 97/98-0015+ re: Howard Stern Show. Ottawa. October 17 & 18, 1997.

Canadian Paediatric Society. (1990, February). *News Bulletin, XII*(1). Sudbury, ON: Author

CBC Radio. (1993a, January 11). *Prime Time with Geoff Pevere.* Toronto, ON: Author.

CBC Television. (1992, November 17). *Adrienne Clarkson presents.* Toronto, ON: Author.

Centerwall, B. (1989). *Exposure to television as a cause of violence: Public communications and behaviour (Vol. 2).* Seattle, WA: University of Washington, Academic Press Inc.

Check, J., Heapy, N., & Iwanyshyn, O. (1985). *A survey of Canadian attitudes regarding sexual content in the media, Report No. 11.* Toronto, ON: LaMarsh Centre, York University and CBC, Toronto, p. 1-29.

Check, J., & LaCrosse, V. (1989). Attitudes and behaviour regarding pornography, sexual coercion, and violence in Metropolitan Toronto high schools (Report No. 34), *The LaMarsh research programme reports on violence and conflict resolution,* York University.

Check, J., & Malamuth, N. (1986). Pornography and sexual aggression: A social learning theory analysis. *Communication yearbook, Vol. 9,* p. 181-213.

Clarke, T. and M. Barlow. (1997). *MAI: The Multilateral Agreement on Investment and the Threat to Canadian Sovereignty.* Toronto, ON: Stoddart.

Commission on Obscenity and Pornography. (1970). *Report of the Commission on Obscenity and Pornography.* Washington, DC: U.S. Government Printing Office.

Comstock, G. (1991). *Television and the American child.* NY: Academic Press, Inc.

Cowan, G. (1992). *Degrading/dehumanizing pornography: The costs of denial.* Paper presented at thea nnual meeting of the Scientific Society for the Study of Sex. San Diego, CA.

Crook, S., Pakulski, J., & Waters, M. (1992). *Postmodernization: Change in advanced society.* London: Sage.

CRTC. (1999, May 17) CRTC WON'T REGULATE THE INTERNET. *News Release.* pp.1-9.

Donnerstein, E., Linz, D., & Penrod, S. (1987). *The question of pornography: Research findings and policy implications.* NY: Collier.

D'Souza, D. (1991). *Illiberal education.* NY: Macmillan.

Duncan, B. (1988). *Mass media and popular culture.* Toronto: Harcourt Brace Jovanovich.

Duncan, B & J. D'lppolito, C. Macpherson, C.Wilson.(1996). *Mass Media and Popular Culture.* Version 2. Toronto: Harcourt Brace Canada.

Dyson, R.A. (1987). *Research findings on media violence and the impact on social policy.* Toronto: Rosendee Corp.

Dyson, R.A. (1988a). *Toronto Star coverage of Bill C-54.* Unpublished manuscript, University of Toronto, OISE.

Dyson, R.A. (1994a, January). New code of TV violence. *Peace Magazine,* X(1), p. 14-15.

Dyson, R.A. (1994c, Spring). Media must weigh freedom of speech against social responsibility. *C-CAVE News,* 4, 5.

Dyson, R.A. (1995). The Treatment of Media Violence in Canada Since Publication of the LaMarsh Commission Report in 1977. Doctoral Thesis, OISEUT, Toronto; National Library, Ottawa.

Eisler, R. (1988). *The chalice and the blade: Our history, our future.* San Francisco: Harper & Row.

Eisler, R. (1996) *Sacred Pleasure.* San Francisco, HarperCollins.

Ellis, D. (1975, September 8-9). Violence and the mass media. *Report of the Proceedings: Workshop on Violence in Canadian Society* (p. 89-119). Toronto, ON: University of Toronto, Centre for Criminology.

Ellis, D. (1992). *Split screen: Home entertainment and the new technologies.* Toronto: Friends of Canadian Broadcasting, Toronto.

Ellul, J. (1987). *Propaganda.* NY: Vintage Books.

Faludi, S. (1992). *Backlash: The undeclared war against American women.* NY: Anchor Books, Doubleday.

Fiske, J. (1985). *Television culture.* NY: Methuen.

Fiske, J., & Hartley, J. (1985). *Reading television.* NY: Methuen.

Franklin, U. (1990). *The real world of technology: CBC Massey lectures series.* Toronto, ON: CBC Enterprises.

Fraser, P. (Chair). (1985). *Pornography and Prostitution in Canada: Report of the Special Committee on Pornography and Prostitution, Vol. 1&2.* Ministry of Supply and Services.

Gerbner, G. (1991a, October). *Media violence as demonstration of power.* Unpublished manuscript, University of Pennsylvania.

Gerbner, G. (1991b, October). The turtles live to ooze again. *Advice: Center for the Study of Commercialism,* 1(3).

Gerbner, G. (1991c, Fall-Winter). The second American revolution. *Adbusters,* p. 8-10.

Gerbner, G. (1993, September). *CEM* (Communique). PA: University of Pennsylvania, Annenberg School for Communication.

Gerbner, G. (1994, Julya). Television violence: The art of asking the wrong question. *The world and I: Currents in modern thought,* p. 385-398.

Gerbner, G., Gross, L.P., & Melody, W.H. (Eds.). (1973). *Communications technology and social policy: Understanding the new "cultural revolution".* NY: John Wiley & Sons.

Gerbner, G., Haigh, R.W., & Byrne, R.B. (Eds.). (1981). *Communications in the twenty-first century*. NY: John Wiley & Sons.

Gerbner, G., Ross, C.J., & Zigler, E. (Eds.). (1980). *Child abuse: An agenda for action*. NY: Oxford University Press.

Gerbner, G., Morgan, M., & Signorielli, N. (1994). *Cultural Indicators*. PA: University of Pennsylvania, Annenberg School for Communication; MA: University of Massachusetts; DE: University of Delaware.

Gerbner, G. (1996, December 19) Ratings System Falls Short, According To Expert On Television Violence. *News Release.*, CEM, Philadelphia, Penn.

Gore, A. (1992). *Earth in the balance: Ecology and the human spirit*. NY: Houghton Mifflin Co.

Gostin, L. (1988). (Ed.). *Civil liberties in conflict*. NY: Routledge.

Gow, K. (1985). *Yes, Virginia, there is right and wrong*. FL: Fidelity House.

Graham, B. and B. Speller. (1997, December). *Canada and the Multilateral Agreement on Investment: Third Report of the Standing Committee on Foreign Affairs and International Trade*.

Gramsci, A. (1971). *Selections from the prison notebooks*. (Q. Hoare, & G.N. Smith, Eds. & Trans.). NY: International Publishers.

Grossman, Lieut. Col. D. (1995). *On Killing: The Psychological Cost of Learning to Kill in War and Society*. NY., Toronto: Little, Brown and Co.

Hall, B.L. (1993b). Learning and global civil society: Electronic networking in international non-governmental organizations. *International Journal of Computers in Adult Education and Training*, 3(3), 5-24.

Herman, E.S., & Chomsky, N. (Eds.). (1988). *Manufacturing consent: The political economy of the mass media*. NY: Random House.

Howitt, D. (1983). *The mass media and social problems*. NY: Pergamon Press.

Huston, A.C., Donnerstein, E., Fairchild, H., Feshbach, N.D., Katz, P.A., Murray, J.P., Rubinstein, E.A., Wilcox, B.L., & Zuckerman, D. (1992). *Big world, small screen: The role of television in American society*. Lincoln, NE: University of Nebraska Press.

ICAVE & NCTV. (1982-1990). *News releases and Bulletins*. Champaign, IL.

Innis, H.A. (1951). *The bias of communication*. Toronto, ON: University of Toronto Press.

Johnson, S. (on behalf of Argyle Communications-Toronto). (1986, June 5). Pro-pornography "leaked" memorandum, distributed by METRAC, *Pornography and free trade: A time for action*, Appendix A, p. 1-6.

Jury awards $25 million in 'Jenny Jones Show' lawsuit. (1999, May 7) *CNN Interactive*. http://www.cnn.com/SHOWBIZ/TV/9905/07/talkshowslaying.02

Kennedy, P. (1993). *Preparing for the twenty-first century*. Toronto: Harper Collins.

Kilpatrick, W. (1992). *Why Johnny can't tell right from wrong*. NY: Simon and Schuster.

Kirby, S., & McKenna, K. (1989). *Experience, research, social change: Methods from the margins.* Toronto: Garamond Press.

LaMarsh, J. (1976). (Ontario Royal Commission on Violence in the Communications Industry.) *Interim Report.* Toronto: Queen's Printer for Ontario.

LaMarsh, J. (1977). (Ontario Royal Commission on Violence in the Communications Industry.) *Report of the Royal Commission on violence in the communications industry. Approaches, conclusions and recommendations (Vol. 1); Violence and the media: A bibliography (Vol. 2); Violence in television, films and news (Vol. 3); Violence in print and music (Vol. 4); Learning from the media (Vol. 5); Vulnerability to media effects (Vol. 6); The media industries: From here to where? (Vol. 7).* Toronto: Queen's Printer for Ontario.

Larsen, O.N. (1968). (Ed.). *Violence and the mass media.* NY: Harper & Row.

Lederer, L. (1980). *Take back the night: Women on pornography.* NY: Bantam Books.

Leyton, E. (1986). *Hunting humans: The rise of the modern murderer.* Toronto: McClelland and Stewart.

MacDougall, J. (1993). Violence in the schools: Programs and policies for prevention. Toronto: Canadian Education Association.

Mackinnon, C.A. (1987). Feminism unmodified: Discourses on life and law. Cambridge, MA: Harvard University Press.

Mander, J. (1978). Four arguments for the elimination of television. NY: Quill.

Mander, J. (1991). In the absence of the sacred: The failure of technology and the survival of the Indian Nations. San Francisco: Sierra Club Books.

Marshall, P.F., & Vallaincourt, M.A. (1993). (Co-Chairs.). Changing the landscape: Ending violenceachieving equality (Executive summary/national action plan). Ottawa, ON: Canadian Panel on Violence Against Women.

Marshall, W.L., & Barrett, S. (1990). Criminal neglect: Why sex offenders go free. Toronto: Doubleday.

Martinez, A. (1992, May). Scientific knowledge about television violence. Ottawa: CRTC.

Martinez, A. (1992, May). *Scientific knowledge about television violence.* Ottawa: CRTC.

McLaren, P. (1993, March). Decentering violence: A U.S. perspective. *Orbit,* p. 10-11.

McLuhan, M. (1964). *Understanding media: The extensions of man.* NY: McGraw-Hill.

McLuhan, M., & McLuhan, E. (1988). *Laws of media: The new science.* Toronto: University of Toronto Press.

Medved, M. (1992). *Hollywood Vs. America.* NY: Harper Collins.

Melody, W.H. (1973). The role of advocacy in policy planning. In G. Gerbner et al. (Eds.), *Communications technology and social policy: Understanding the new "cultural revolution"* (p. 165-180). NY: John Wiley & Sons.

Miedzian, M. (1991). *Boys will be boys: Breaking the link between masculinity and violence.* NY: Doubleday.

Montgomery, K.C (1989). *Target: Prime time: Advocacy groups and the struggle over entertainment television.* NY: Oxford University Press.

National Council of Churches. (1994, October 19). J. Kilbourne (Narrator), *Proceedings of the National Council of Churches Teleconference: The killing screens, discussion with George Gerbner* [Video recording]. Toronto: United Church of Canada and Kinetic Inc.

Nelson, J. (1988) *The Colonized Eye: Rethinking the Grierson Legend.* Toronto: Between the Lines.

Nelson, J. (1989). *Sultans of sleaze: Public relations and the media.* Toronto: Between the Lines.

NIMH. (1982). *Television and behavior: Ten years of scientific progress and implications for the eighties. Vol. 1, Summary report.* Washington, DC: U.S. Government Printing Office.

Obmascik, M. (1999, May 28) Violent video games pulled from DIA. *Denver Post.* Local P.

O'Connor, D. (1985). *The pervasiveness of military themes in the early male culture.* Unpublished doctoral dissertation, University of Toronto, Toronto.

OECD. (1997, October 6). *Multilateral Agreement on Investment: Consolidated Text and Commentary.* Ottawa.

Ontario. (1993, April 27, July 19, May 3, May 11, June 17, July 5, July 13, July 19). Trading cards and slasher films, Ontario Film Review Board. *Legislative Assembly, official record of debates (Hansard), third session, thirty-fifth parliament,* p. 311-2555. Toronto, ON: Publications Ontario.

OTF & Ontario Ministry of Education. (1989). *Media Literacy.* Toronto: Author.

Ouellet, G. (1990, January). The health and social effects of television viewing on children. *Ontario Medical Review,* p. 20-24.

PAT. (1994, April). *The street of the Pied Piper: A survey of teachers' perceptions of the effects on children of the new entertainment technologies.* England: Author.

Postman, N. (1986). *Amusing ourselves to death.* NY: Penguin Books.

Provenzo, E.F. (1993, October 25). Violence, video games, and interactive TV. *Conference on electronic child abuse: Problems and solutions* [Video recording]. Toronto, ON: IPCA.

Pungente, J., & Duncan, B. (1994, Spring). An exclusive Mediacy interview with Len Masterman. *Mediacy,* 16(2), 16-20.

Raboy, M. (1998, April). Public Broadcasting and the Global Framework of Media Democratization. *Gazette: The International Journal For Communications Studies.* London, Thousand Oaks &New Delhi, Sage Publications. 60(2), 167-180.

Radecki, T. (1990). *TV and other forms of violent entertainment: A cause of 50% of real-life violence.* Champaign, IL: I-CAVE.

Rapoport, A. (1989). *The origins of violence.* NY: Paragon House.

Razack, S.H. (1989). *Feminism applied to law: The women's legal education and action fund.* Unpublished doctoral dissertation, University of Toronto, Toronto.

Sauvageau, F., Atkinson, D., & Gourdeau, M. (1991, June). *Summary and analysis of various studies on violence and television.* Canada: Quebec Institute of Research on Culture and CRTC.

Schiller, H. (1989b). *Culture Inc.: The corporate takeover of public expression.* Oxford: Oxford University Press.

Scott, D.A. (1985). *Pornography: Its effects on the family, community and culture.* Washington, DC: Child and Family Protection Institute.

Sedley, S. (1988). The spider and the fly: A question of principle. In L. Gostin (Ed.), *Civil liberties in conflict.* NY: Routledge.

Snow, N. (1998) *Propaganda, Inc.: Selling America's Culture To The World.* New York. Seven Stories Press.

Solomon, J. (1988). *The signs of our time.* NY: Harper & Row.

Spencer, M. (1995, January-February). The politics of Noam Chomsky. *Peace Magazine*, p. 16-21.

Status of Women, Canada. (1994, May 26). *Film classification in Canada.* Ottawa, ON: Author.

Sullivan, E.V. (1982). *Mass media and political integration: Thematizing three major dailies in a Canadian city.* Unpublished manuscript, University of Toronto, OISE.

Sullivan, E.V. (1987). Critical pedagogy and television. In D. Livingstone & contributors (Eds.), *Critical pedagogy and cultural power.* MA: Bergin & Garvey Publishers.

Toffler, A. (1970). *Future shock.* NY: Bantam Books.

UNESCO. (1991). *New Communications Technology Research Trends*, Jouet & Coudray, eds., France.

Vipond, M. (1989). *The mass media in Canada.* Toronto: James Lorimer & Co.

Wertham, F. (1968). Is television hardening us to the war in Vietnam? In O.N. Larsen (Ed.), *violence and the mass media.* NY: Harper & Row.

Winn, M. (1977). *The plug-in drug.* NY: Viking Press.

Withey, S., & Abeles, R.P. (Eds.). (1980). *Television and social behavior: Beyond violence and children.* Hillsdale, NJ: Erlbaum Ass.

Wolf, N. (1992). *The beauty myth.* Toronto: Vintage Books.

Youth News Network. (1994, March). *The YTV Newsletter.* Toronto: YTV Canada Inc.

INDEX

ALSO PUBLISHED BY

DEMOCRACY'S OXYGEN *How the Corporations Control the News*
James Winter
2nd printing, revised edition, updated

A book that presents the hard facts that illustrate the complicity between government and corporate media interests as it asks the questions 'who owns newspapers in Canada and what influence have they on content?'

Once the hinge of democracy, the media now specialize in 'junk food news'—Winter's analysis is strong. *Globe and Mail*

Particularly strong in the profiles of Black, his fellow baron Paul Desmarais, and the publishing giant Québecor. *Quill & Quire*

A deep desire for fundamental political and media reforms backed up by facts, figures and quotations. *Barrie Zwicker, Vision TV*

294 pages, bibliography, index
Paperback ISBN: 1-55164-060-0 $23.99
Hardcover ISBN: 1-55164-061-9 $52.99
1997 revised edition, updated

MANUFACTURING CONSENT *Noam Chomsky and the Media*
Mark Achbar, editor

Charts the life of America's most famous dissident, from his boyhood days running his uncle's newsstand in Manhattan to his current role as outspoken social critic. Included are exchanges between Chomsky and his critics, historical and biographical material, filmmakers' notes, a resource guide, more than 270 stills from the film, and, 18 "Philosopher All-Stars" Trading Cards!

Bristling and buzzing with ideas. *Washington Post*

You will see the whole sweep of the most challenging critic in modern political thought. *Boston Globe*

One of our real geniuses...an excellent introduction. *Village Voice*

Intellectually challenging crash course in the man's thought in a package that is clever and accessible. *Los Angeles Times*

...challenging, controversial. *Globe and Mail*

...a rich, rewarding experience, a thoughtful and lucid exploration of the danger that might exist in a controlled media. *Edmonton Journal*

A gem of a biography. *The Sunday Times*

264 pages, 270 illustrations, bibliography, index
Paperback ISBN: 1-55164-002-3 $24.99
Hardcover ISBN: 1-55164-003-1 $53.99
1996

ALSO PUBLISHED BY

BLACK
ROSE
BOOKS

METHOD IS THE MESSAGE
Rethinking McLuhan through Critical Theory
Paul Grosswiler

This book examines McLuhan's work in the light of many theorists, including Theodor Adorno, Walter Benjamin, Raymond Williams, James Carey, Jean Baudrillard and Umberto Eco.

...a profoundly intelligent and original fusion of McLuhan and Marx. With this book McLuhan's position as an ingenious innovator in critical, cultural and postmodern theory is restored.

James W. Carey, CBS Professor of International Journalism, Columbia University

McLuhan strikes many media historians as perverse; this book reminds us why he's also so damned interesting. It is must reading.

John Nerone, Professor of Communications, University of Illinois

The book's provocative thesis will certainly ignite controversy on all sides of the political and intellectual spectrum.

Liss Jeffrey, Executive Producer, The McLuhan Program in Culture and Technology

...makes a compelling argument that McLuhan has a great deal to offer. This thoughtful book should be read carefully by students of communication everywhere.

Robert McChesney, Associate Professor of Journalism and Mass Communication, University of Wisconsin

Paul Grosswiler is an Associate Professor in the Department of Communication and Journalism at the University of Miane, Orono. He worked for several years as a journalist in Maine and Missouri.

256 pages, bibliography, index
Paperback ISBN: 1-55164-074-0 $24.99
Hardcover ISBN: 1-55164-075-9 $53.99
1998

A Cure of the Mind, *by Theodore Sampson*
Aphra Behn, *by George Woodcock*
Balance: Art and Nature, *by John Grande*
Beyond O.J., *by Earl Ofari Hutchinson*
Beyond Boundaries, *by Barbara Noske*
Communication, *by Marc Raboy*
Common Cents, *by James Winter*
Every Life Is a Story, *by Fred H. Knelman*
Fateful Triangle, *by Noam Chomsky*
Humerous Sceptic, *by N.Anthony Bonaparte*
Military in Greek Politics, *by Thanos Veremis*
Murray Bookchin Reader, *by Janet Biehl and Murray Bookchin*
Oscar Wilde, *by George Woodcock*
Perspectives on Power, *by Noam Chomsky*
Peter Kropotkin, *by George Woodcock*
Public Place, *by Dimitrios Roussopoulos*
Rethinking Camelot, *by Noam Chomsky*
Russian Literature, *by Peter Kropotkin*
Writers and Politics, *by George Woodcock*
Women Pirates, *by Ulrike Klausmann, Marion Meinzerin, Gabriel Kuhn*
Zapata of Mexico, *by Peter Newell*

send for a free catalogue of all our titles
BLACK ROSE BOOKS
C.P. 1258, Succ. Place du Parc
Montréal, Québec
H3W 2R3 Canada

or visit our web site at: http://www.web.net/blackrosebooks

To order books in North America:
(phone) 1-800-565-9523 (fax) 1-800-221-9985
In Europe: (phone) 44-0181-986-4854 (fax) 44-0181-533-5821

Printed by the workers of
VEILLEUX IMPRESSION À DEMANDE INC.
Longueuil, Québec
for Black Rose Books Ltd.